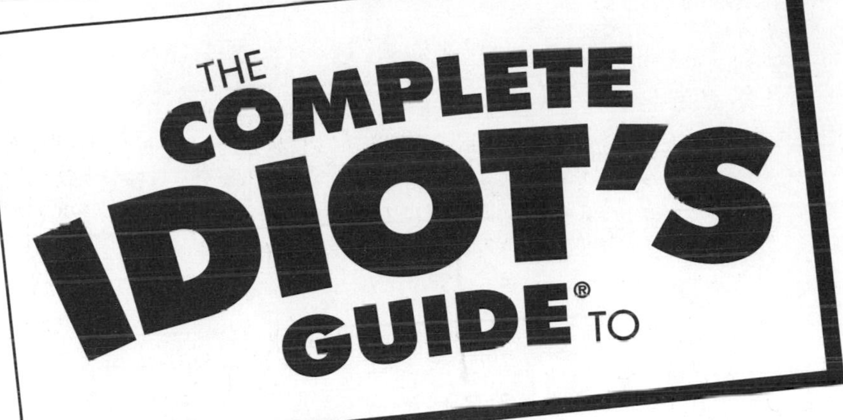

The Perfect Resume

Fourth Edition

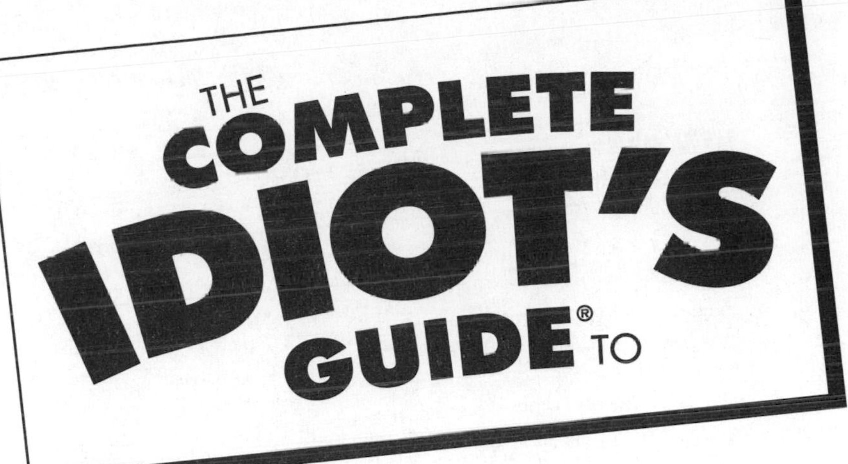

The Perfect Resume

Fourth Edition

by Susan Ireland

A member of Penguin Group (USA) Inc.

To my dad, who taught me at an early age the value of building character through work.

ALPHA BOOKS

Published by the Penguin Group

Penguin Group (USA) Inc., 375 Hudson Street, New York, New York 10014, U.S.A.

Penguin Group (Canada), 10 Alcorn Avenue, Toronto, Ontario, Canada M4V 3B2 (a division of Pearson Penguin Canada Inc.)

Penguin Books Ltd, 80 Strand, London WC2R 0RL, England

Penguin Ireland, 25 St Stephen's Green, Dublin 2, Ireland (a division of Penguin Books Ltd)

Penguin Group (Australia), 250 Camberwell Road, Camberwell, Victoria 3124, Australia (a division of Pearson Australia Group Pty Ltd)

Penguin Books India Pvt Ltd, 11 Community Centre, Panchsheel Park, New Delhi—110 017, India

Penguin Group (NZ), cnr Airborne and Rosedale Roads, Albany, Auckland 1310, New Zealand (a division of Pearson New Zealand Ltd)

Penguin Books (South Africa) (Pty) Ltd, 24 Sturdee Avenue, Rosebank, Johannesburg 2196, South Africa

Penguin Books Ltd, Registered Offices: 80 Strand, London WC2R 0RL, England

International Standard Book Number: 1-59257-463-7
Library of Congress Catalog Card Number: 2005933833

07 06 8 7 6 5 4 3

Interpretation of the printing code: The rightmost number of the first series of numbers is the year of the book's printing; the rightmost number of the second series of numbers is the number of the book's printing. For example, a printing code of 05-1 shows that the first printing occurred in 2005.

Printed in the United States of America

Publisher: *Marie Butler-Knight*
Editorial Director: *Mike Sanders*
Senior Managing Editor: *Jennifer Bowles*
Senior Acquisitions Editor: *Randy Ladenheim-Gil*
Development Editor: *Lynn Northrup*
Senior Production Editor: *Billy Fields*
Copy Editor: *Keith Cline*
Cartoonist: *Richard King*
Cover/Book Designer: *Trina Wurst*
Indexer: *Brad Herriman*
Layout: *Becky Harmon*
Proofreading: *Donna Martin*

Contents at a Glance

Contents

Foreword

A book is a good book, even a great book, if you keep saying to yourself as you go through it: "Now, how did they learn *that*?"

A continual sense of wonder in you, the reader. That's the key. That's how you measure whether a book is really helpful, or not. And what I've learned over the years is that such wonder is not produced simply by a writer's experience. It's produced by experience plus one other ingredient, harder to find: wisdom. If you're puzzled about what I mean by "wisdom," I mean learning to separate the important from the unimportant. I mean learning to separate the wheat from the chaff. I mean learning, as Susan Ireland herself says in this most helpful book of hers: What is the least you need to know? Ah, there is wisdom, right there!

Books about resumes—of which there are hundreds, if not thousands—often are "yawners," I regret to report—after reading them for 35 years. On and on and on, they go. While visions of sugarplums, or at least of soft pillows, dance in their readers' wee little heads.

The authors of books about resumes commonly seem to feel there is so much to tell, and so little time. *You must remember this, you must remember that, and oh yes, you must remember this also.* They believe we live in the Information Age, as is commonly said. Well, that's not exactly true. We live in the Too-Much-Information Age. Most of us wander, as David Shenk first pointed out back in 1998, in a kind of overwhelming *Data Smog.*

Hence, "what is the least you need to know?" is the true place, the wise place, where a book on resumes needs to start.

There is a lot of wonder and wisdom in this book. When I came across Susan's words—like "If your resume generates job interviews for work you're not interested in, something is wrong with your resume"—I found myself thinking, "Now, how did she learn *that*?" And, in fact, I found myself thinking this continually, throughout the book.

But the point of a book, of course, is not "how did *she* learn that?" but "how can *I* learn that?" That's easy. Put yourself in Susan's hands. Trust her. Trust this book. I recommend it highly, for the obvious reasons: its wisdom and your wonder.

—Richard Bolles

Richard Bolles is the most widely read and respected leader in the whole career development world. His book, *What Color Is Your Parachute? A Practical Guide for Job-Hunters & Career-Changers*, is now in its 35th annual revision, and has sold more copies (8 million) than any other career book in the world.

Introduction

Success in finding your ideal job depends largely on having a dynamite resume. Changes have taken place in the way resumes are reviewed by managers and human resource professionals. Would you believe that the number of applicants per job has increased to such a point that each resume is given only about eight seconds to grab the reader's attention?

Many companies want resumes sent to them via e-mail, or they simply download them from an online resume bank. In other organizations, resumes are put into resume scanners and electronically entered into databases for automated selection.

Knowing how to create a resume for today's job market could make or break your job search. But don't panic! Just follow the guidelines in this book and you'll create a resume that will be considered by a hiring manager of any job you sincerely believe you're qualified for.

The Complete Idiot's Guide to the Perfect Resume, Fourth Edition, explains the ins and outs of how to prepare and send hardcopy and electronic resumes so that you'll be ready to hit the ground running in your job hunt.

As a professional resume writer who has helped thousands of job seekers, I've seen how well-written resumes (not boilerplate forms) lead to promising interviews and job offers. I've also seen how a carefully crafted resumes can help a job seeker (such as you) get through the seemingly impossible task of finding career satisfaction. In other words, a great resume can help you find a position that you enjoy with a paycheck that supports your lifestyle.

As the proud owner of *The Complete Idiot's Guide to the Perfect Resume, Fourth Edition*, you have me as your personal resume coach. Imagine that I'm sitting right at your elbow as you work at your desk or kitchen table. My job is to guide you through the entire process as you:

- Develop a winning resume strategy.
- Write each line to make the most of your qualifications.
- Create a great format for your resume.
- Distribute your new resume to employers.

To illustrate my points, I've included over 100 sample resumes that reflect goals and challenges similar to what you're facing. These samples may spark some ideas that you can use in your resume.

The secret to success in using this book is to relax and take one step at a time. You'll be surprised how painless the process of writing a resume is!

Between the Covers

Because helping you craft a top-notch resume is the goal of *The Complete Idiot's Guide to the Perfect Resume, Fourth Edition*, let's talk about what's inside.

Advice Along the Way

Whether you read this book from cover to cover or open it to specific points to get help with your job search, you'll notice the following sidebars throughout:

Terms of Employment

These sidebars will keep you informed about buzzwords in the job hunt business.

Career Casualty

Don't miss these important warnings. They'll save you lots of work, angst, and time.

Job Hunt Hint

With the job search tips you'll find in these sidebars, you'll get your new job in no time!

Bonus Check

For that extra kick in your job hunt, check out these sidebars. They're filled with juicy tidbits you probably didn't think of.

Part 1, "Plan to Succeed," explains why you need a good resume and what that resume can do for you. You'll also find the "Resume Commandments," which are my secrets to creating a compelling resume.

Part 2, "Six Steps to a Perfect Resume," is where you'll find my straightforward, six-step resume writing process. Before you know it, you'll be finished with your resume.

Part 3, "So You Need a Special Resume," shows you variations on a typical resume, including the achievement resume, hybrid resume, and curriculum vitae.

Part 4, "Wrapping It Up," gives you tips on how to get your resume out of your printer and into an employer's hands. You also learn how to write effective cover letters and thank-you notes that will keep your job search going in the right direction.

Part 5, "The Electronic Job Search," teaches you how to create a successful electronic resume that won't get lost in cyberspace! You'll become a pro at preparing resumes that can be e-mailed, posted on websites, and put through resume scanners.

As if all that wasn't enough, I've also included a "Portfolio of Sample Resumes" at the end of the book, jam-packed with resumes for just about every type of job seeker.

Acknowledgments

I'd like to thank Beth Brown, Catherine Sutton, Nancy Rosenberg, and Ruth Schwartz (professional resume writers on my team) for the resumes they contributed to this book. Special gratitude and remembrance goes to my mentor and friend, Yana Parker (author of *The Damn Good Resume Guide*). My thanks to Andreé Abecassis (my agent at Ann Elmo Agency), Randy Ladenheim-Gil (my senior acquisitions editor), Lynn Northrup (my development editor), Billy Fields (my senior production editor), Keith Cline (my copy editor), and, of course, Mom and my husband, Charlie.

Trademarks

Part 1

Plan to Succeed

It's been a long, hard day at the office for Ms. Hiring Manager. Her eyes are glazed over from looking at 75 resumes, trying to find the right person for an opening in her department. She's about to put on her coat and head for home when something on her desk catches her eye. It's another resume—yours. "At last!" she announces, after spending less than a minute scanning the page. "Someone who fits the bill!"

That's the kind of immediate recognition you can expect from your resume once you grasp and employ the principles presented in these chapters. After reading this section, you'll be miles ahead of your competition. The principles in Part 1 alone are well worth the price of this book. So turn the page and find out what most job seekers don't know about writing a job-winning resume. Before you know it, your resume will be sitting pretty on your next employer's desk!

Chapter 1

Winning Resume Wisdom

In This Chapter

- Designing a resume that creates the future you want
- Using past successes for future rewards
- Keeping secrets from the employer
- Making your resume quick and inviting to read
- To lie or not to lie

Writing the perfect resume takes a little time and concentration, but when you finish it, you'll feel like a million bucks—or as if you could *make* a million bucks!

Trust me, time spent working on a resume is time well spent. I've seen lots of people walk away with finished resumes, saying they never knew they could look so good on paper; they never thought their work history could appear so impressive; or they never thought they could look qualified for something they'd never done in the past.

A few principles lie behind the kind of job-winning resume I'm talking about. This chapter discusses key concepts that will not only provide you with resume wisdom, they'll also solve every resume problem you'll encounter. At the end of this chapter you'll find sample resumes that demonstrate these principles.

The Commandments

Before you boot up your computer (or get your ballpoint pen and paper if you're sitting at your kitchen table), I want to impart a few tricks that even most professional resume writers don't know. (Your competition surely doesn't!) These concepts can make the difference between a boring resume that just sits on a manager's desk (or, even worse, gets thrown away) and one that demands "Read me, read me! Call me, call me!" These resume tips are so important I've dubbed them "The Resume Commandments."

The Resume Commandments

I. Thou shalt not write about your past; thou shalt write about your future!

II. Thou shalt not confess.

III. Thou shalt not write job descriptions; thou shalt write achievement statements.

IV. Thou shalt not write about stuff you don't want to do again.

V. Thou shalt say less rather than more.

VI. Thou shalt not write in paragraphs; thou shalt use bullet points.

VII. Thou shalt not lie.

Now let's look at each of these commandments to understand why they are so important.

Thou Shalt Not Write About Your Past

Because your resume is a marketing piece for your next job, it concerns your future, not your past. If you're writing a chronological resume (explained in Chapter 2), don't write your resume as if it were a historical document. Even though the body of your chronological format is structured around your work history (your past), the achievement statements should support your job objective statement (your future).

"My resume is about my future?" you ask. "But it talks about my work history and what I did at my previous jobs. Doesn't that mean it's about my past?"

That's exactly what most people think, but the secret to getting a new and exciting job is to build your resume around the job you're striving for, not the ones you've previously held. So before you even start writing your resume, you need to plan what kind of work you want to do next.

> CAUTION
>
> **Career Casualty**
>
> Some folks think a list of statements should end with the best one. Not on a resume! What if an impatient or busy reader never gets to the end of the list? Always start a list with your best item.

Create a resume that's about your future by imagining that you're an artist with an empty canvas (such as your computer screen) in front of you. Your assignment is to paint a picture of yourself at your next job, using any of the following four tools:

- Your experience (such as previous job titles, volunteer work, or school projects)
- Your skill areas (such as management, computer knowledge, or sales)
- Your concerns (such as the environment, homelessness, or human rights)
- Your personality (such as dependability, sense of humor, or ability to communicate)

When you're finished, you should have a word-picture of you working for your next employer.

What will the employer think of your future-oriented resume? At first glance, she may assume she's reading about your past, but as she gets drawn into it, she'll find herself imagining that you're working for her. And that's what will make her want to call you for an interview.

Thou Shalt Not Confess

"Forgive me, Father, it's been a year since I last updated my resume," you cry. Have no fear, my friend; I'm here to fill you in on all the tips, including this one: Don't let one trace of that confessional tone leak onto your resume!

Why? Because your resume is not a confessional—you don't have to tell all. Don't waste space or distract the reader by putting anything on your resume that doesn't support your job objective or cast you in the best light possible with regard to experience, ability, age, and personality. (In Part 2, I talk about how to work with these issues specifically.)

Be selective. Pick through all your information and choose only what's relevant to your job objective. The resumes later in this chapter show you how to apply this commandment.

Shooting Yourself in the Foot

Teresa Smith was having trouble finding a position as a marketing director. She needed a job desperately and decided to go for a position as an administrative assistant. If she listed her MBA degree under her Education heading, she knew she would look overqualified for a clerical job. Take a look at her resume. Notice that she decided not to include her degree in order to improve her chances of getting an interview.

If you're applying for a job for which you might appear overqualified, consider leaving the heavyweight qualifications off of your resume. Remember, your resume is not a confessional; you aren't obligated to disclose all.

Get Your Priorities Straight

Trudy Caldwell had been a secretary and receptionist for a number of years and wanted to move into the field of human resources. In preparing for her career change, she had gone back to college and earned a degree in human resources while continuing her occupation as a secretary.

Notice how Trudy prioritized information on her resume to make the most marketable items pop out at the reader. Because her degree was more marketable than her work history, she decided to show it off by positioning her Education section near the top of her resume. This organization helps the reader of this resume quickly see that she's a new graduate in human resources who worked her way through school. Trudy then de-emphasized her former job titles by placing Work History at the bottom of the page and listing the job titles after the company names.

When a busy manager receives your resume, she'll skim it very quickly to see whether she's interested in reading it word for word. For that reason, it's vital that you place your material according to how relevant it is to your job objective. Prioritizing correctly will make your resume declare, "I'm the one you're looking for!" (You'll read more about this concept in Part 2.)

Job Hunt Hint

Don't be afraid to leave things off your resume if you're worried those items might make you look like the wrong candidate for the job. It's acceptable to delete information that isn't relevant to your job objective, as long as you don't create gaps in your work history.

By prioritizing the sections of your resume, you can highlight aspects that are most relevant to your job objective. For instance, you might wish to move your volunteer experience near the top of your resume if it's particularly meaningful to the job you're applying for.

> **Bonus Check**
>
> If your resume generates job interviews for work you're not interested in, something is wrong with your resume! Before sending your resume to another employer, revise it according to the following points to ensure that it markets you for the type of work you want to pursue.
>
> - Use a resume format that highlights the appropriate skills and experience.
> - Don't mention responsibilities you don't want to hold on your next job.

Drop Irrelevant Info

For the past two years, Christopher Bond spent most of his time managing a family crisis, a situation he decided was not appropriate to put on his resume. During that time span, he did some freelance catalog production for a former colleague.

Notice how Christopher constructed the Work History section on his resume without mentioning his personal situation, even though it consumed about 80 percent of his time and energy.

Like Christopher, you may have a situation in your work history that you don't want to mention on your resume. As long as you don't create a void in your work history, it's perfectly fine not to bring up the sticky matter on your resume. To find creative ways to deal with tricky issues in your work history, turn to Chapter 7.

Understate Too Much Experience

When applying for a specific position, use the job posting as a checklist for what should appear on your resume. Without copying the ad's exact wording, try to match each of the qualifications the employer is seeking in his candidate.

Sara Cartwright had 15 years of experience as an auditor and accountant. Because jobs were scarce in her field, she was compelled to take a lower position than she would have liked. In creating her resume, she thought that if she put "15 years as an accounting professional" in her Summary of Qualifications section, she might seem too high-powered because the job announcement asked for 5 to 7 years of experience.

As you can see from her resume, Sara decided to write "More than seven years as an accounting professional." Sara's revised statement is true (because 15 years is certainly more than 7 years) and makes her look more suitable for the job she's seeking.

You may choose to generalize your qualifications on your resume to downplay them. This is perfectly acceptable as long as your statements are honest.

The second commandment is going to come in handy in Part 2 when you figure out the following:

- How far back to go in your work history
- What to say about gaps in your employment
- Whether to present your volunteer work
- How to list sensitive issues

Your resume should serve as a teaser. It should contain statements that say enough to spark the manager's interest without giving away all the details, especially when those details are about a sensitive issue that would be better addressed in the job interview, if at all.

Until you get to Part 2, let this commandment give you peace of mind, knowing that you don't have to write a complete autobiography.

Thou Shalt Not Write Job Descriptions

If you were an employer, what three questions would you ask a job candidate? You would probably ask …

- Do you have any experience?
- Are you good at what you do?
- Do you like this kind of work?

Don't be shy—answer "Yes" to all of these questions by writing about achievements instead of job duties on your resume. Achievement statements are the most powerful way to say "I'm good at what I do!"

Make sure your achievements are stated appropriately for the type of work you're interested in. For example, a salesperson's achievement statements will probably be much more dramatic (for example: Exceeded sales quotas by 300 percent) than the ones that appear on an accountant or technician's resume (for example: Used spreadsheet applications to analyze reports for upper management).

Examine the two resumes for Diane Short. The first is a job-description resume (blah!); the second is an achievement-oriented resume (yes!). See how much more enticing the second one is? Diane's achievement statements provide the following information:

- She has particular experiences.
- She's good at what she does.
- She believes in and likes her work.

She's given the employer three good reasons to call her for an interview.

I expand on this commandment in Part 2 when you write your achievement statements. At this point, I want you to understand the concept of using your resume to brag a little (or a lot) about your successes.

Thou Shalt Not Write About Stuff You Don't Want to Do

Writing your resume is like writing your next job description, because everything you put in your resume suggests what you're eager to do in your new job. Never write about duties you don't want to do again, no matter how good you are at them! *Nondisclosure* on your resume could be the ticket to landing a job you really love.

Terms of Employment

Nondisclosure (not mentioning something) is not the same as lying (telling something that isn't true). Nondisclosure is acceptable on a resume. Lying is not!

For example, when George was applying for a database programming position at a high-tech firm, he specifically did not want to supervise any staff. Even though in his previous job he had been in charge of a department and had been commended for his ability to build team spirit under adverse conditions, he was determined not to acquire that kind of responsibility in his next job. In his resume, he spoke about his many programming projects, but never once mentioned that he had managed anyone. Consequently, he attracted a programming job he loves with no supervisory responsibilities.

I remind you about this commandment as you go through the steps in Part 2. For now, just keep in mind that you are in the seat of power: you get to create your future by choosing what to put in and what to leave out of your resume!

Thou Shalt Say Less Rather Than More

Ah, the oxymoron that works so well in marketing: Less is more. Let's consider why it has withstood the test of time.

When it comes to things we all value, time sits near the top of the list, along with wealth and health. We say things such as, "Time is money" and "It's not worth my time." Because time is at a premium in today's hectic world, it stands to reason that a promotional piece that takes less time to read is more likely to succeed than a lengthy one. Therefore, less text is more effective at grabbing the reader's attention.

Following the "less is more" theory has another advantage. By distilling all of your skills and experience into a minimum of words on one or two sheets of paper, you automatically put down only the very best stuff. So less is more in the sense that even though you provide less information, it's all high-quality information, which makes the resume more impressive.

The Eight-Second Test

In today's job market, your resume has only about eight seconds to catch an employer's attention. In eight seconds, an employer scans your resume and decides whether she will invest more time to consider you as a job candidate. The secret to passing the eight-second test is to make your resume look inviting and quick to read. That's why I recommend having a one-page resume if possible. Having a one-pager says, "I'm organized, and I'm not a motor-mouth."

Goody Two-Pages

For those who have a beefy career history or lengthy list of must-read accomplishments, one page may not be enough. If you're one of those people, go for it—just don't exceed two pages unless you're sure the reader is expecting more. For instance, if you're applying for an academic or scientific position, you'd probably have a seven- or eight-pager called a curriculum vitae (which I discuss in Chapter 13).

If your resume is just a little more than a page, do your best to get it down to one page by using your editing and computer graphics skills. Then ask yourself, "Does it look easy to read?" If the print is too small or dense, you're better off with a two-page resume that's easy to read.

Thou Shalt Not Write in Paragraphs

Many resumes have long paragraphs filled with juicy information. The problem is that a busy manager is unlikely to read a resume made up of long paragraphs. A paragraph demands too much time to read.

Do the reader (and yourself) a favor by using bullet points to break your material into bite-sized pieces. A bullet at the beginning of a statement effectively says, "Here's an independent thought that's quick and easy to read," whereas a paragraph implies that one has to read the whole thing to get the full meaning.

For the best effect, start each achievement statement on a new line so that all the bullet points line up on the left, like the following:

- Made classroom presentations to students K–8, demonstrating the importance of art to man's physical and mental survival.
- Tutored high school students of Project Read, integrating reading and writing to offer new perspectives and respect for their own life stories.
- Conducted cultural field trips to sites including businesses, performing arts centers, and museums.

In case you're not convinced that bullet statements are a good idea, take a look at the two versions of Marty Ramirez's resume. You'll see the same resume in two graphic layouts: the first uses paragraphs; the second uses bullet points to break up the blocks of print. Which do you think looks quicker to read?

Thou Shalt Not Lie

I'm starting to sound like your mother, aren't I? I have to say it anyway: Never tell a lie on your resume.

If you're wondering what kinds of lies I'm talking about, here are some that frequently appear on resumes and are apt to catch an employer's attention:

- Stating experience at a particular place of employment where you never worked
- Misrepresenting the level of responsibility you held (for example, listing "Art Director" when you were really a graphic designer)
- Listing a school that you didn't attend
- Claiming to have a degree that you didn't obtain
- Taking credit for someone else's achievement
- Overstating skill levels in a technical field

Lying on your resume can cause more damage to your career than you may realize. Here are two good reasons to create a resume that contains only the truth:

- A lie on your resume can undermine your self-confidence during a job interview. If you're anything like me, just knowing that the interviewer might ask a question about your fib will make you nervous. To make matters worse, noticeable anxiety will most likely make a bad impression on your potential employer.
- After you're hired, a falsehood on your resume can be grounds for termination. If your resume is examined as part of your promotion review, you could lose your job if someone discovers a lie.
- A lie on your resume may indicate that you don't believe you're qualified for the job. Maybe you need to rethink your job objective or perhaps you need counseling to build your self-esteem.

As you can see, it's in your short- and long-term interest not to lie on your resume.

The Least You Need to Know

- Write about your future on your resume, not about your past.
- You don't have to tell everything in your resume. Stick to what's relevant and marketable.
- Use your resume to talk about your achievements, not monotonous job descriptions.
- Don't write about anything that you don't want to do again.
- Grab the reader's attention by being concise and using bullet point statements.
- Be creative but honest in your resume.

Teresa Smith
123 Serendipity Lane
Pierre, SD 12345
(123) 555-1234
teresasmith@bamboo.com

JOB OBJECTIVE

Administrative Assistant

HIGHLIGHTS OF QUALIFICATIONS

- Seven years combined administrative and research experience.
- Adept at handling sensitive business issues with discretion and professionalism.
- Cited as one of the top administrative assistants at Kramer Associates, Inc.

PROFESSIONAL EXPERIENCE

2001-pres. Kramer Associates, Inc., Pierre, SD
ADMINISTRATIVE ASSISTANT

- Charged with organizing and generating correspondence for major clients involved in confidential government activities.
- Re-designed the office computer system, enabling 125% more work to be processed.
- Commended for creating weekly "Casual Day," which brought a friendlier and more cooperative atmosphere to the workplace.
- Prepared legal and business documents using word processing and spreadsheet applications.

1999-2001 **University of South Dakota,** Pierre, SD
RESEARCH ASSISTANT

- Conducted bibliographic research that contributed to paper delivered at the National Psychology Symposium in Washington, D.C.
- Word-processed voluminous notes and provided accurate transcriptions of university and professional lectures.
- Translated German scientific text and compiled readers for undergraduate and graduate classes.

EDUCATION

B.A., Business Administration & German
University of South Dakota, Pierre, SD, 1999

Trudy Caldwell
123 Fremont Avenue • San Francisco, CA 12345
(123) 555-1234 • tcaldwell@bamboo.com

Human Resources Professional

SUMMARY OF QUALIFICATIONS

- More than five years of experience in business office work with recent assignments in personnel administration.
- Competent project manager with an eye for added results.
- Eager to pursue a career in human resources.

EDUCATION

M.S., Human Resources, University of California, San Francisco, CA, 2004

RELEVANT ACCOMPLISHMENTS

PERSONNEL ADMINISTRATION

- Processed a minimum of 100 applications per week, using a database to file and sort data accessed by 12 managers. (Barstow & Bigelow, Inc.)
- Conducted orientations for new hires: explained company policies and gave employee tours of company. (Goodman Lumber)
- Coordinated payroll data by compiling information from time card machine and tallying employee vacation calendars. (Barstow & Bigelow, Inc.)

PROJECT MANAGEMENT

- Redesigned the mail system to expedite sorting and delivery. (Williams Sonoma Co.)
- Managed a 4,000-piece direct mail effort that met seasonal marketing deadlines despite heavy in-house workloads. (Barstow & Bigelow, Inc.)
- Initiated a company-wide recycling program that resulted in excellent publicity for the firm. (Goodman Lumber)

WORK HISTORY

2003-present	Executive Assistant, Barstow & Bigelow, Inc., San Francisco, CA
2000-2003	Administrative Assistant, Williams Sonoma Co., San Francisco, CA
1994-2000	Receptionist, Goodman Lumber, Daly City, CA

Christopher Bond

123 Piedmont Avenue
Atlanta, GA 12345
123-555-1234
chrisbond@bamboo.com

Catalog Production Coordinator

SUMMARY OF QUALIFICATIONS

- Seven years as a print production professional, working in corporate and independent settings.
- Degree in journalism with additional training at daily news publication.
- Noted for accelerating production through strong managerial skills.

PROFESSIONAL EXPERIENCE

2005-pres. **Thomas Govington** (independent artist), Atlanta, GA
BROCHURE PRODUCTION SPECIALIST

- Designed and coordinated production of a four-color brochure that portrayed the artist's talent in three media: paint on canvas, ceramics, and bronze.

2000-05 **Johnson Paper, Incorporated,** Atlanta, GA
CATALOG PRODUCTION COORDINATOR

- Managed full production of a 400-page catalog distributed to more than 1,000 retailers and 80 distributors.
- Coordinated deadlines among six departments that sprinted from creative to shipping in less than two months per run.
- Supervised 35 artists and technicians; handled relations with more than 15 vendors.
- Represented the Production Department at management meetings.
- Instructed local college interns in print production techniques and systems.

1997-99 **Emory University Press,** Atlanta, GA
PRINT PRODUCTION INTERN

- Gained hands-on experience in every aspect of print production, working under the press's most senior printer.
- Frequently assisted in technically demanding assignments for major clients.

EDUCATION AND AFFILIATIONS

B.A., Journalism, Emory University, Atlanta, GA, 1991
Junior year abroad in Madrid for work-study program at prominent newspaper
American Printers Association
International Paper and Print Production Institute

SARA CARTWRIGHT, CPA
123 Turandot Street • Oakland, CA 12345
(123) 555-1234 • scartwright@bamboo.com

OBJECTIVE

A position in Audit Management

SUMMARY OF QUALIFICATIONS

- More than seven years as an accounting professional with particular strength in conducting audits.
- Skilled at gaining cooperation from internal and external professionals.
- Experienced consultant to executive management on sensitive financial issues.

PROFESSIONAL EXPERIENCE

2005-pres. Auditing Operations Manager, Anderson Electronics, San Leandro, CA

- Realized $40,000 in six months for the company by discovering several major unnoticed past due collections.
- Audited expense reports to verify compliance with company and governmental policies.
- Implemented CEO- and CFO-directed projects to restructure accounting procedures.

1999-05 Senior Auditor, Internal Accounting, Dartmouth Enterprises, Oakland, CA

- Conducted quarterly and annual audits for headquarters and 15 branch offices.
- Guided management through setup of accounting departments in four new business units located in separate Western states.
- Facilitated external audits that showed 100% compliance with professional standards.
- Authored analysis sections of SEC annual 10K and quarterly 10Q corporate reports.
- Designated Senior Auditor after four months with company as Internal Auditor.

1991-99 Accountant, Brokaw, Farnsworth & Associates, CPAs, San Francisco, CA

- Provided auditing services to corporate clients engaged in international manufacturing.
- Served as financial consultant to one of the nation's largest banking institutions.
- Prepared federal and state tax forms for a wide range of corporate structures.

EDUCATION AND CERTIFICATION

B.S., Accounting, California State University, Hayward, CA
CPA since 1998

(Job-Description Resume)

DIANE SHORT
Marketing Communications Director

123 Walnut Avenue, #2, Berkeley, CA 12345, d_short@bamboo.com (123) 555-1234

SUMMARY OF QUALIFICATIONS

- More than 10 years in marketing with recent experience as Director, Marketing Communications for the largest manufacturer in its classification.
- Creative thinker whose ideas have directly increased profitability.
- Manage multiple projects at once, with strict adherence to time and budget constraints.

PROFESSIONAL EXPERIENCE

2001-pres. Macy's, San Francisco
Director, Marketing Communications, 2005-pres.
Director, Public Relations & Licensing, 2002-2005
Marketing Consultant, 2001-2002

- Created sales collateral and ran creative aspects for advertising campaign.
- Developed and managed a national publicity program.
- Authored and designed press kits.
- Developed GWPs (gift with purchase).
- Collaborated with University of San Francisco Medical Center to design a promotion.
- Currently developing a merchandise strategy for a TV program.
- Analyzed competition, oversaw product development, approved prototypes, and managed business relations with licensees.
- Designed merchandise packaging and displays; negotiated with licensees to use visuals.

1997-2001 Delaney Advertising, Inc., New York City
Director, Marketing Communications Services

- Directed the New York office.
- Supervised staff and managed photographic production and budgets.

1993-1997 Gap, Inc., San Francisco
Media Coordinator

- Developed and implemented advertising campaigns. Managed creative development and execution. Monitored media budget.

EDUCATION

B.A., Communication Studies, with a minor in Business Administration
San Francisco State University, San Francisco, CA

Multimedia Program, University of California, San Francisco, currently enrolled

(Achievement-Oriented Resume)

DIANE SHORT
Marketing Communications Director
123 Walnut Avenue, #2, Berkeley, CA 12345, d_short@bamboo.com (123) 555-1234

SUMMARY OF QUALIFICATIONS

- More than 10 years in marketing with recent experience as Director, Marketing Communications for the largest manufacturer in its classification.
- Creative thinker whose ideas have directly increased profitability.
- Manage multiple projects at once, with strict adherence to time and budget constraints.

PROFESSIONAL EXPERIENCE

2001-pres. MACY'S, San Francisco **Director, Marketing Communications,** 2005-pres.
Director, Public Relations & Licensing, 2002-2005
Marketing Consultant, 2001-2002

- Created sales collateral (including videos) and ran the creative efforts for national advertising campaign that established Macy's as the manufacturer of quality products.
- Developed and managed a national publicity program that increased retail sales more than 5% and dramatically enhanced brand recognition.
- Authored and designed the first press kit that clearly defined the company's image and product range.
- Enhanced product value and increased sales by developing GWPs (gift with purchase).
- To position company as an advocate for women's health, collaborated with University of San Francisco Medical Center to design a promotion that shared proceeds.
- Currently developing a merchandise strategy for an hour-long cable television program to air Christmas of next year.
- Analyzed competition, oversaw product development, approved prototypes, and managed business relations with national and international licensees.
- Designed merchandise packaging and displays, and successfully negotiated with licensees and retailers to utilize these visuals to maintain consistent image.

1997-2001 DELANEY ADVERTISING, INC., New York City, **Director, Marketing Communications**

- Directed the New York office for this national full-service advertising company.
- Supervised staff and managed high-volume photographic production and budgets.

1993-1997 GAP, INC., San Francisco, **Media Coordinator**

- Developed and implemented advertising campaigns. Managed all phases of creative development and execution. Monitored media budget.

EDUCATION

B.A., Communication Studies, with a minor in Business Administration
San Francisco State University, San Francisco, CA

Multimedia Program, University of California, San Francisco, currently enrolled

(Resume with Paragraph Formatting)

Marty Ramirez
123 Antelope Avenue
Boston, MA 12345
(123) 555-1234
mramirez@bamboo.com

OBJECTIVE

Field Representative for Local 510

DEMONSTRATED EFFECTIVENESS

Effectively negotiated and arbitrated grievances and contracts. Served on three contract negotiating committees, each strengthening the union shop. Co-developed first steward training classes for Local 510. Enforced collective bargaining agreements, health and safety standards, and grievance procedures as Rotating Floor Steward or Permanent Shop Steward since 1987. Chaired strike committees in 2000 and 2003, developing picketing plans, choosing picket captains, and informing membership of legal behavior on the picket line. Co-developed and led Local 510 affirmative action workshops, using bilingual and bicultural skills to stress commonalities among people. Conducted training and strategy sessions for U.N.H. labor and academic professionals, resulting in Partnership Programs.

WORK HISTORY

1984-pres. **Journeyman Installer**
SIGN, DISPLAY, AND ALLIED CRAFTS, LOCAL 510, I.B.P.A.T.

2001 **Primary Campaign Manager**
WILSON RILES, JR., MAYORAL CANDIDATE, BOSTON, MA

1998-01 **Teacher, World Cultures/Spanish/Bilingual**
OAKLAND UNIFIED SCHOOL DISTRICT

EDUCATION

B.A., Comparative Culture, University of New Hampshire, 1984
Graduate Studies, Latin American Culture, Harvard University

MEMBERSHIPS

West County Central Labor Council
Local 510 Political Action Committee
Boston Direct Action Committee
Former Member, A.P.R.I. & C.B.T.U.

(Resume with Bullet-Point Statements)

Marty Ramirez
123 Antelope Avenue, Boston, MA 12345
(123) 555-1234, mramirez@bamboo.com

OBJECTIVE

Field Representative for Local 510

DEMONSTRATED EFFECTIVENESS

- Effectively negotiated and arbitrated grievances and contracts.
  - Served on three contract negotiating committees, each strengthening the union shop.
  - Co-developed first steward training classes for Local 510.
  - Enforced collective bargaining agreements, health and safety standards, and grievance procedures as Rotating Floor Steward or Permanent Shop Steward since 1987.
- Chaired strike committees in 2000 and 2003, developing picketing plans, choosing picket captains, and informing membership of legal behavior on the picket line.
- Co-developed and led Local 510 affirmative action workshops, using bilingual and bicultural skills to stress commonalities among people.
- Conducted training and strategy sessions for U.N.H. labor and academic professionals, resulting in Partnership Programs.

WORK HISTORY

1984-pres. **Journeyman Installer**
Sign, Display, and Allied Crafts, Local 510, I.B.P.A.T.

2001 **Primary Campaign Manager**
Wilson Riles, Jr., mayoral candidate, Boston, MA

1998-01 **Teacher, World Cultures/Spanish/Bilingual**
Boston Unified School District

EDUCATION

B.A., Comparative Culture, University of New Hampshire, 1984
Graduate Studies, Latin American Culture, Harvard University

MEMBERSHIPS

West County Central Labor Council
Local 510 Political Action Committee
Boston Direct Action Committee
Former Member, A.P.R.I. & C.B.T.U.

Chapter 2

Chronologically Speaking

In This Chapter

- Why choose a chronological format?
- When a conservative approach is the way to go
- How a chronological resume highlights the strengths of a work history
- How to accelerate a vertical or horizontal career move by using a chronological resume

Have you ever heard the real-estate adage: "location, location, location"? In resume writing, the adage is "format, format, format." The format of your resume is so crucial that it can make or break your chances for a job interview. The right format will tell the reader right away that you're a top-notch candidate for the job.

The two basic resume formats are chronological and functional. This chapter covers the guidelines, templates, and samples for the chronological resume. Chapter 3 describes the ins and outs of the functional resume. In a very short time, you'll have made one of the most important decisions in the resume writing process: choosing the best format.

Highlighting Your History

The chronological resume is the most traditional resume format. It's been around for years and has done well for millions of job seekers.

The following template for the chronological resume outlines the content of a resume in this format. Notice that this format highlights a job seeker's dates of employment, places of employment, and job titles (the chronology of the person's work history) by using them as headings. Achievements are then listed under these headings.

(Chronological Resume Template)

Name
Street
City, State Zip
Phone, Fax, E-mail

JOB OBJECTIVE

The job you want next

SUMMARY OF QUALIFICATIONS

- How much experience you have in the field of your job objective, in a related field, or using the skills required for your new position.
- An overall career accomplishment that shows you'd be good at this job.
- What someone would say about you as a recommendation.

PROFESSIONAL EXPERIENCE

20xx-pres. **Company Name, City, State**
Job Title

- An accomplishment you are proud of that shows you're good at this profession.
- A problem you solved and the results.
- A time when you positively affected the organization, the bottom line, your boss, your co-workers, your clients.
- Awards, commendations, publications, etc., you achieved that relate to your job objective.

20xx-xx **Company Name, City, State**
Job Title

- A project you are proud of that supports your job objective.
- Another accomplishment that shows you're good at this line of work.
- Quantifiable results that point out your skill.

19xx-xx **Company Name, City, State**
Job Title

- An accomplishment you are proud of that shows you will be valued by your next employer.
- An occasion when someone "sat up and took notice" of your skill.

EDUCATION

Degree, Major (if relevant), 20xx (optional)
University, City, State

Many employers (especially those in conservative fields such as law and finance) like chronological resumes for the following reasons:

- They're used to reading chronological resumes and, therefore, feel comfortable with an applicant who uses this conventional approach.
- They can see a job seeker's work history in a flash because it's highlighted in the body of the resume.

If you are applying for a job in a conservative industry or company, use the chronological format. You should also use this format if you want to emphasize your work history for any of the following reasons:

- You want to make a horizontal career move within your current field.
- You'd like to make a vertical career move within your current field.
- Your most recent (or current) position is one you are proud of.
- You have no major gaps in your work history.

Keep in mind that the templates in this book are not boilerplates! The bullet point statements are ideas that I might suggest if I were with you as you create your resume. Because not all of these statements will apply to your situation, use only the ones that give you the opportunity to support your job objective. If these prodders aren't enough, check out the brainstorming exercises in Chapter 7.

Now let's look at some sample resumes (found at the end of this chapter) from real job seekers that demonstrate situations in which the chronological resume is the best choice.

The Horizontal Slide

Andrew Gregory had been in audit management for a number of years and wanted to remain in that line of work. His chronological resume clearly showed that he had a stable history as an audit professional with experience in management. Without reading the small text of the bullet point statements, the employer could see from the headings of his chronological resume that Andrew was a likely candidate for the job.

If you're making a horizontal career move and have no gaps in your work history, the chronological format is an excellent way to market yourself.

> CAUTION
> **Career Casualty**
> There is a mistaken impression among job seekers that the chronological format is old fashioned and should not be used. Don't fall for this faulty thinking! The chronological format is still the most widely accepted type of resume and should be used if its criteria fits your career goals.

Vertical Climb

In Stacy Vernon's resume, her job titles alone told the story of her gradual climb from administrative assistant to events coordinator/executive assistant. Her chronological format easily demonstrated that moving up the ladder one more rung to event planner was a logical step.

If you're seeking a vertical career move, promote yourself with a chronological resume. It's the surest way to highlight the thread of success that runs through your career.

A Strong Start

Although Roger First was a volunteer project coordinator in an educational setting for six years, his recent paid experience was the most impressive to a potential boss. Roger's chronological format highlighted his recent position by listing that job first in his work history. You can include volunteer experience in the body of a chronological resume if you entitle the section Relevant Experience instead of Employment Experience or Professional Experience.

> **Job Hunt Hint**
>
> Here's a way to emphasize that you have experience in the industry you're applying to: Put your company names in bold or all caps and place them before your job titles in your work history.

If your most recent positions are highly relevant to your job objective, the chronological resume is definitely the format for you. Also, if your recent position or positions are more impressive than the others in your work history, give them greater resume real estate by listing more bullet point statements under those job headings. The other job titles can follow with just a few or no statements under them.

Getting Labeled

One quick glance at Gina Schultz's chronological resume told a hiring manager that Gina had a strong foothold in retail business. Her work history headings screamed sales, and her bullet statements pointed to visual merchandising. Gina's chronological resume made the employer's decision to call her for an interview a no-brainer!

If, like Gina, the job titles in your work history reflect what you want to do in your next job, the chronological resume is a great way to get labeled as a qualified candidate. A quick scan of your job titles and related bullet points (which are highlighted in the chronological format) will reveal that you want to continue in the same line of work.

Background Check

Jonathan Turner's resume presented his strong background in executive management, leaving no question that he was qualified to take his expertise to a similar position in an Italian firm. Although the small print rang of wonderful achievements, it was the work history headings that immediately informed the employer that Jonathan was well worth considering for the job.

When your job titles support your job objective especially well, use the chronological resume. You may also want to highlight the titles by putting them in bold print.

Conservative Line

Because the railroad industry is rather conservative, Roger Smythe chose the chronological format for his resume. Although he had never held a management position (as he was requesting in his job objective statement), the subheadings under his Professional Experience section clearly reflect that he's an intelligent man with a love of the rail industry. The employer saw that Roger's seven-year career in the field was a suitable foundation for a promotion into management.

If you have experience in an industry and you want to make a big leap ahead within that industry, take advantage of the chronological resume. By accenting your industry experience through your work history, you can demonstrate that you're ready for a step up into the position you seek.

Get It Together

Now that you've seen several sample chronological resumes, can you picture your own resume in that format? Do you fit the guidelines mentioned earlier in this chapter? If so, you're ready to move on to Chapter 4, where you'll start to put your words into print. If you're uncertain as to whether the chronological resume is the best format for you, turn to the next chapter, where you can check out the functional resume.

The Least You Need to Know

- The chronological resume is the most traditional resume format.
- Use the chronological format if you are making either a vertical or horizontal career move.
- Because the chronological format highlights your work history, use it if your history is stable and your job titles are relevant to your job objective.
- Choose between the chronological and functional formats based on your situation, not on hearsay about what's trendy.

Andrew Gregory, C.P.A.

123 Trenton Place • Newark, NJ 12345 • (123) 555-1234 • agregory@bamboo.com

JOB OBJECTIVE: Position in Audit Management

SUMMARY OF QUALIFICATIONS

- More than five years as an internal and external auditor with a strong financial and operational background in industries including manufacturing.
- Confident professional who facilitates cooperation among parties.
- Knowledge of data processing and spreadsheet applications.
- Personal activity in futures and options trading.

PROFESSIONAL EXPERIENCE

2005-2006 **Senior Auditor**
HOME AND MORTGAGE, INC., Newark, NJ

- Saved company $4,000 - $12,000 a month by analyzing project needs and recommending improved utilization of contractual and full-time staff.
- Audited management and employee expense reports to verify compliance with company policies and procedures.
- Originally contracted to perform field operation audits that led to CEO- and CFO-directed projects.

2002-2005 **Manager, Internal Audits**
NORTH AMERICAN BUILDING SUPPLY, Morristown, NJ

- Attained functional level of audit manager, reporting to Senior Corporate Controller.
- Conducted extensive due diligence and auditing of more than 15 prospective company and customer contract acquisitions (up to $20 million).
- Made numerous productive recommendations to senior management, based on operational benefits and numerical findings.
- Coordinated participation of external auditors to complete timely audits according to professional standards.
- Co-wrote the management discussion and analysis sections of the SEC annual 10K and quarterly 10Q corporate reports.

1999-2002 **Senior Accountant**
SMITHERS & WONG (Formerly Smithers and Troutt), Florham Park, NJ

EDUCATION

B.S., Accounting, Magna Cum Laude, New Jersey State University, Morristown, NJ, 1998
Recipient of First New Jersey Accounting Scholarship Award

Stacy E. Vernon

123 Stonestown Road • Fremont, LA 12345 • (123) 555-1234 • eventshappen@bamboo.com

JOB OBJECTIVE: Position in Event Planning

SUMMARY OF QUALIFICATIONS

- Over 12 years' experience planning business and social events, including conferences, celebrations, parties, dinners, and luncheons.
- Skilled at leading and working within a team to produce events that promote the organization's image, mission, and objective.

PROFESSIONAL EXPERIENCE

2004-present **Events Coordinator/Executive Assistant to General Manager**
TRAFALGAR & SONS, INC., Fremont, LA

- Coordinated the company's 20th Anniversary Celebration at the Fremont Museum of Modern Art for more than 200 top investors. This black-tie event included dinner and dancing to Martin Andrews' Orchestra.
- Planned and produced an executive business retreat at a California winery.
- Orchestrated a 150-person private party in Manhattan. Arranged invitations, entertainment, accommodations, and transportation.
- Set up numerous live national and international videoconferences requiring special equipment, rooms, meals, and information packets.

2001-2004 **Administrative Assistant to President and to Vice President, Consumer Products**
WESTINGHOUSE, INC., South Fremont, LA

- Served on the UNICEF Campaign event planning committee that promoted and produced the 1,800-person kickoff rally and closing party with celebrity speakers, entertainment, food, and contests.
- Organized 9 Board and 45 officers' luncheons per year; planned menus and floor plans.
- Served as liaison to Board members, stockholders, staff, and general public on behalf of President and Vice President.

1994-2001 **Administrative Assistant to CEO and to Executive Vice President**
THOMAS FOODS CORPORATION, West Bend, LA

- Planned annual Christmas parties at major West Bend hotels for 200 employees and guests. Collaborated with hotel caterers on all aspects.
- Commended for producing the company's first outdoor employee events on very limited budgets, which boosted morale during merger.

EDUCATION

B.S., Business Administration, Louisiana State University, New Orleans, LA
Independent Study: Cooking, Southern Cuisine School, New Orleans

Roger E. First

123 Franklin Street • Cleveland, OH 12345 • (123) 555-1234 • rfirst@bamboo.com

Educational Program Coordinator

SUMMARY OF QUALIFICATIONS

- More than seven years of experience coordinating projects in academic environments.
- Excellent at generating new ideas and improving upon existing systems to further the administration of an organization.
- Success at motivating staff through clear communication and outstanding organizational skills.

RELEVANT EXPERIENCE

2005-pres. **Children's Day School,** Cleveland, OH
Project Coordinator

- Currently creating a promotional multimedia presentation that reflects the high standard of this private preschool-elementary school with a socioeconomically diverse student body.
- Promoted school allegiance and parent participation by:
  - Actively networking among parents, faculty, and students.
  - Re-evaluating current goals, strategies, and financial management to support extracurricular activities.
- Chaired the Academic Endowment Fund and Annual Giving Fund Committees.

1999-05 **St. Mary's Elementary School,** Lakewood, OH
Volunteer Project Coordinator

- Played key role in restructuring volunteer activities. Collaborated with administration to prioritize need for volunteers, re-evaluate programs, and make improvements to optimize volunteer participation in light of today's family structure.
- Successfully initiated enhancements to academic programs by surveying needs and facilitating discussion between administration and parents.
- Started Creative Arts Projects which, for the first time, enabled students to gain recognition for their creativity while generating over 17% of annual funds raised.
- Directly supervised 10 parents and indirectly managed 40 volunteers, who organized educational, extracurricular, and fundraising activities.

1994-99 **Time-Warner, Inc., Educational Division,** New York, NY
Research Associate

- Conducted research of subject matter to be used for educational films distributed to high schools nationwide.
- Compiled photographs for *Now Is Our Time*, a hardback book to accompany films.

EDUCATION

B.A., Sociology & Urban Studies, 1996, Boston University, Boston, MA

Gina R. Schultz

123 Sacramento Street • St. Louis, MO 12345 • (123) 555-1234 • ginas@bamboo.com

JOB OBJECTIVE

Position in Visual Merchandising

SUMMARY OF QUALIFICATIONS

- Experienced in merchandising for two of the nation's most successful retailers, as a sales associate for over 10 years.
- "Your sense of design is so good, you should be doing my job." — Visual Merchandiser for Macy's nationwide.
- Knowledge of:

Fashion accessories	Sportswear
Housewares	Tabletop products
Gift items	Decorative pieces

RELEVANT PROFESSIONAL EXPERIENCE

2003-2006 MACY'S, St. Louis Sales Associate

- Executed special holiday window and floor displays, using plan-a-grams and personal creativity.
- Maintained displays and floor stock, frequently changing presentations to accommodate inventory and seasonal trends.
- Demonstrated product enthusiasm that generated extremely high sales and numerous customer commendations. Achieved three regional customer service awards.
- Monitored inventory and delivery systems to ensure timely in-store placement of products.

1994-2002 EMPORIUM, St. Louis Sales Associate

- Merchandised clothing and accessories, following schematics and block plans for a department that generated 35% of store's sales.
- Tracked sales trends and collaborated with department manager to determine effectiveness of POPs and displays.
- Provided excellent service to a wide range of customers. Won several "Employee of the Month" awards.
- Conducted classroom and on-the-job training for new employees.

EDUCATION

Merchandising & Design Program, Washington University, St. Louis, MO

JONATHAN S. TURNER

123 Terrano Street • Salvatore, 1234 • Milan, Italy • (01) 555-1234 • jonturner@bamboo.com

OBJECTIVE

Executive management position in Finance and Accounting for an Italian firm

SUMMARY OF QUALIFICATIONS

- More than 10 years as an accounting/audit professional with more than 5 years in management.
- Extensive experience in international accounting and finance.
- Fluent in Italian; conversant in Italian and U.S. accounting and reporting requirements.
- Successful at designing, implementing, and completing projects to the satisfaction of senior management in a goal-oriented and deadline-driven profession.

PROFESSIONAL EXPERIENCE

2002-06 **Controller,** FINANCIAL MANAGEMENT, INC., San Francisco, CA

A high-growth company, which in the last two years has expanded from U.S. $3 billion to over U.S. $9 billion in retail, closed-end, and institutional funds under management.

- Oversaw all accounting and reporting for five subsidiaries: an investment management company, a transfer agency, a broker dealer, an insurance company, and a holding company.
- Significantly increased efficiency of accounting and reporting by computerizing manual processes and instituting accounting controls.
- Achieved high integrity in financial reporting with a four-day deadline for submission of final consolidated reporting packages to the parent company.
- Maintained a perfect record of zero proposed audit adjustments through four annual audits. Served as liaison to external auditors.
- Trained and directly supervised five accounting professionals, and indirectly oversaw additional support staff of six.
- Designed and implemented accounting procedures for new products such as Contingent Deferred Sales Charges and Variable Annuity Funds.
- Supervised preparation of quarterly and annual regulatory reports, including:
  - Focus reports for the National Association of Securities Dealers and the Securities and Exchange Commission.
  - Investment Management Regulatory Organization reports for the regulatory authorities.
- Controlled and supervised the department's development of computer systems, as the general ledger systems administrator.

— Continued —

JONATHAN S. TURNER
Page 2

2000-01 **Director, Financial Markets Accounting,** EURO SECURITIES, LTD., Rome, Italy
One of the largest merchant banks in Italy, which began closing operations in 2000.

- Reviewed monthly accounts and reconciliations for Corporate, Property, and Leasing divisions and off-shore subsidiaries.
- Managed U.S. and Italian regulatory reporting to the U.S. Securities and Exchange Commission and the Reserve Bank of Italy.
- Prepared the annual financial statements and assisted in preparing tax returns for the Italian parent company, the main operating company, and eight subsidiaries.

1994-00 **Supervising Senior,** KPMG ITALY, LTD., Milan, Italy, 1998-00
Audit Manager, KPMG & ASSOCIATES, San Francisco, CA, 1994-98
A professional audit firm with locations worldwide.

- Promoted from Audit Assistant to Audit Manager in three years' time.
- Managed multi-audit engagements for publicly and privately owned companies, including financial services, oil and gas, real estate, and government agencies.
- Prepared financial statements, incorporating the requirements of U.S. Generally Accepted Accounting Principles and Italian Accounting Standards.
- Delivered presentations to audit staff as a trainer in the firm's national and local training programs. Topics included technical accounting, auditing, and management training.
- Interviewed and assessed potential new-hires. Conducted annual performance evaluations for professional staff.

EDUCATION AND AFFILIATIONS

American Institute of Certified Public Accountants, member since 1998
California State Board of Accountancy, member since 1998

University of California at Santa Cruz, Santa Cruz, California
Bachelor of Science in Economics & Finance, 1994

Italian Securities Institute, Milan, Italy
Money Market and Fixed Investment Securities and Financial Futures, 2001

Proficient in Lotus for Windows, Excel for Windows, and Sunsystems General Ledger Accounting packages

— Currently hold Permanent Resident Visa for Italy —

ROGER F. SMYTHE

123 Alvarez Street, #2 • San Diego, CA 12345 • (123) 555-1234 • rfsmythe@bamboo.com

JOB OBJECTIVE

A management position within the railroad industry
with a focus on network design or strategic planning

SUMMARY OF QUALIFICATIONS

- A thorough understanding of the railroad industry, with a strong interest in the analysis of trends and the integration of marketing and operations to meet future demands.
- A quick study: able to easily gain new skills, ask the right questions, and apply knowledge to work effectively, both independently and in teams.
- Skilled in building relationships and communicating clearly with individuals at all organizational levels.

PROFESSIONAL EXPERIENCE

2001-pres. **CENTRAL PACIFIC RAILROAD,** San Diego, CA *Maintainer*

- Performed installation and maintenance of centralized traffic control systems, within a safety-sensitive and deadline-driven environment.
- Planned and executed daily construction programs during foreman's absences, providing leadership to team members to ensure quality and timeliness.
- Designed, coordinated, and facilitated the department's regional commercial driver training program, resulting in logistical flexibility and improved productivity.

1999-01 **NEVADA RAILROAD,** Wells, NV *Trackworker*

- Performed quality control on production tie gang, serving as leadman on backwork crew and on spot maintenance projects.
- Quickly earned the respect of supervisors and crew members alike, based on versatility, technical expertise, an in-depth understanding of work processes, and a commitment to quality and safety.

1998-99 **UNIVERSITY OF ALASKA,** Anchorage, AK *Research Fellow*

- Specialized in the history of industrialization, with a focus on systems theory, research, and analysis of business, labor, and technology.

1996-98 **RAILROAD MUSEUM, INC.,** Jarbridge, NV *Conservator*

- Supervised track department: planned and implemented maintenance activities and construction projects; collaborated with departmental superintendents to create and administer budgets.

EDUCATION

B.A., American History, University of California, Santa Barbara, CA, 1998
Coursework included Economics, Business, and Civil Engineering studies.

Chapter 3

Get Functional

In This Chapter

- How resume writing has adapted to new job trends
- When to use a functional resume
- What magic is behind a skills-based resume
- How to make sore points in your history look healthy

First impressions are crucial and lasting whether you're introducing yourself to your new mother-in-law or your boss-to-be. I'll let you figure out how to win over your mother-in-law, and I'll stick to what I know best: helping you make a stunning impression with your potential employer. In this chapter, you'll discover how to rope in a new boss with a functional resume, before she reads even one word of the small print.

The Times Are a Changin'

Work trends have changed dramatically in the past 50 years. It used to be that someone got a job shortly after graduating and kept it for the rest of his life. If things went well, he might move up the ladder within the company, but he usually felt sentenced to the same boss for 20 years to life. Loyalty to the company equaled stability, something greatly valued by employers (and by mothers-in-law, too, for that matter). An applicant who had job-hopped—not to mention changed careers—was considered unstable and therefore a risk for a would-be employer.

But since the early 1980s, the rate of job and career change has increased to such a point that it's now typical for a professional to shift careers three or four times during his adult life and to move to a new job once every three years. In this new climate, job-hopping is now called diversity, and many employers consider diversity an asset as long as the job seeker's rate of change is in line with the average for the industry.

How did this employment trend affect resume writing? It brought about the need for a new format: the functional resume (also referred to as the skills resume). If you want to be defined by your skills instead of your work history, the functional format is an effective one to use. As an alternative to the chronological format, the functional format works wonders for adventurous professionals such as the following:

- Career changers
- Parents re-entering the workforce
- People who took time off to travel or pursue a personal project
- Heavy-duty volunteers
- Students fresh out of school
- Survivors of recent or not-so-recent bouts of unemployment
- Entrepreneurs making the transition back into the corporate world
- Folks who've had the same responsibilities for years and years at multiple job sites

Job Hunt Hint

To shorten a resume that has a lengthy work history filled with repetitious experiences, switch from a chronological to a functional format. The employer will appreciate your ability to organize material efficiently.

Do you fit into any of these categories? If so, read on to find out how you can present yourself in a functional resume that will float your potential employer's boat.

The functional format presents your accomplishments under skill headings (instead of under job title headings, as in the chronological format), giving you the freedom to prioritize your accomplishments by significance rather than by chronology.

Thus, the functional resume format enables you to show off your skills to a potential employer. By placing your achievement statements front and center, you put your best foot forward. This format enables you to define yourself by your skills instead of your work history.

As you can see from the following template, Work History is a very concise section at the bottom of the resume, and achievement statements are placed in the body of the resume according to skill headings.

In short, use the functional format if you meet one of the following criteria:

- You are changing careers.
- You are re-entering the job market.
- You need to emphasize skills or experience from an early part of your work history.
- Your volunteer experience is relevant and needs to be highlighted.
- Your most recent position is not impressive.
- You have one or more awkward gaps in your employment history.

Take a look at the resumes (found at the end of this chapter) from the following job seekers to see how the functional format worked with their experience. Maybe you'll find that you have similar reasons for using a functional resume.

The Career Changer's Dream

Thomas Horton wanted to change careers from law to nonprofit management, so he used the functional format for his resume. This format emphasized his transferable skills (management, development, and motivation) in the body of his resume so that the employer would see him as a manager with a legal background rather than a lawyer trying to get into management.

If you're a career changer with a work history that may lead a potential employer to pigeonhole you into your previous line of work, use the functional format. The functional resume allows you to define yourself according to your skills instead of your former job titles.

Bonus Check

More new graduates use functional resumes than chronological resumes. That's because functional resumes increase the perceived value of unpaid experiences by spotlighting them in the body of the resume.

Skills Up Front and Center

Beverly Jensen was an accomplished language instructor with years of experience teaching at the college level. The functional resume worked well for her because it presented the skills she had used in her many teaching positions in concise statements under skill headings. In a chronological format, she would have been forced to repeat these statements for each position she held.

If you've held many positions that carried similar responsibilities (for instance, as a teacher or therapist), and you need an efficient way of presenting your experience, the functional resume may be the way to go. By grouping statements under the functional resume's skill headings, you eliminate redundant statements in each job listing throughout your work history. The functional resume can also be a good choice if you feel embarrassed about your current or last position, because you can tuck that job title away in the Work History section at the bottom of the resume and emphasize the jobs you're proud of.

Re-Entry with Force

After being a full-time mom for three years, Chris Montoya felt she was ready to go back into the workforce. She had filled her three unemployed years with volunteer work (in addition to parenting) and wanted to continue in a nonprofit environment, this time for pay. Her functional resume shows how she presented her relevant achievements in the body of the resume and referred to her volunteerism and parenting in her Work History section.

Don't let anyone tell you that you didn't do anything for the last so-many years because you were a full-time parent. You worked hard and developed many useful skills. So use a functional resume that includes parenting in your Work History section to fill an employment gap with dignity. After all, parenting is a full-time job, even though you didn't draw a salary from it.

(Functional Resume Template)

Name
Street
City, State Zip
Phone, Fax, E-mail

JOB OBJECTIVE

The job you want next

SUMMARY OF QUALIFICATIONS

- How much experience you have in the field of your job objective, in a related field, or using the skills required for your new position.
- An overall career accomplishment that shows you'd be good at this job.
- What someone would say about you as a recommendation.

RELEVANT EXPERIENCE

MAJOR SKILL

- An accomplishment you are proud of that shows you have this skill.
- A problem you solved using this skill, and the results.
- A time when you used your skill to positively affect the organization, the bottom line, your boss, your clients.
- Awards, commendations, publications, etc., you achieved that relate to your job objective.

MAJOR SKILL

- A project you are proud of that supports your job objective.
- Another accomplishment that shows you're good at this line of work.
- Quantifiable results that point out your skill.
- An occasion when someone "sat up and took notice" of your skill.

WORK HISTORY

20xx-present	Job Title	COMPANY NAME and city
20xx-xx	Job Title	COMPANY NAME and city
20xx-xx	Job Title	COMPANY NAME and city
19xx-xx	Job Title	COMPANY NAME and city

EDUCATION

Degree, Major (if relevant), 20xx (optional)
University, City, State

Long, Long Ago

Donald Toni wanted to combine the sales skills he'd developed at the beginning of his career with the administrative skills he'd used in his recent set of jobs. By using a functional resume, he was able to highlight his early career achievements by placing them under the prominent Sales skill heading. Notice that his two skill headings (Administration and Sales) added up to his Job Objective (Sales Service Administrator). Pretty cool, huh?

If you have valuable experience that would get buried at the bottom of a chronological resume, create a functional resume so that you can prioritize that experience near the top of your skills sections.

Best Foot Forward

Rex Robinson's career in financial services was running full speed ahead until he landed his current job. After giving it a good try, he had to admit that it just wasn't working out because of some personal conflict with his co-workers. So in the winter of 2002, he decided to look for a position in a different financial institution.

His functional resume allowed him to list his current position in the Work History section without saying anything more about it. He then spotlighted his best jobs by writing achievement statements under relevant skill headings in the body of his resume. In this clever way, his resume made him look like a star performer without drawing attention to his less-desirable position.

If you're currently stuck in a job you hate and don't want to highlight it on your resume, don't use the chronological format. Instead, create a functional resume where you can quietly mention your current job title and company in the Work History, while highlighting achievements from other positions under skill headings in the body of the resume.

Into the Real World

Sean Rosen's functional resume is a great example of how a student can present his limited experience to an employer. By creating relevant skill headings, Sean announced what he could do as a graphic designer (his job objective). By stating "concurrent with education" in his Work History heading, he explained that he's an industrious fellow who worked his way through school. And the potential employer could pick up on this information before reading any of the small print!

If you're a student, don't worry that your resume is going to be a blank page—the functional format enables you to draw on your school activities, internships, volunteerism, and other unpaid experience.

Fill In the Gap

Frank Jacoby had a very complicated work history with lots of job-hopping and gaps in employment. To smooth things over, he used a functional format that concentrated on the skills he brought to the table rather than his work history. He then grouped his positions near the end of his page, placed the dates to the far right so they wouldn't be easily noticed, and filled in his gaps with short-term projects and schoolwork. In the end, his functional resume made him look appropriate for a position where short project assignments were common.

This clever technique for listing short-term employment could come in handy for you if you have a tricky work history like Frank's.

Decisions, Decisions!

At this point, you need to decide which resume format you're going to use. If you know which format is best for your situation, you're ready to charge ahead. If you're teetering on the fence between the chronological and functional resumes, try creating your resume in both formats. Then see which one you think works best for you. For variations on the chronological and functional resumes, try one of the hybrid formats mentioned in Part 3.

When you've made your choice, you're ready to follow the directions in Part 2 for creating the perfect resume, applying the six steps to the type of resume that you selected.

The Least You Need to Know

- A functional resume frames your experience according to skills rather than job titles.
- The functional format is more widely accepted than it used to be because job and career changes are more common.
- A functional resume allows you to prioritize your achievements according to impact rather than chronology.
- Use a functional resume if you are changing careers or re-entering the workforce after a time of unemployment.
- Consider choosing the functional resume if you are a new graduate and have little paid experience in the field of your objective.

THOMAS HORTON

123 Danville Road, Cleveland, OH 12345
(123) 555-1234 thomashorton@bamboo.com

OBJECTIVE

Executive Director of a nonprofit organization

HIGHLIGHTS

- Over five years' management experience emphasizing a collaborative yet decisive style.
- Adept at building productive relationships to further the organization's goals.
- Persuasive skills, both written and verbal.

PROFESSIONAL EXPERIENCE (at Caldwell, Stevenson & Horton)

MANAGEMENT

- Achieved a revenue growth from $600K to $1.5M per year within my area of management, while keeping overhead low.
- Planned and adhered to a budget of up to $750K.
- Supervised a staff of 15, involving training, work flow, quality control, conflict resolution, and review processes.
- Directed the acquisition, installation, and maintenance of a 40-workstation system.

DEVELOPMENT/MOTIVATION

- Built a large loyal client base through personal attention, quality service, and consistent follow through.
- Assisted clients in identifying their interests, and motivated them to act accordingly.
- Wrote persuasive letters and documents, frequently influencing decision makers.
- Involved personnel in goal sharing, resulting in dramatically increased productivity.

WORK HISTORY

2003-2006	Law Offices of Caldwell, Stevenson & Horton, Cleveland	Partner
2001-2003	Prudential Insurance Company, Cleveland	Claims Examiner

EDUCATION

J.D., Boalt College of Law, Berkeley, CA, 1999
B.A., Finance & Administration, Georgetown University, Washington, DC, 1993

AFFILIATIONS

Board of Directors, Cleveland Symphony
Advisory Council to the Cleveland AIDS Project

BEVERLY JENSEN
123 Pine Street San Francisco, CA 12345
(123) 555-1234 • bevjensen@bamboo.com

OBJECTIVE

English as a Second Language Instructor

HIGHLIGHTS OF QUALIFICATIONS

- LIFE California Community College Instructor Credential in Basic Education.
- TESL Certificate with coursework in reading, writing, listening, and speaking.
- Proficient in French, Spanish, and German.
- More than 10 years of experience as an ESL teacher at the community college level.

PROFESSIONAL AND RELATED EXPERIENCE

CLASSROOM TEACHING

- Taught English language skills (listening, speaking, reading, writing) at all levels to non-native speakers:
  - Community college and university students
  - French residents in France
- Approached classroom teaching as a facilitator of student learning, providing a wide range of learning activities in a warm, supportive environment.
- Integrated computer training (IBM and Macintosh) with English language instruction in the computer lab.
- Instructed adult students in basic education skills required for vocational training.
- Implemented an individual reading program for students, third grade through high school.

CURRICULA DEVELOPMENT AND COURSE EVALUATION

- Designed and implemented an ESP class in business English and marketing at Aspect ILS (International Language School).
  - Evaluated student needs through informal testing, discussion, and observation.
  - Formulated lessons to meet specific learning objectives.
- Developed three mini-courses for ESL students at Aspect ILS on ethnic art of San Francisco, and the culture of English language communication through music.
- Improved existing Basic Education Curricula at San Francisco State University.
- As member of Excelsior Reading Clinic instructional team, participated in on-going course evaluation and curricula development of reading program.

(Continued)

Beverly Jensen, Page 2

MULTI-CULTURAL / MULTI-ETHNIC COMMUNICATIONS

- As an ESL teacher:
  - Lived in France for three years, teaching adolescents, university students, and adults.
  - Taught an extremely diverse student population in the San Francisco area for more than 10 years.
- As a Peace Corps Volunteer in Ghana for two years:
  - Taught physical education classes in French.
  - Participated in cross-cultural studies with four African teachers and seven other volunteers.
- Worked as an au pair for one year in Germany.

WORK HISTORY

Teacher, ESL, 1993-present
City College of San Francisco, San Francisco, CA 1993-00, 2002-present
John F. Kennedy University, Orinda, CA 1999-01, 2004-present
Aspect International Language School, San Francisco, CA 2003-present
ACHNA-American Language Program, Paris & Nancy, France, 1996-99

Teacher, Basic Education, 1992
San Francisco Community College, San Francisco, CA

Reading Resource Teacher, 1992-05
Excelsior Reading Clinic, San Francisco, CA

EDUCATION

TESL Certificate, University of California, Berkeley, 1996
MA, Secondary Education, San Francisco State University, 1993
BA, French, University of California, Berkeley, 1988
Education Abroad Program, Madrid, Spain, Summer 1983

CREDENTIALS

Lifetime California Community College Instructor Credential: Basic Education
Lifetime California Teaching Credentials: Standard Secondary, Reading Specialist

PROFESSIONAL AFFILIATIONS

Teachers of English to Speakers of Other Languages (TESOL)
California Teachers of English to Speakers of Other Languages (CATESOL)
Northern California Council of Returned Peace Corps Volunteers (NCCRPCV)

Chris Montoya

123 Holk Street, Apt. 6 • Las Vegas, NV 12345 • (123) 555-1234 • chrismontoya@bamboo.com

JOB OBJECTIVE: Position in Development

SUMMARY OF QUALIFICATIONS

- More than four years' experience developing strategies and proposals for generating revenue.
- Comfortable initiating and building rapport with affluent individuals.
- Excellent research and writing capabilities. Articulate ideas clearly and concisely.

RELEVANT EXPERIENCE

DEVELOPMENT

- As liaison to individual donors, cultivated ongoing relationships and encouraged donor involvement in fundraising activities. (Environmental Resource Center)
- Collaborated in grant proposal formulation by compiling and summarizing supporting data. (Environmental Resource Center)
- As campaign fundraiser, produced promotional events at celebrity homes that raised funds and generated public support. (Nevada gubernatorial campaign)

COMMUNICATION

- Used listening and verbal skills to resolve countless technical, political, and interpersonal problems among individuals from diverse backgrounds. (Seacoast Investments, Inc.)
- Persuaded decision makers within the government and business sectors through proposals, reports, and correspondence. (Seacoast Investments, Inc.)
- Increased revenue more than 10% by drafting mutually beneficial contracts that frequently led to renewals. (Seacoast Investments, Inc.)
- Handled media relations, providing an accurate and concise portrayal of the organization's positions on current issues. (Environmental Resource Center)

WORK HISTORY

2004-present Las Vegas Symphony, Las Vegas, NV
Volunteer, Assistant to Development Database Manager

2003-2005 Full-time Parent

2000-2003 Seacoast Investments, Inc., Las Vegas, NV
Portfolio Manager

1998-2000 Environmental Resource Center, Las Vegas, NV
Regional Development Associate

PROFESSIONAL DEVELOPMENT AND EDUCATION

Center for the Support of Nonprofit Organizations, Las Vegas, NV
Successful Fundraising Strategies
Writing Successful Grant Proposals

B.A., cum laude, English Literature, University of Pennsylvania, Philadelphia, PA, 1997

Donald H. Toni

123 Bernardino Avenue • Seattle, WA 12345 • (123) 555-1234 • dhtoni@bamboo.com

OBJECTIVE: Sales Service Administrator

SUMMARY OF QUALIFICATIONS

- More than 12 years of administrative experience at the executive level.
- Keen understanding of business concepts in working with budgets and financial presentations.
- Able to manage a vast array of responsibilities including corporate meeting planning.
- Communicate clearly and persuasively; effective in contract negotiations.

PROFESSIONAL ACCOMPLISHMENTS

Administration

- Coordinated events for Arundel Corporation with up to $50K budgets. Negotiated contracts for catering, equipment, entertainment, and accommodations.
- Arranged Arundel's luncheon for more than 200 journalists and politicians to introduce Seattle stadium plan. Produced six-page accompanying booklet.
- Managed KQDD's annual awards program, determining awards and selection process.
- Improved speed and accuracy of president's sales reports, budget development and reconciliation, and expense tracking by computerizing Wide Road Sporting's accounting.
- Supervised work of eight administrative and customer service staff at Clydesdale Travel.

Sales

- As sales agent, successfully persuaded airline representatives to clear space on overbooked flights and make special arrangements for clients.
- Managed Arundel's sales forecasting and development of sales-support collateral.
- Handled customer relations and business correspondence for KQDD's General Manager.

WORK HISTORY

2002-pres. **Arundel Corporation,** Seattle, WA, *Assistant to the President & CEO*

2000-02 **Wide Road Sporting Goods,** Seattle, WA, *Executive Office Assistant*

1999-00 **Hyatt Regency, American Airlines,** Seattle, WA, *Contractual Sales Administrator*

1995-98 **KQDD-TV,** Seattle, WA, *Assistant to the General Manager*

1993-95 **Clydesdale Travel,** Seattle, WA, *Sales Agent*

EDUCATION

B.S., Business Administration, Duke University, Durham, NC, 1992

REX T. ROBINSON

123 Vermont Street • Casper, WY 12345 • (123) 555-1234 • rexrobinson@bamboo.com

OBJECTIVE: A Senior Management position in a credit union with responsibilities in branch administration and lending

HIGHLIGHTS OF QUALIFICATIONS

- 15 years' experience in financial environments, including mortgage and consumer lending.
- Successfully turned around two credit union operations and three bank branches.
- Continuously achieved designated profitability and market share growth goals.
- "A strong community leader and team member" — Former Mayor of Casper.

PROFESSIONAL ACHIEVEMENTS

MANAGEMENT

- Managed Maplewood Savings' new branch in Casper, turning a deficit of $93,000 to a profit of $450,000 and increasing loan base by $8.3M and deposits by $4.6M.
- Administered all aspects of daily operations at Union Credit.
- Projected Maplewood's budgets for staffing, loan demands, and deposit growth.
- Developed a reporting system to keep Union's senior management abreast of achievements.
- Motivated staff at each institution to extend their best effort in meeting customers' expectations.

LENDING

- Managed loan portfolios of up to $55M at First Interstate.
- Hired, trained, and supervised staff of up to 25 in credit analysis, presentations, lending regulations, and product development and marketing at Maplewood Savings.
- Utilized lending expertise in real estate (secondary market sales/servicing), consumer lending, and VISA credit and debit cards to achieve Union's profitability and market share growth.

WORK HISTORY

2005-pres.	**Senior Branch Manager**	Maritime Credit Union, Casper, WY
2000-05	**Vice President/Manager**	Maplewood Savings, Casper, WY
1996-00	**Senior Development Lender**	Union Credit, Casper, WY
1995-96	**Business Development Lender**	First Interstate Bank, Orinda, CA
1993-95	**Commercial Loan Officer**	Bank of America, Oakland, CA
1991-93	**Commercial Loan Officer**	Wells Fargo Bank, Lafayette, CA

SPECIALIZED TRAINING AND EDUCATION

Certificates:	Maplewood Savings: Management Training Program, Consumer Lending
AIB Training:	Beginning & Advanced Financial Statement Analysis, Tax Return Analysis
Seminars:	Negotiating Skills, Communication, Bank Management, Quality Control
B.A./A.B.	University of California, Los Angeles, CA, 1991

Sean M. Rosen

123 Fillmore Street • San Francisco, CA 12345 • (123) 555-1234 • smrosen@bamboo.com

Objective

Graphic Designer

Summary

- Experienced with design concepts for packaging, advertising, and corporate communications.
- Photographer with skills in evaluating prints for reproduction.
- Familiar with print preparation and production.
- Understanding of video shooting and editing for television.
- Experienced in: Photoshop, FreeHand, Illustrator, Quark Xpress, PageMaker, FileMaker Pro, Persuasion, MS Word

Experience

GRAPHIC DESIGN

- Created consumer packaging using PMS and four-color processing; prepared designs for photo shoots.
- Produced ad campaign strategies for a variety of products and services.
  - Designed thumbnails, roughs, and final comps for print advertising.
  - Wrote copy for television and print media.
- Communicated corporate identity through design of logo and collateral.
- Created mechanicals; proofed blue lines and color keys.
- Used a wide range of typography to appeal to specific audiences.

PHOTOGRAPHY

- Photographed fashion and food compositions in studio settings.
- Developed portfolio of color landscape prints from across the U.S.
- Exhibited photos in two Bay Area locations.
- Won award in black-and-white community photo contest.
- Black and white darkroom and other technical experience.

Relevant Work History (Concurrent with Education)

2003-pres. **Freelance Computer Graphic Designer/Writer**
San Francisco, CA

2001-03 **Marketing & Graphics Assistant**
Smith & Co., San Francisco, CA

Education

B.F.A., Graphic Design & Marketing, anticipated spring 2007
San Francisco Art Institute, San Francisco, CA

Marketing Program, summer 2003
Emory University, Atlanta, GA

— Portfolio Available —

Frank Jacoby

123 Alamo Avenue • Salt Lake City, UT 12345 • (123) 555-1234 • fjacoby@bamboo.com

JOB OBJECTIVE: A position in Video Production with focus on Editing, Research, and Writing

SUMMARY OF QUALIFICATIONS

- More than 15 years as an editor in documentary film and television, including 4 years with CBS's *60 Minutes.*
- Ability to create interesting visuals to demonstrate concepts.
- Experienced researcher and interviewer for production projects.
- Continuing professional development in video and multimedia technology.

PROFESSIONAL EXPERIENCE

EDITING

- As editor for *60 Minutes*, worked with producers and writers to meet deadlines for weekly shows. Emmy Award-winning segments: "Wall Street" and "Farewell to China."
- Edited PBS documentaries on controversial topics such as the accident at Love Canal and the arms race.
- Completed editing projects for corporate clients including Kellogg's, Xerox, and Mazda.

RESEARCH AND WRITING

- For several documentary assignments, located archival footage, conducted historical research, interviewed subjects, and wrote evaluations.
- As coordinating editor for the "*60 Minutes* Retrospective," an hour-long special, retrieved 35 to 50 hours of footage and coordinated distribution to editing teams.
- Performed library research, compiled relevant information, and wrote summaries as a paralegal in a corporate law firm.

WORK HISTORY

Paralegal	Parsons, Fitch, Jones & Birmingham, Salt Lake City, 2001-present
Student	Film Arts Foundation, Salt Lake City, 1999-2001
Editor	Cable TV-27, *Consumer Reports Documentary*, New York City, 1998-1999
Editor	CBS, *60 Minutes*, New York City, 1994-1998
Asst. Editor	*Bill Moyers' Journal*, New York City, 1992-1994
Sound Editor	ABC, *20/20*, New York City, 1990-1992
Editor	German Television, Mediafilm, New York City, 1989-1990
Asst. Editor	WGBH Documentary, Boston, 1988-1989

EDUCATION

B.F.A., New York University, Institute of Film and Television, New York City

Continuing Professional Development:
Non-Linear Editing/AVID, Video Coalition, Salt Lake City
Video Editing and Interactive Multimedia, Film Arts Foundation, Salt Lake City

—Resume reel available—

Part 2

Six Steps to a Perfect Resume

Picture Christopher Columbus standing at the bow of his ship looking out at the horizon, about to embark upon his famous voyage of 1492. Not knowing how vast the Atlantic Ocean was or exactly what he was getting into, he probably had a major anxiety attack, which is a normal response to a seemingly impossible task. To keep his sanity, he must have taken this monumental trip one knot at a time until he finally spotted land some 34 days after setting sail.

Like Columbus, you're probably feeling a little overwhelmed as you set out to put your life on paper. Most job seekers feel this way. To keep your stress level down and help you reach your destination (getting a perfect job) as quickly as possible, I've divided the process into manageable pieces, which I talk about in this part of the book.

Turn the page and read about the first of six steps for writing your resume. Set aside about three hours (that's an average length of time to write a resume if all goes smoothly). Follow each step, and, like Columbus, you'll reach land. If you get stuck on one step, don't worry about it—just go on to the next step and come back to the hard one later.

Chapter 4

Step One: Name That Resume

In This Chapter

- Designing a heading that makes your name stand out
- How to state your name if it's nongender-specific
- Including a degree or credential immediately after your name
- Listing a fax number and website address

When you introduce yourself at a social, business, or networking event, your name is frequently a springboard for conversation. It's the thing you most want people to remember, because it's what they'll use to find you again. For that reason, clever folks say their name clearly and, if possible, make it stand out. (I often say "Susan Ireland, like the country.")

The same principle applies to your resume: You want your name to stand out. Whether you're writing a chronological or functional resume, the guidelines in this chapter for creating the Heading section apply.

Putting Things in Place

The Heading section of a resume appears at the top of the page, as highlighted in the following template. The heading includes your name and contact information.

You've been putting your name at the tops of papers since you learned how to write in first grade. It's so automatic you probably just plop it there without thinking. Before you do that on your resume, read these tips on how to make your name and other contact information stand out.

- Your name and contact information should appear at the top of your resume, not at the bottom of the page. This information is traditionally placed at the top of the page, and that's where an employer will expect to find it.
- Place your name in the top middle or the upper-right corner of the page. Why? After your resume is read, it will probably go into a filing cabinet with the left-hand side of the paper placed against the spine of the folder.

Your name will be noticed easily if it's in the top middle or in the upper-right corner of the page.

- Consider incorporating a horizontal line or shaded bar into the design of your heading to set it apart from the rest of the resume. To get ideas, browse throughout the book, in the "Portfolio of Sample Resumes" at the back of this book, and at my website, www.susanireland.com. All of the resumes in these sources were created in MS Word, using techniques you can learn from the program's Help menu.

What's in a Name?

If you have a nongender-specific first name (such as Chris, Pat, or Robin), you can use some tricks to indicate whether you're male or female. But before you let your secret out, be sure that you want the employer to know. The following two scenarios may help you decide whether you want to keep your gender a mystery.

Giving a Clear Signal

In some cases, it's to the job seeker's advantage for the employer to know the applicant's sex. For instance, Robin Harris (a man) knew that even though sex discrimination is illegal in the job placement process, the company for whom he wanted to work gave its most productive sales territories to men. Therefore, he wanted the employer to know right off that he was a man, because that would put him ahead of all the women candidates in the stack of resumes.

> **Bonus Check**
>
> Contrary to what you might think, your resume is not a formal document—it's a marketing piece that introduces you. So refer to yourself the way you would like to be addressed. If your first name is Elizabeth, but you want to be called Beth, use Beth in your Heading section. Middle initials are optional.

Here are a few ways you can clarify your gender on paper:

- Use a gender-specific nickname instead of your given name (for example, Rob Harris instead of Robin Harris).
- Include a middle name if it's clearly male or female (for example, Robin Frank Harris).
- Start your name with Mr. or Ms. (for example, Mr. Robin Harris).

If you're considering this last option, think twice. This technique is seldom used and looks somewhat awkward. However, if you're applying within the United States and have an unusual or non-American name that probably won't be recognized as male or female no matter what you do to it, the Mr. or Ms. technique would work.

Keep 'Em Guessing

Now let's look at a situation where it might not be to the job hunter's advantage for his or her gender to be known. Terry Hoover (a woman) was after the same job that Robin (in the last scenario) wanted. In order to be considered for the job, she chose not to add anything to her name—she simply put Terry Hoover on her resume, knowing the employer would have to guess whether she was a man or a woman until Terry met the employer in person. At that point, she'd be at the interview and able to sell herself as a fully qualified candidate.

(Resume Heading)

Name
Street
City, State Zip
Phone, Fax, E-mail

JOB OBJECTIVE

The job you want next

SUMMARY OF QUALIFICATIONS

- How much experience you have in the field of your job objective, in a related field, or using the skills required for your new position.
- An overall career accomplishment that shows you'd be good at this job.
- What someone would say about you as a recommendation.

PROFESSIONAL EXPERIENCE

20xx-pres. **Company Name, City, State**
Job Title
- An accomplishment you are proud of that shows you're good at this profession.
- A problem you solved and the results.
- A time when you positively affected the organization, the bottom line, your boss, your co-workers, your clients.
- Awards, commendations, publications, etc., you achieved that relate to your job objective.

20xx-xx **Company Name, City, State**
Job Title
- A project you are proud of that supports your job objective.
- Another accomplishment that shows you're good at this line of work.
- Quantifiable results that point out your skill.

19xx-xx **Company Name, City, State**
Job Title
- An accomplishment you are proud of that shows you will be valued by your next employer.
- An occasion when someone "sat up and took notice" of your skill.

EDUCATION

Degree, Major (if relevant), 20xx (optional)
University, City, State

Showing Off Credentials

If you have a degree or credential that indicates your profession, you could put the initials of your degree or credential next to your name in the Heading section. For example, Francine Wilks was going for a position as a CPA in an accounting firm where her credential was extremely important to the job. She showed it off nicely by placing it in her heading.

Warren Samuels wanted the reader of his resume to immediately see that he's a physician. He got the message across quickly by placing his degree next to his name in the Heading section of his resume.

Job seekers respond differently to seeing their credential or degree letters next to their names. Some folks like the look of it; others aren't at all comfortable having them there. It's entirely up to you—do what feels appropriate for your field and personality.

Job Hunt Hint

Make the font size of the letters of your credentials one or two point sizes smaller if you place them immediately after your name. In this way, they maintain importance without graphically overpowering your name.

Home Sweet Home

Putting your street address in your heading is preferable to listing a PO Box number, because a home address conjures up a more stable image. If you have a specific reason not to give out your street address, however, it's acceptable to use a post office address.

Following are some examples of addresses in headings. Patricia Ferrari used her home address in her Heading section. Juanita Cuellar didn't feel comfortable giving out her street address, so she chose to use her PO Box number in her Heading. Both Headings are permissible, but Patricia's address made her look a little more stable than Juanita.

Francine Wilks, CPA

123 Linden Place • Tempe, AZ 12345 • (123) 555-1234 • fwilks@bamboo.com

Warren Samuels, M.D.

123 Franklin Avenue, #2, St. Paul, MN 12345 (123) 555-1234 w_samuels@bamboo.com

Patricia Ferrari

123 Rippling Rock Avenue
Memphis, TN 12345
(123) 555-1234
pferrari@bamboo.com

Juanita Cuellar
P.O. Box 123, Charlotte, NC 12345-1234
(123) 555-1234
jcuellar@bamboo.com

I've Got Your Number

Your phone number is critical in your resume heading because your first contact from an employer will probably be by phone. Depending on your situation, you may want to list one or two phone numbers—but don't go overboard by listing every contact number you have (home, office, cell, and pager). Give only the one or two needed to reach you or to leave a message.

By putting a phone number on your resume, you automatically give your potential employer permission to do the following:

- Call that number
- Leave a message about your job search
- Expect you to speak freely if you pick up the phone

Be sure you're okay with all three of these assumptions for each phone number in your heading. Following are a few cases in point.

Gretchin Hendley didn't want any job search phone calls at her place of work, so in her heading, she listed only her home number where she had an answering machine that she could check from work. Larry Picasso, on the other hand, was being laid off, and everyone in his department was aware that he was looking for a new job. Therefore, it made perfect sense for him to list his office phone number in his heading, because he could receive messages and speak freely about his job search during business hours.

If you list only one phone number in your heading (as Gretchin did in the previous example), it will be assumed that it's your home or personal line. If you give more than one phone number, you need to indicate the difference between them (as Larry did in the second example).

Career Casualty

Avoid listing your work e-mail address on your resume, because doing so would send your prospective employer the message that you use company resources for personal pursuits—in this case, your job hunt. Instead, fork out the dough for a personal e-mail account (if you don't already have one) and put that address in the Heading section.

Gretchin Hendley
123 Green Lane • Harristown, VA 12345 • (123) 555-1234 • ghendley@bamboo.com

Employers hardly ever fax a response to a job applicant, so putting a fax number on a resume is a waste of valuable space.

Larry Picasso
123 Fountine Blvd. • Denver, CO 12345
Office: (123) 555-1234 • Home: (123) 555-5678
lpicasso@bamboo.com

E-Mail Giveaway

Yahoo!, Hotmail, and other online services offer free e-mail accounts with local access around the world. If you don't already have a personal e-mail account, consider getting one of these freebies for your job search.

Listing your e-mail address (if you have one) in the Heading section is beneficial, because it can do two things:

- Expedite the employer's response
- Demonstrate that you're online savvy (a must when applying for most positions today)

Don't clutter up your heading with unnecessary stuff. When writing your e-mail address in your heading, there's no need to prefix the address with *e-mail:* because most readers know that an e-mail address contains an @ sign.

Alice Friend put her e-mail address on her resume, showing that she's easy to reach and is comfortable online.

Alice Friend
123 Fruit Tree Blvd.
Omaha, NE 12345
(123) 555-1234
alice_friend@bamboo.com

Job Objective: Software Engineer

Job Hunt Hint

If you're a professional consultant with a website about your services, be sure to include your site's URL in your resume heading. You don't need to prefix the address with website address: because most readers know that URLs have http:// or www in them.

Hot URLs

URLs (website addresses) are not commonly found in headings for two reasons:

1. Most people don't have a personal website (and most people don't need one for their job search).
2. Personal websites often contain private information and other stuff a potential employer shouldn't see.

However, if you're in website development, multimedia, or any field where your image might be enhanced because you have a spiffy personal website, put your URL in your heading along with your other contact information.

Dawson Peroni, for instance, was applying for assignments as a web game developer. Because his personal website had links to some of his projects, he included his URL in his resume's heading.

Dawson Peroni

123 Highland Ave.
Santa Fe, NM 12345

(123) 555-1234
d_peroni@bamboo.com
www.dawsonp.com

Job Objective: Web-Game Developer

Deborah Lord's research found that the small nonprofit where she was applying was planning to establish a presence on the Internet. Therefore, she put her website address on her resume to suggest that she could help them out with that process.

Deborah Lord
123 Moody Beach Lane
Mobile, AL 12345
(123) 555-1234
DDLord@bamboo.com

Job Objective: Volunteer Coordinator

The Least You Need to Know

- When designing your resume Heading section, place your name at the top of the page, either in the center or on the right-hand side of the page.
- Create a stable image by providing a street address instead of a PO box number.
- List only those phone numbers where employers can leave messages and where you can speak freely.
- Use a personal e-mail account for your job search and include that e-mail address in the heading of your resume.
- If you're a consultant or website professional, you may find it advantageous to include your personal website address next to your e-mail address.

Chapter 5

Step Two: Ask for What You Want ... You Just Might Get It

In This Chapter

- The importance of having a Job Objective statement on your resume
- What to do if you have more than one job objective
- How to write a concise Job Objective statement to get the job you want
- When to substitute a professional title for the Job Objective statement

Whether you're a world traveler or a job seeker, it's important to know where you're going in order to get there. (At least Columbus *thought* he knew where he was going when he set sail.) And when asking for help in getting there, you need to tell the guide where you're headed.

On your resume, this destination is shown through the Job Objective statement that appears just below your Heading. In this chapter, you'll learn why it's important to have a Job Objective section, how to create it, and where to place it. You'll also learn a clever alternative that could set you ahead in salary negotiations.

It's All Marketing

Your resume is effectively your career brochure because it markets you for your next career move. Just like any other marketing piece, your resume needs to be created with an objective in mind.

A marketing professional for an event production company would never create a poster for a concert until she knew what type of music was going to be performed, where it was being held, and who the target audience was. It's the same with your job search. Before you can produce your powerful marketing piece, you need to know what job you're going after, what skills are required for the job, and, if possible, who the reader of your resume is. After you have that information, you can put together a resume that'll get your foot in the door.

If you aren't sure what your job objective is, do some career planning to decide what role (for example: outside sales or marketing communications) you want to play for an employer. Second, investigate the job market to learn what positions you want to apply for. Then write your resume with a Job Objective statement on it.

Multiple Choice

If you find yourself with a list of two or more job objectives, don't make the mistake so many job seekers make by trying to create a generic resume to cover all possible job objectives. A generic resume is likely to fall flat on its face because it will make you look like a jack of too many trades, a weak contender against other candidates who are specialized in their fields.

Instead of developing a generic resume, follow these guidelines to create more than one targeted resume:

1. Make a list of your job objectives.
2. Prioritize that list so that your number one choice is first.
3. Create a resume that's focused on your first-choice job objective.
4. When your first resume is completed, make a copy of that resume on your computer.
5. Replace the objective statement with your second-choice job objective.
6. Go through the resume line by line, targeting it for your new objective.

In this way, you can create multiple resumes, each of which can stand strong against specialized competition in today's job market.

The Weight of a Job Objective

By starting your resume with a Job Objective statement, you immediately tell your potential employer …

- What position you're looking for.
- Who needs to get your resume. A human resources clerk will probably be the first person to see your resume. Your Job Objective statement will indicate to that clerk which hiring person should receive your resume.
- How to interpret your resume. Your Job Objective statement tells the reader, "Everything that follows is relevant to this position." That's an important point to make, because this is a marketing piece, not your life history!

Job Hunt Hint

The Job Objective section of your resume could be titled any one of the following:

- Job Objective
- Objective
- Career Objective
- Goal
- Career Goal

In short, a Job Objective statement makes it easier for a potential employer to understand what you have to say in your resume. A resume without a Job Objective statement effectively says, "This is what I've done. Could you figure out what I should do next?" That's a weak approach! A job objective gives your resume focus and strength, and makes a powerful first move toward title and salary negotiations.

The highlighted section of the following resume template shows where your Job Objective statement should be placed. (To learn about alternatives to having a Job Objective section on your resume, see "Breaking the Rules" later in this chapter.)

(Job Objective Section)

Name
Street
City, State Zip
Phone, Fax, E-mail

JOB OBJECTIVE
The job you want next

SUMMARY OF QUALIFICATIONS

- How much experience you have in the field of your job objective, in a related field, or using the skills required for your new position.
- An overall career accomplishment that shows you'd be good at this job.
- What someone would say about you as a recommendation.

PROFESSIONAL EXPERIENCE

20xx-pres. **Company Name, City, State**
Job Title

- An accomplishment you are proud of that shows you're good at this profession.
- A problem you solved and the results.
- A time when you positively affected the organization, the bottom line, your boss, your co-workers, your clients.
- Awards, commendations, publications, etc., you achieved that relate to your job objective.

20xx-xx **Company Name, City, State**
Job Title

- A project you are proud of that supports your job objective.
- Another accomplishment that shows you're good at this line of work.
- Quantifiable results that point out your skill.

19xx-xx **Company Name, City, State**
Job Title

- An accomplishment you are proud of that shows you will be valued by your next employer.
- An occasion when someone "sat up and took notice" of your skill.

EDUCATION

Degree, Major (if relevant), 20xx (optional)
University, City, State

Wording with an Objective

I've said it before, and I'll say it again: Less is more! You need to say everything as concisely as possible, starting with your Job Objective statement.

Putting your Job Objective statement near the top of your resume is the clearest way to tell the reader what you want for your immediate future.

Some resumes have flowery opening statements with job objectives buried deep inside them. They use phrases such as "challenging position," "room for advancement," and "opportunity to grow." Give the reader of your resume a break—cut out all the fluff because it doesn't say much anyway. Stick to what's important:

- The job title you'd like next, if you know it (for example, Manager or Sales Representative).
- The area of work you want to be in (for example, Marketing or Sales). On rare occasions, this might include an area of specialization (for example, "with an emphasis on new business development" or "focusing on graphic design").

> CAUTION
>
> **Career Casualty**
>
> Don't include "entry-level" in your Job Objective statement. Why tell the reader you want the lowest-level job, with pay to match? Leave it out, and you may be given a position that's a little higher up the food chain.

Challenge yourself to write your job objective in 10 words or less. (Of course, the employer won't count, so it's okay to exceed 10 words if you have to.) Give yourself a bonus check if you can narrow it down to just a few words.

Take a look at the following examples of Job Objective statements:

> **Not so good:** A challenging position that will utilize my skills and experience as Director of Marketing

Yawn! Everyone wants to be challenged, and of course you'll be using your skills and experience.

> **Much better:** Director of Marketing
>
> **Not so good:** An administrative position in a growth-oriented company where I can use my background in finance to promote the firm

This statement sounds like you're judging the company's ability to provide for your future.

> **Much better:** Administrative position with a focus on finance
>
> **Not so good:** A position as Associate Field Producer in TV Programming that offers room for advancement and high rewards

Bad idea! It sounds like you want the job of the person reading the resume!

> **Much better:** Associate Field Producer, TV Programming

Want to see this concept at work? Review the concise Job Objective statements in the sample resumes at the end of this chapter.

Straight as an Arrow

Jack Kraus knew exactly what position he was going after at the university, so he listed the precise title that was in the job posting he was responding to in his job objective. His concise statement had no frills—it went straight to the point and didn't waste the reader's time.

If you know the exact title of the job you're applying for, by all means use that as your job objective. Doing this leaves no doubt as to what position you want. If you later apply for a job with a slightly different job title, you can always change your job objective to match.

Spreading Your Umbrella

Like an umbrella, David Goldstein's job objective covered a number of things: his prospective job title and his three areas of expertise. By creating a column with eye-catching bullet points, he suggested to the employer several ways he could fit into the organization. Smart guy!

The approach David used is a good one for professionals such as the following:

- Consultants who offer several services
- Generalists who want to show off their special skills
- Administrators who need to say they can wear several hats
- Technical folks who have expertise in a number of areas

Do you fall into one of these categories? If so, you might benefit from the umbrella technique David used.

Breaking the Rules

Now that you've learned the rule of having a Job Objective statement, I'm going to tell you about a technique that breaks, or at least bends, that rule.

If you're continuing in a profession in which you have substantial experience, consider putting your *professional title* next to your name or near the top of your resume. This can be a stronger approach than using a Job Objective statement. A title effectively says, "This is what my profession is." A Job Objective statement says, "This is what I want to be." If you have enough experience to give yourself a title, it can be a more forceful introduction.

Using your professional title instead of a Job Objective statement can do the following:

- Give you an edge on your competition by presenting you as an established professional in your field
- Set a strong foundation for title and salary negotiations

Look at the resumes for Robert McFarland and Katrina Lambros. Do you see how the professional-title technique makes each job seeker look accomplished in his or her career?

Terms of Employment

Your **professional title** could be an official job title you've held or simply the professional role you're qualified to fill. For instance, a resume writer (such as myself) could use any of the following professional titles at the top of her resume:

- Resume Writer
- Resume Consultant
- Job Counselor
- Career Development Professional

She would choose her professional title based on what type of work she was looking for.

Titles That Talk Big

Robert McFarland had been a construction dispute consultant for a number of years and was using his resume to move to another consulting firm. By placing his professional title immediately under his heading, he established himself as someone grounded in his field. This assertive approach not only won him an interview, it also paid off big when he negotiated his salary.

Do you have a professional title that would tell the employer which role you want to play in his organization? If so, consider using it on your resume instead of a Job Objective statement.

Heading Within a Heading

In her resume heading, Katrina Lambros inserted her professional title right under her name. Notice how confident Katrina looked with her title up top and stunning achievement statements in the body of her resume. Her whole presentation made her look like the type of salesperson the employer wanted on his team!

Whether your professional title is incorporated into your heading or positioned immediately under your heading, it's bound to stand out and impress a potential employer.

The Least You Need to Know

- To have a perfect resume, you must make it targeted to a job objective.
- Your Job Objective statement should appear immediately below the Heading section of your resume.
- This section can be called Job Objective, Career Objective, or simply Objective.
- If you have more than one job objective, create a separate resume for each objective.
- Keep your Job Objective statement concise and to the point.
- Instead of using a Job Objective statement, you can use a professional title.

Jack Kraus

123 Godfrey Avenue, #2, Philadelphia, PA 12345 **(123) 555-1234** **jkraus@bamboo.com**

JOB OBJECTIVE

Student Affairs Officer II, Housing & Dining Services: Residential Programs

SUMMARY OF QUALIFICATIONS

- 19 years as a professional educator with strengths in program development and administration.
- Enthusiastic team leader and outstanding communicator, both one-to-one and before groups.
- Creative in solving problems and maximizing resources. Computer literate.

EDUCATION

M.A., Educational Administration, Temple University, Philadelphia, PA, 1996

B.A., History, St. John's College, Santa Fe, NM, 1986

RELEVANT ACCOMPLISHMENTS

PROGRAM ADMINISTRATION

Philadelphia Unified School District

- Developed new educational programs, including:
  - Tutoring program for ESL students that achieved highest recommendations.
  - "Future System" curricula, a hands-on approach that included a computer lab.
  - $12,000 ham radio station project for high-achieving students.
- As Teacher-in-Charge, supervised 45 teachers in principal's absence and assisted in administrative decision-making and program development.
- Chaired ESL Advisory Committee comprised of parents, administrators, and teachers, which served as a forum for student issues.

TEACHING

Church Street School

- Currently teach basic college courses (English, history, and writing) to students, ages 18-50 and from diverse educational and cultural backgrounds.
- Tutor and advise students regarding study skills and career development.

Philadelphia Unified School District

- Instructed adults in basic education skills, GED preparation, and ESL, in addition to holding a full-time elementary teaching position.

TXN Newsroom Guest Speaker

- Delivered presentations to school groups and cable companies on new technologies in the classroom.

WORK HISTORY

2004-present	Instructor	Church Street School, Philadelphia, CA
2002-2004	Guest Speaker	TXN Newsroom, Philadelphia, PA
1986-2004	Educator	Philadelphia Unified School District, Philadelphia, PA

David Goldstein

123 Lincoln Avenue • West Hollywood, CA 12345 • **(123) 555-1234** • daveg@bamboo.com

OBJECTIVE: Sales Trainer in the areas of: Interpersonal Communication
Sales Techniques
Product Knowledge

SUMMARY OF QUALIFICATIONS

- 15 years as a successful sales professional.
- Experienced at teaching others how to improve interpersonal communication.
- Skilled at training sales associates in proven sales techniques.
- Ability to develop presentation and training materials.

PROFESSIONAL ACCOMPLISHMENTS

TRAINING

Jewel Junction

- Trained 24+ franchisees regarding: Product knowledge, Projected trends, Merchandising, Proven selling techniques
- Trained City Center sales staff including 23 associates and one assistant manager.
- Led staff meetings to introduce lines and instill respect and enthusiasm for products.
- Served on the product development committee charged with determining seasonal merchandise and promotions.
- Diffused numerous conflicts among sales staff through group and individual counseling.
- Designed employee incentive program that rewarded improved performance.

Clearwater, Inc.

- Trained sales staff in numerous department stores nationwide for short-term promotional sales of Clearwater accessories.

SALES

- Consistently ranked among the highest in sales at Jewel Junction, using strong presentation skills to sell luxury items in a slow economy.
- Commended for achieving above-average sales and for developing strong rapport with customers at Grove Jewelry Distributors.
- Exceeded sales record 20% in a 10-state, 20-store region of Clearwater, Inc.

WORK HISTORY

2003-present Merchandising Manager, Jewel Junction, Inglewood, CA
2001-2002 Customer Service/Sales Associate, Grove Jewelry Distributors, Long Beach, CA
1998-2000 Sales Associate, Beemans (department store), Miami Beach, FL
1997 Promotional Representative, Clearwater, Inc., Santa Monica, CA
1991-1996 Sales Representative, Frost's Fifth Avenue, Hollywood, CA

EDUCATION

Liberal Arts, Quincy College, Key West, FL
Professional development courses: Interpersonal Communications, Sales Training, Product Knowledge and Presentation

Robert McFarland

123 Middlesex Street • Wethersfield, CT 12345 • (123) 555-1234 • rmcfarland@bamboo.com

Construction Dispute Consultant

HIGHLIGHTS OF QUALIFICATIONS

- 16 years as construction consultant and owner of mid-size construction firm.
- Extensive experience in woodframe construction.
- Skilled at resolving contract disputes.

RELEVANT EXPERIENCE

CONSTRUCTION BUSINESS MANAGEMENT

- Built a prominent construction business that grew from 0 to 250 employees and from annual gross of $25K to $9M in six years.
- Managed approximately 300 construction projects, including:
  New commercial buildings
  Commercial tenant improvement
  New and remodel residential work
  Structural rehabs
- Oversaw 500,000 sq. ft. per year wood framing operation.

PROBLEM RESOLUTION

- Successfully negotiated numerous contract and labor disputes, initiating compromises that led to resolutions of up to $125K
- Collaborated with architects and owners to create most cost-effective designs on projects up to $2.5M in value, frequently requiring resolution of competing interests.
- Continually generated technical and interpersonal solutions that met tight budget and time constraints.

PRESENTATIONS

- Wrote hundreds of analyses for construction projects, focusing on financial, safety, and time issues.
- As guest lecturer at local community college, spoke on resource-efficient construction.

WORK HISTORY

2003-present	Construction Consultant/Contractor, Cosgrove Contractors, Hartford, CT
1993-2003	President/Operations Manager, Golly Co., West Hartford, CT
1987-1993	General Contractor, Ruby Construction, Hartford, CT

EDUCATION

B.A., Religious Studies, Springfield College, Springfield, MA

Katrina Lambros

International Sales Representative / Sales Manager

123 Lee Avenue • Pikesville, Maryland 12345 • (123) 555-1234 • katrinal@bamboo.com

SUMMARY OF QUALIFICATIONS

- 12 years successful direct sales and sales management career in corporate culture.
- Courageous selling style that results in: Win-win gains for client and company
  Achievement of unlikely sales
  Reversal of lost sales
- Skilled at closing sales through ingenious and spontaneous "packaging" of products.

PROFESSIONAL ACCOMPLISHMENTS (at VM Tech)

Personal Quota Attainment

- Consistently attained top national rankings out of 110 managers:
  - 125-150% of quota, five out of six years
  - #2 Sales Manager
  - #1 Female Sales Manager
  - #3 Sales Manager
- Won annual awards including "Top Systems Sales Performer."
- Ranked #1 out of 475 sales representatives.
- Exceeded annual quota 125% the first year, with no previous sales experience.

Selected Achievements

- As an outsider in an established market, closed a $150,000 sale of a newly launched product.
- Increased business substantially with a major client and exceeded average monthly sales quotas by 43%.
- As District Manager, increased sales force productivity by 25%.
- Introduced training to develop each salesperson's abilities in proven sales techniques.

Promotions

- One of eight women nationwide promoted to District Manager.
- Promoted to Sales Manager out of field of 17 candidates.
- Advanced to Manager, Key Accounts due to mastery of technical system selling.
- Out of 723 Sales Representatives, chosen as coach for training center.

WORK HISTORY

2006	RENWICK, INC., Baltimore, MD	Organizational Consultant
2005	PHONE SERVICE SYSTEMS, Washington, DC	Sales & Marketing Consultant
1993-2004	VM TECH, Bethesda, MD	District Manager (2002-2004) Sales Manager (1996-2002) Manager, Key Accounts (1994-1995) Sales Representative (1993)

EDUCATION

B.S., Psychology, 1992, Catholic University of America, Washington, DC

Chapter 6

Step Three: Knock 'Em Off Their Feet

In This Chapter

- Kicking off your resume with a strong Summary of Qualifications
- Figuring out what to say and how to say it
- Avoiding resume clichés that put the employer to sleep
- Facilitating a smooth career change with effective phrases

Experienced players in the marketing game know it's important to create a splash right away in a promotional piece. The way to do that on your resume is to give top billing to qualifications that will knock the employer off her feet. In this chapter, you'll learn how to choose and compose opening statements that will draw in employers and make them start itching to call you.

Right from the Start

Kick off your resume with a Summary of Qualifications section. This section is a list of the top three or four reasons you're qualified for the job you're seeking. The following resume template shows where the Summary of Qualifications section appears on the resume.

For example, the opening section of Christopher Columbus's resume might have read as follows:

Summary of Qualifications

- First European to make verified contact with Americans since the Vikings five centuries before.
- Christened six Caribbean islands (whose names now signify choice vacation spots).
- Noted captain and navigator of four Atlantic crossings who set contemporary world sailing records.

(Summary of Qualifications Section)

Name
Street
City, State Zip
Phone, Fax, E-mail

JOB OBJECTIVE

The job you want next

SUMMARY OF QUALIFICATIONS

- How much experience you have in the field of your job objective, in a related field, or using the skills required for your new position.
- An overall career accomplishment that shows you'd be good at this job.
- What someone would say about you as a recommendation.

PROFESSIONAL EXPERIENCE

20xx-pres. **Company Name, City, State**
Job Title
- An accomplishment you are proud of that shows you're good at this profession.
- A problem you solved and the results.
- A time when you positively affected the organization, the bottom line, your boss, your co-workers, your clients.
- Awards, commendations, publications, etc., you achieved that relate to your job objective.

20xx-xx **Company Name, City, State**
Job Title
- A project you are proud of that supports your job objective.
- Another accomplishment that shows you're good at this line of work.
- Quantifiable results that point out your skill.

19xx-xx **Company Name, City, State**
Job Title
- An accomplishment you are proud of that shows you will be valued by your next employer.
- An occasion when someone "sat up and took notice" of your skill.

EDUCATION

Degree, Major (if relevant), 20xx (optional)
University, City, State

Wouldn't you want this guy to captain your next transoceanic sailing trip?

You may not be able to tout mind-blowing achievements like Columbus, but you can look pretty terrific with three or four smashing statements that set you apart from the crowd. Talk about anything that makes you stand out in your field. That something could be any of the following:

- Your experience
- Your credentials
- Your expertise
- Your personal values
- Your work ethics
- Your background
- Your personality

Terms of Employment

The **Summary of Qualifications** section is a brief set of points that say you're qualified for your Job Objective. This section can also be called:

- Highlights of Qualifications
- Qualifications
- Highlights
- Summary
- Profile

There's room to be creative in naming this section, so go for it!

In the *Summary of Qualifications*, you're free to make claims, drop names, and do your best to entice the employer to call you for an interview. Remember, all claims must be substantiated later when you write the body of your resume, so be honest while giving yourself full credit.

Say It with Style

Whatever you do in your Summary of Qualifications, don't use hackneyed phrases such as "Excellent written and oral communication skills," "Outstanding organizational abilities," "Goal-oriented individual," or other overused, vague lines.

Columbus's resume would have gotten lost in the pack if it had read as follows:

Summary of Qualifications

- Exceptional organizational and people skills
- Goal oriented, self-motivated individual
- Excellent communication skills

Don't get me wrong—the meanings behind most of those phrases are wonderful and may be perfectly true for you. But because these clichés appear on almost everyone's resume, they don't have punch and, frankly, are not taken seriously.

Bonus Check

Throughout the resume, write in the first person without using pronouns. In other words, phrase your statements as though you were talking about yourself without saying "I." For example, write "Understand the art of conflict resolution" instead of "I understand the art of conflict resolution."

Before you put a statement in your Summary of Qualifications, ask yourself: Is it a grabber? Is it news to the reader? If it's what everyone else says, it's not news, and it won't grab the reader. It has to be said in a way that's remarkable and memorable.

Always make your point as concretely as possible. Use facts to create credibility and to instill a sense that you are unlike any other candidate applying for the job. Ask yourself the following questions:

- What specifically have I done that demonstrates that I have the desired quality?
- How will my skills translate into success at my next job?

Here are some examples of what I mean:

- Fred was applying for a pizza delivery position. Because this type of employment has a high no-show rate, he felt his reliability was a marketable asset. So instead of writing "Excellent record of attendance," he wrote, "Never missed a day of work in 11 months."
- When Sandy was going for a customer service position, she knew the potential employer was looking for someone with excellent communication skills. She wrote "Deemed Customer Service Rep of the Month for resolving problems diplomatically."
- Instead of "Goal-oriented professional," Frank wrote "Exceeded quotas for four consecutive years" on his resume for a sales position.

For more ideas on Summary of Qualifications statements, see what the following two job seekers wrote on their resumes (found at the end of this chapter).

Keeping Up with the Fast Trackers

Jamie Choi designed a Summary of Qualifications section in his resume that told his potential employer that he's experienced in his field and valued by those who work with him. Notice his clever technique of getting someone else to say he was a good employee relations specialist: He quoted one of his former clients. His summary statements alone made the employer want to read his entire resume.

Look through your evaluation forms and letters of recommendation from former employers to see if you have a quotable quote for your resume.

On the Lines of a Career Changer

The Summary of Qualifications is one of the most important sections on a career changer's resume because it becomes a bridge between the job seeker's past and future. In his resume, Charles Humphries used just three statements to provide the following information:

- He had experience in the field he was moving into (even though he'd never held the job title he was going after).
- He had the required skills and motivation for the position.
- He had a technical background, which was something his competition might not have.

His Summary of Qualifications section packaged Charles as a low-risk, high-value candidate.

Your Summary of Qualifications statements should so strongly paint a picture of you at your next job that there appears to be little or no transition into your new job, even if you're making a big career change.

Go Figure

Now it's time to write your Summary of Qualifications statements. To help you come up with three or four strong statements, answer the following questions. If one doesn't apply to your situation, skip it and move on to the next.

1. How much experience do you have in this profession, in this field, or using the required skills?

   Example: Someone staying in the field of financial management might write, "I've worked as a financial manager for a mid-size company for the last 14 years."

   Summary statement: Fourteen years as the financial manager of a company with current sales of $75 million.

   Example: A job seeker making the transition from teaching to corporate training might write, "I spent the last seven years teaching things to all kinds of kids."

   Summary statement: Seven years of professional experience using strong communication skills to enhance learning of children from diverse backgrounds.

2. Imagine that your best friend is talking to the hiring person about the job you want. What would your best friend say about you that would make the employer want to call you for an interview?

   Example: The best friend of a job hunter desiring an editorial position with a newspaper might say, "She even won the Pulitzer Prize! I don't think anyone from the *Examiner* has ever done that before."

   Summary statement: First syndicated journalist from the *Examiner* to receive the Pulitzer Prize.

   Example: The colleague of a CEO seeking a membership on the Board of Directors of a crisis-prevention nonprofit organization might say, "He led a group that helped the community recover from the 1989 earthquake."

   Summary statement: Known for leading a committee that took the first step toward community rehabilitation after the 1989 earthquake.

3. How is success measured in the position mentioned in your Job Objective? How do you measure up?

   Example: A salesperson reaching for a sales management job might write, "I have always sold more than my quota and tried to motivate other salespeople so my team could meet group goals."

   Summary statement: Consistently exceeded personal quotas and inspired sales team members to meet group goals.

   Example: A software developer wishing to make a move into technical writing might write, "Many different users have told me that my explanations are easy to understand."

   Summary statement: Reputation for writing clear and concise explanations for technical and nontechnical users.

4. What credentials do you have that are important for this job?

   Example: A fashion buyer looking for a position as a graphic designer might write, "My college degree was in design."

   Summary statement: Bachelor of Fine Arts with an emphasis on design.

   Example: A geology teacher seeking a position at a community college in California might write, "I have a Lifetime California Community College Teaching Credential in Earth Science."

   Summary statement: California Community College Teaching Credential, Earth Science, Lifetime.

5. What is it about your personality that makes this job a good fit for you?

   Example: A customer-service representative staying in the same field might write, "I am very diplomatic, so I get good results."

   Summary statement: Outstanding diplomacy that consistently produces win-win results for customers and the company.

   Example: An architect applying for a post in a professional organization could write, "I have natural problem-solving skills that lead to good solutions."

   Summary statement: Natural problem-solving skills that create both practical and agreeable solutions.

6. What personal commitments or passions do you have that would be valued by the employer?

   Example: Someone wanting to lead an environmental organization could write, "I am committed to educating people about industrial waste hazards that are endangering the environment."

   Summary statement: Strong commitment to preserving nature through education about hazards to the environment.

   Example: A psychologist going for a job in human resources might say, "I like to help others achieve their potential through evaluation of their personal skills."

   Summary statement: Dedicated to maximizing others' potential through careful assessment and acknowledgment of their personal skills.

> **Career Casualty**
>
> Be careful not to list tasks you don't like to perform. Mentioning them is a sure way of finding them in your next job description.

7. What other experience do you have that will be a bonus to the employer?

   Example: A new graduate seeking her first job as a nurse could write, "I volunteered in a medium-size clinic."

   Summary statement: Volunteer experience in a clinic with an interdisciplinary staff of 12.

   Example: Someone trying for a position on the mayor's administrative staff might mention, "My family includes three generations of political professionals, so I'm used to debating controversial issues."

   Summary statement: Developed talent for debating controversial issues as a member of a family with three generations of political professionals.

8. Do you have any technical, linguistic, or artistic talents that would be useful on the job?

   Example: Someone applying to be a teacher in a multilingual school might write, "I can speak Spanish, Italian, and Russian."

   Summary statement: Fluent in Spanish, Italian, and Russian.

   Example: An artist seeking a commission from the city's museum could write, "I have worked in just about every kind of medium."

   Summary statement: Adept at working in a range of mediums, including paint, pen and ink, clay, metal, collage, and wood.

Not all of these questions will work for your situation. Just answer the ones that do, and you're bound to come up with three or four good statements for your resume.

The Least You Need to Know

- A strong Summary of Qualifications section will grab an employer's attention and make him or her think, "Here's the person for the job."
- Your Summary of Qualifications summarizes your qualifications for your next job (your future); it doesn't summarize your past.
- Don't write overused phrases such as "Excellent communication skills."
- Prioritize your Summary of Qualifications statements so that the strongest one comes first.

Jamie Choi

123 Montecito Street, #1 • Santa Cruz, CA 12345 • (123) 555-1234 • jchoi@bamboo.com

OBJECTIVE: Employee Relations Specialist

SUMMARY OF QUALIFICATIONS

- More than 10 years as an expert in:
  The Psychology of Work
  Wholeness in the Workplace
- Skilled at assisting people from all levels of employment and cultural backgrounds.
- "You've changed my understanding of work. I now find it a dynamic and energizing principle." — Manufacturing Manager

TRAINING AND DEVELOPMENT ACCOMPLISHMENTS

2004-pres. Chrysalis, Santa Cruz, CA **Instructor,** Wholeness in the Workplace

- Taught professionals, managers, office workers, and tradespeople from multicultural backgrounds. Topics include:
  - Dealing with Stress
  - Responsibility and Commitment
  - Dynamics of Teamwork
  - Concentration
  - Organizational Skills
  - Dealing with Difficult People
- Turned around a failing institutional library and, with no previous professional librarian experience, produced an efficient system within four weeks.
  - Trained volunteers.
  - Organized holdings and standardized procedures.
- Managed building renovation project, training and supervising a crew of student volunteers with no experience in construction. Finished project within time constraints.

1996-2003 MacMillan Institute, Albuquerque, NM **Trainer/Manager**

- Trained professionals, artists, tradespeople, and students in productive work habits that increased proficiency, work satisfaction, and income.
- Created a "work laboratory" that provided hands-on experience in development of:
  - Teamwork
  - Conflict Management Skills
  - Dynamic Work Style
  - Self-Esteem
  - Client Relations
  - Time Management Skills

1994-1996 Center for Humanistic Studies, Santa Fe, NM **Full-Time Student,** Human Development

1989-1991 Los Alamos Properties, Los Alamos, NM **Co-Manager**

- Trained and supervised renovation staff working on residential projects.

EDUCATION

M.A., Human Resources, University of California, Santa Cruz, CA

Charles E. Humphries

123 Baytown Avenue • Jacinto, TX 12345 • (123) 555-1234 • c_humphries@bamboo.com

JOB OBJECTIVE: Technical Sales Account Manager

SUMMARY OF QUALIFICATIONS

- 13 years as an engineer collaborating on key marketing/sales strategies for one of the nation's largest corporations.
- Enjoy making sales presentations that motivate audiences to "buy into" new products.
- Technical versatility: construction, computer systems, telecommunications, and safety.

PROFESSIONAL ACCOMPLISHMENTS

SALES / MARKETING

- Increased premium product sales 15% ($4.1 million) by designing a $2.7 million advertising and point-of-sale strategy. Led team of sales experts, merchandising specialists, market researchers, P.O.S. vendors, and product engineers.
- Made winning "sales" presentation regarding a $37 million retail automation project. Built consensus among company divisions with competing interests by facilitating needs assessment, goal setting, and cooperative strategy planning.
- Increased revenue $12 million annually by convincing 8,300 retailers to use electronic funds transfer system.
- Led several testimonial and training presentations that "sold" new technologies to audiences with resistance to change.

TECHNICAL PROJECT MANAGEMENT

- Led technical development of customer-activated credit/debit card payment system implemented at AP stations nationwide. Increased corporate annual sales $154 million.
- Led development of computerized maintenance dispatch system for 8,250 retail outlets and 60 bulk facilities that eliminated down time, increasing sales $8.4 million per year.
- Directed the $49 million construction of 40 service stations, designing architectural plans that met environmental regulations and local government demands.

WORK HISTORY

1993-present American Petroleum Inc., Houston, TX

Environmental Safety Fire and Health Specialist, 2005-present
Trading Analyst, 2003-2005
Project Manager, Market Place Development, 2002-2003
Project Manager, Electronics Systems - Service Stations, 1999-2002
Analyst for Product Order and Delivery, 1998-1999
Project Manager, Service Station Construction, 1995-1998
Staff Engineer, 1993-1995

EDUCATION

B.E., Chemical Engineering, Massachusetts Institute of Technology, Cambridge, MA, 1993
Professional Development: American Demographics Annual Marketing Conference
Sales and negotiations seminars

Chapter 7

Step Four: Make History

In This Chapter

- Creating a Work History that shows off your strengths
- Using dates on your resume to fight age discrimination
- Disguising gaps in your employment history
- Adding volunteer experience to your Work History section
- Making your promotions noticeable at a glance

Employers give a lot of attention to the Work History section of a resume. It's one of the first things they look for after they see your job objective. They want to know about your track record, where you've been and how long you stayed there. What they're trying to figure out is: Are you a stable person? What are your demonstrated talents? And most important, would you be a good fit for the job opening they have?

A well-presented Work History section is clearly important. Building one that maximizes your experience is what this chapter is all about.

Location, Location, Location

Where you list your previous positions depends on what type of resume format you're using. If you're a chronological resume writer (remember that lesson in Chapter 2?), your Work History will be distributed throughout the midsection of your resume. The following chronological template shows you exactly where it would appear.

If you're a functional resume writer (see Chapter 3), Work History will be listed in one section at the bottom of your resume. This chapter's functional resume template highlights the area I'm talking about.

(Work History in Chronological Resume)

Name
Street
City, State Zip
Phone, Fax, E-mail

JOB OBJECTIVE

The job you want next

SUMMARY OF QUALIFICATIONS

- How much experience you have in the field of your job objective, in a related field, or using the skills required for your new position.
- An overall career accomplishment that shows you'd be good at this job.
- What someone would say about you as a recommendation.

PROFESSIONAL EXPERIENCE

20xx-pres. **Company Name, City, State**
Job Title

- An accomplishment you are proud of that shows you're good at this profession.
- A problem you solved and the results.
- A time when you positively affected the organization, the bottom line, your boss, your co-workers, your clients.
- Awards, commendations, publications, etc., you achieved that relate to your job objective.

20xx-xx **Company Name, City, State**
Job Title

- A project you are proud of that supports your job objective.
- Another accomplishment that shows you're good at this line of work.
- Quantifiable results that point out your skill.

19xx-xx **Company Name, City, State**
Job Title

- An accomplishment you are proud of that shows you will be valued by your next employer.
- An occasion when someone "sat up and took notice" of your skill.

EDUCATION

Degree, Major (if relevant), 20xx (optional)
University, City, State

(Work History in Functional Resume)

Name

Street
City, State Zip
Phone, Fax, E-mail

JOB OBJECTIVE

The job you want next

SUMMARY OF QUALIFICATIONS

- How much experience you have in the field of your job objective, in a related field, or using the skills required for your new position.
- An overall career accomplishment that shows you'd be good at this job.
- What someone would say about you as a recommendation.

RELEVANT EXPERIENCE

MAJOR SKILL

- An accomplishment you are proud of that shows you have this skill.
- A problem you solved using this skill, and the results.
- A time when you used your skill to positively affect the organization, the bottom line, your boss, your clients.
- Awards, commendations, publications, etc., you achieved that relate to your job objective.

MAJOR SKILL

- A project you are proud of that supports your job objective.
- Another accomplishment that shows you're good at this line of work.
- Quantifiable results that point out your skill.
- An occasion when someone "sat up and took notice" of your skill.

WORK HISTORY

20xx-present	Job Title	COMPANY NAME and city
20xx-xx	Job Title	COMPANY NAME and city
20xx-xx	Job Title	COMPANY NAME and city
19xx-xx	Job Title	COMPANY NAME and city

EDUCATION

Degree, Major (if relevant), 20xx (optional)
University, City, State

Writing History

Of all the sections of your resume, your Work History is the most likely to be verified by a potential employer. Be sure your entries in this section coincide exactly with the information your former employers will give.

As you read through this chapter, remember Resume Commandment II: Thou shalt not confess. (The Resume Commandments were listed in Chapter 1.) In other words, you don't have to tell everything. Stick to what's relevant and marketable. Rely on this commandment when resolving issues in your Work History section.

The next step is to put the Work History section in your resume. Sounds easy enough, doesn't it? But what if you have a situation that's tricky to present in your employment history? This situation could be any of the following:

- Dates that go back so far that they trigger age discrimination.
- So little employment history that you appear too young for the job.
- Gaps in your work history.
- Multiple positions at the same company.

Let's take a closer look at some Work History issues and figure out ways you can resolve them. Be sure to reference the sample resumes at the end of this chapter.

Fight Age Discrimination

Job Hunt Hint

Dates in your Education section are optional. List them if they make you look the right age for the job you are going for. Delete them if they lead the reader to deduce that you are older or younger than you want to appear for the job application.

"How far back should I go in my work history?" is a good question to ask yourself as you set out to document your history. In general, you're not expected to go back more than 10 years, but you can if it's to your benefit. To help you figure out how far back to go in your work history, consider the following:

- How relevant your earliest positions are to your job objective
- How old you want to appear on your resume

Age discrimination works in two ways. An employer may disqualify a job candidate because he is either too old or too young. Age discrimination is illegal, but like it or not, employers usually try to figure out your age using the dates you give. Most employers have an age range they consider to be ideal for a particular job, based on the following factors:

- Salary expectations
- Skill level
- Ability to supervise or be supervised
- Amount of life experience needed
- Company or industry image

A well-written resume uses dates to lead the employer to deduce that you are the ideal age for the job you're after, regardless of your actual age. The following two sections show you how to work with dates on your resume to create the ideal image.

Putting Your Younger Foot Forward

Sally, 35 years old, was applying for a job as a sales clerk in a clothing store that catered to teenagers and young adults. She thought the employer was probably looking for a woman in her mid-20s because the employer wanted someone who fit the image of the store and who wouldn't expect wages as high as someone who had been in the field for many years.

To present herself as the ideal candidate, Sally decided to go back only five years in the Work History on her resume, because the employer most likely to …

1. Take 20 years of age as a starting point.
2. Add the five years of work experience shown in her work history.
3. Conclude that Sally was at least 25 years old.

Likewise, in her Education section, she stated her degree but did not give her graduation date because doing so would give away her age.

The dates on Sally's resume were all honest, they just didn't tell all. In the interview, she would have the opportunity to sell herself with her enthusiasm, professional manner, and appropriate salary request, thereby fulfilling the employer's expectations of the ideal candidate.

If you feel at all uncomfortable about abbreviating your Work History in order to avoid age discrimination, you may want to call that section Relevant Work History or Recent Work History.

Older Is Better

Sam is a new graduate who worked in his dad's business all through high school and college. He was a remarkable achiever and was ready for more responsibility in the workforce than most people his age. He applied for a position as a store manager, knowing that if he could just get his foot in the door he could convince the owner he could handle the job.

He thought that the employer was probably expecting to hire someone in his late 20s. So on his resume, Sam went back in his Work History section eight years to when he started working for his dad in low-level positions, and showed his progression over the following years. He stated that he had a degree, but he did not give the date of completion, because it might indicate that he was only 22. Everything on Sam's resume honestly painted the picture of someone who had the experience and maturity of a 30-year-old without ever revealing his age.

CAUTION

Career Casualty

If you've owned a business, don't say so on your resume. In the hiring world, it's often thought that once people have worked for themselves, they'll never make good employees again, because self-employed people like being the boss and are driven by the profit motive. A way around revealing your self-employment is to give yourself a job title in your business, choosing a title that supports your current job objective, if possible.

Down and Dirty Formula

Here's a quick and easy method for understanding how dates on your resume make an impression about your age. I call it my EPT (Experience Plus Twenty) formula. Subtract the earliest date on your resume from today's date (using years only, no months). Add that number of years to 20 (as a ballpark figure for how old you might have been when your experience started) to get a total. Your perceived age is equal to or greater than this total. For example, a resume written in 2006 with a Work History that starts in 1990 tells the employer that the job applicant is at least 36 years old (16 years of experience + 20 = 36).

Unsightly Unemployment Blemishes

Bonus Check

If your potential employer isn't likely to recognize a company you list in your Work History, you may want to give some explanation as to what industry it is in or what product it sells. You can do that by writing a short overview statement immediately beside or under the company name.

"What's wrong with a few gaps in my work history?" you might ask. "Isn't everyone entitled to a little time off?" Many responsible professionals have taken breaks in their careers to travel, take care of ill parents, recover from personal illnesses, or for other legitimate reasons. But for some reason, employers don't like to see gaps in your work history. Unexplained gaps may cause an employer to think that you're hiding something or that you might have a past or current problem (such as substance abuse, incarceration, laziness, or instability) that would affect your ability to work. They would rather see the unemployed time explained, especially if the explanation is somehow connected to your job objective or at least shows strength of character. To gain the employer's trust, it's important to justify your employment gaps. If you have a period of unemployment in your history, the following sections explain some ways of dealing with it.

Years Go Solo

Use only years, not months, when referring to spans of time in your Work History. Using years makes it quicker for the potential employer to grasp the length of time and can eliminate the need to explain gaps of less than one year.

Notice the gap in this presentation:

12/02-3/06	Manager	Friendly's Ice Cream Parlor, Trenton, NJ
2/99-12/01	Manager	Lyon's Restaurant, Milbrae, CA

Without the months, there is no apparent gap:

2002-2006	Manager	Friendly's Ice Cream Parlor, Trenton, NJ
1999-2001	Manager	Lyon's Restaurant, Milbrae, CA

Months complicate the presentation and make it harder (and therefore longer) for someone to figure out. Remember the eight-second scan I talked about in Chapter 1? Providing just the years will help you pass that eight-second test.

Filling In the Gaps

If your unemployment covers two calendar years or more, you need to explain the void. Consider all the things you were doing during that time (volunteer work, school activities, internships, schooling, travel, and so on) and present it in a way that's relevant to your job objective, if possible. You may have two or three "job titles" that could fill an employment gap on your resume. If so, choose the title that is most relevant to your job objective.

Someone looking for a medical sales position who took care of an ill parent for two years might list the following:

2002-04 Home Care Provider for terminally ill relative

An applicant for a travel agent position could refer to a vacation:

2004-05 Independent travel: Europe, Asia, and South America

A mother wanting to re-enter the job market as a teacher's aide might say:

2001-06 Full-Time Parent and PTA Volunteer, St. John's Academy

Character That Counts

Even if your activities during your unemployment have no apparent relevancy to your job objective, you need to account for the gap. Explain what you were doing in a way that is honest and feels comfortable to you. If your main activity was something you don't want to talk about, think of something else you were doing during that time, even if it doesn't relate to your job objective, and refer to that activity instead of using a job title in your Work History. Don't refer to personal illness, unemployment, or rehabilitation. These topics usually raise red flags, so avoid mentioning them at all cost.

Some suggested substitutes for a job title include the following:

Full-Time Parent

Home Management

Family Management

Family Financial Management

Independent Study

Personal Travel

Adventure Travel

Travels to (fill in the place you traveled to)

Professional Development

Freelance Work (replace Work with the type of work you did, such as writer, artist, or plumber)

Student

Consultant

Contractual Work (replace Work with the type of work you did, such as administrator, accountant, hair stylist)

> **Bonus Check**
>
> Employers must be very careful about what questions they ask in a job interview, because they can be sued for asking questions that suggest illegal hiring practices. Therefore, an employer might choose not to interview you rather than risk a lawsuit by asking about unexplained employment gaps on your resume.

Relocation from abroad
Volunteer
Civic Leader

There's no need to elaborate on your "filler" job title, unless doing so will support your job objective. For instance, if your Job Objective statement reads "Fundraiser," you might say "Volunteer (emphasis on fundraising)" in your Work History section.

The Gapless Resume

Janet Bennett had a long period of recent unemployment. For that reason, she chose to use the functional format and filled in her gap with two job titles:

- Childcare Teacher (which was a volunteer position at her church)
- Full-Time Parent (for her two children)

These two titles not only demonstrate that she's a stable citizen, they also qualify her for her job objective. Can you see how she used both experiences in the achievement statements in the body of the resume?

If you include unpaid experience in your Work History section as Janet did, be sure that you call this section either Work History or History, not Employment History, because the word *employment* implies that you were paid.

Promoting Your Promotions

You can be especially proud of your work history if you've been promoted within a company. So go ahead, this is your chance to brag!

Potential employers will be impressed by your promotions because they indicate employment stability and high performance. Let's look at ways to show off your promotions in your Work History section.

Imagine that you have been promoted three times within a company called Harrison Productions. Notice what kind of impression you might make if you used this format:

2004-present	President, Harrison Productions, Chicago, IL
2003-2004	Vice President, Harrison Productions, Chicago, IL
2000-2003	Producer, Harrison Productions, Chicago, IL

At first glance, the employer is likely to think you are a job-hopper who had three jobs in four years. (Ouch!) Only upon closer examination might she understand that your three jobs were at the same company. But what if the employer doesn't take the time to figure that out? You will have made a negative impression when you had an excellent opportunity to make a positive one.

I suggest organizing the same information in this way:

2000-present	HARRISON PRODUCTIONS, Chicago, IL
	President, 2004-present
	Vice President, 2003-2004
	Producer, 2000-2003

Notice how this second version makes it immediately clear that you were a loyal employee who had multiple promotions.

The good news is that this concept applies to both the chronological and functional formats, as demonstrated by the following three job seekers.

Grass Underfoot

Dianne Woo was concerned that a potential employer would view her as stagnant because she'd worked at General Electric for so many years. To avoid creating such a negative image, she separated her job titles under the company heading and inserted achievements for each one, as you can see in her resume. Doing so made it obvious the grass hasn't been growing under her feet!

If you have many years at the same organization, emphasize your promotions by placing bullet point achievement statements under each job title. Doing so will give your Work History a sense of dynamism and diversity, thereby countering the image of being a stick-in-the-mud that sometimes comes from exceptional longevity at one company.

Straight Up

Barry Rizkallah presented his comprehensive career at Chevron in a concise list in the Work History section of his functional resume. At a glance, the reader could see that Barry was an accomplished marketing professional—why else would he have been promoted through such a healthy tenure?

When listing your promotions at one place of employment, organize the dates of your job titles so the reader understands at a glance that they are a subset of the overall dates at the company. In each of the following two resumes, the overall dates are flush left, and the job title dates are on the right, making it obvious that the job title dates are detailing the overall time at the company.

Zipping Along

When Shane Mathews wrote his resume in 2002, he wanted to show off his promotions at his last two companies. By grouping his job titles as subsets under each company heading, he achieved two things:

- He made it easy for employers to see that he'd been promoted.
- He avoided having to go into detail about each job title.

The employer surely appreciated this smart move.

The Happy Job-Hopper

Temporary employment or short-term assignments can make your Work History look complicated and sometimes create gaps in employment. If that's the case for you, don't worry. You have two solutions to choose from.

The first solution is to list the name of the employment agency you worked for, followed by a subset of impressive clients, as in the following example:

Creative Employment Agency, Graphic Designer, 2001-pres.

Clients included: Xerox Corp.
IBM
First Bank

The second option is to justify the span of time with a professional title preceded or followed by a term such as *contractor, freelance*, or *consultant*, whichever is appropriate for your field. The following examples show this strategy:

Creative Employment Agency, Freelance Graphic Designer, 2001–pres.

Clients included: Xerox Corp.
IBM
First Bank

Marketing Consultant, 2000–present
McMillan Financial Services
Lewiston National Bank
Prosperity Trust

By bundling your short-term assignments under a professional title in your Work History, you'll no longer look like a job-hopper.

Formatting Tricks

In addition to the tips mentioned so far in this chapter, here are a few you might need to know about:

- Because there is no prescribed order in which to list your work history components (date, job title, employer's name, city), you are free to prioritize the elements according to your job objective's relevance. For instance, the President of Universal Studios might present his work history in any one of these ways:

  2005–pres., President, Universal Studios, Los Angeles

  President, Universal Studios, Los Angeles, 2005–pres.

  Universal Studios, Los Angeles, President, 2005–pres.

  Universal Studios, Los Angeles, 2005–pres., President
- You may state your date ranges either with the century digits in both years (for example: 2002–2003) or with the century digits in the first year and not in the second (for example: 2001–03). The key is to be consistent throughout your resume.

- If your list of job titles at one company is so long you think it might overwhelm the employer, you can list only the ones that support your job objective. In that case, preface your list with something such as "Relevant Positions" or "Positions included," and don't list dates for each job. The following example shows this strategy:

2000–present	TransAmerica State Insurance, Wilmington
Relevant Positions:	Marketing Manager Business Analyst Marketing Specialist

- Depending on what you list in the Work History section of your functional resume, consider naming this section one of the following:

Work History	History
Employment History	Experience
Relevant History	Career History

The Least You Need to Know

- Use only years, not months, when presenting your work history.
- Avoid age discrimination by using the EPT formula.
- Disguise gaps in your Work History by giving yourself a job title that explains the unemployed span.
- Arrange your Work History section to show off your promotions within a company.

Janet Bennett

123 Amboy Street • Little Rock, AR 12345 • **(123) 555-1234** • jbennett@bamboo.com

JOB OBJECTIVE: A position teaching preschool and elementary-age children.

SUMMARY OF QUALIFICATIONS

- More than 20 years teaching preschool and elementary-age children.
- Good communication skills with children and adults.
- Capable of leading projects. Supportive team worker.
- Experience working in low-economic settings.

EXPERIENCE

WORK WITH CHILDREN

- Taught children of low-income families at State of Arkansas Preschool Program, a parent participation program.
- Incorporated parents into the preschool program, being sensitive to the parents' needs for shared responsibility.
- Planned the preschool's parent education programs and trained them in effective communications with children.
- Collaborated with fellow preschool teacher to share ideas and solutions, as well as to train teacher aide in classroom management style and curriculum.

SCHOOL-COMMUNITY RELATIONS

- Served on PTA Board as president (four years) and coordinator of parent services in the classroom (four years) of Briarcliff Elementary (my children's school).
- Taught Parent Educator Program (five years) at Briarcliff. Co-planned curriculum, and facilitated discussions on prevention of drug/alcohol abuse and self-esteem.
- Volunteered extensively for classroom activities, field trips, etc. at Booker Baptist Church.
- As member of School Site Council, planned use of state funds for school.
  - Identified the area of need; built a consensus of how to address it.
  - Applied for funding.

WORK HISTORY

Childcare Teacher	Booker Baptist Church, North Little Rock, AR	2006
Full-Time Parent	Little Rock, AR	1990-06
Classroom Teacher	State of Arkansas Preschool Program, Sherwood, AR	1983-90
Classroom Kindergarten Teacher	Pine Bluff Public Schools, Pine Bluff, AR	1981-83

EDUCATION AND CREDENTIALS

B.S., Elementary Education, University of Arkansas, Little Rock, AR, 1980
State of Arkansas Teaching Credential, K-9 and Early Childhood, lifetime

DIANNE WOO

123 Hollister Place, St. Louis, MO 12345 (123) 555-1234 diannewoo@bamboo.com

OBJECTIVE

Office Manager

SUMMARY OF QUALIFICATIONS

- 12 years office management experience in one of the nation's leading corporations.
- Consistent record of increasing productivity by maintaining effective interdepartmental relations and office systems.
- Excellent IBM and Macintosh skills.
- International background. Bilingual: Mandarin/English.

PROFESSIONAL EXPERIENCE

1994-present GENERAL ELECTRIC, INC., St. Louis, MO

Administrative Secretary to Director, Corporate Communications, 1999-present

- Independently streamlined this fast-paced department that generates annual, quarterly, and monthly publications with individual circulation of up to 120,000.
- Devised electronic network that facilitates immediate written communications with over 200 remote locations.
- Managed budgets totaling $1 million. Prepared estimates and proposals for new publications.

Secretary to Vice President, Merchandising, Office Products, 1997-1999

- Set up and managed office procedures for the Merchandising Department, which produced a national wholesale office products catalog.
- Provided office support for 13 managers.

Secretary/Assistant to Manager, Office Services, 1994-1997

- Increased quality of office services for the 750-person headquarters building by improving customer service and inventory systems.

Assistant to Managing Director, Missouri Training Academy, 1994

- Assisted Director in setting up training program for technical and media professionals.

1986-1994 FOREIGN OFFICE, REPUBLIC OF CHINA

Administrative Secretary to Consul General, St. Louis, MO, 1989-1994

Secretary to Ambassador, Beijing, China, 1986-1988

- Represented Republic of China to foreign diplomats and maintained strict confidentiality as "right-hand" to the Consul General and the Ambassador.
- Served as translator to Chinese officials during state visits.

EDUCATION

B.S. equivalent, University of Beijing, China, 1986

Certificates, Foreign Language Correspondent, Beijing, China

Barry M. Rizkallah

123 Banana Drive • Wheeling, WV 12345 • (123) 555-1234 • rizkallah@bamboo.com

Marketing Professional

Summary of Qualifications

- 13 years as a marketing professional for one of the nation's leading corporations.
- Expertise in project management, marketing, and vendor relations.
- Computer proficient: Excel, PowerPoint, MS Word, Vizio, Lotus Notes, Microsoft Project.

Selected Accomplishments

at Chevron U.S.A. Products, Inc.

PROJECT MANAGEMENT

- Led a team of operations, advertising, and product development managers for the $200,000 launch of a new product.
- Coordinated analytical team efforts to standardize quality of service in 8,500 retail sites.
- Increased sales and improved customer relations by developing Chevron International's first co-op advertising program.
- Organized sales retreats in U.S. and overseas resorts for 50 agents from around world.
- Trained regional coordinators and outside consultants in new computer programs.

MARKETING

- Created "Who's Who," a 12-page, four-color brochure distributed worldwide that promoted Chevron as a valuable international player.
- Designed a $15,000 booth for international trade shows for Chevron's cultural diversity.
- Produced "Technical Tables and Charts," a detailed 50-page publication used in the shipping industry. Updated content and image, dramatically increasing demand.

Work History

1993-present **Chevron U.S.A. Products, Inc., Wheeling, West Virginia**

Business Analyst, 2006-present
Marketing Specialist, 2002-2006
Senior Marketing Assistant, 1999-2002
Marketing Help Desk Representative, 1998-1999
Collections Representative, 1997-1998
Customer Representative, 1993-1997
Administrative Assistant, 1993

1992-1993 **Saudi Research & Marketing, Inc., Houston, TX**

Publication Subscription Manager

Education

B.A., Public Relations, minor: Business, West Virginia State College, Wheeling, WV, 1991

Shane Mathews

123 Bay Court • Columbus, OH 12345 • (123) 555-1234 • shanem@bamboo.com

JOB OBJECTIVE: Collections Administrator

SUMMARY OF QUALIFICATIONS

- Ten years of business experience, including eight years in the financial services industry.
- Proficient at utilizing computer systems to produce analytical reports.
- Enhance operations through strong organizational and problem-solving skills.

EXPERIENCE

THE BANK OF OHIO, Columbus, OH, 2002-pres.
Corporate Operations Manager
Banking Officer
Banking Assistant

- Retrieved data, analyzed information and spread financial reports for management, using mainframe and PC systems. LAN Administrator for two years.
- Bank-certified to respond to credit inquiries using Robert Morris Associates criteria.
- Administered operational systems that satisfied auditors for four consecutive years.
- Reduced liability and standardized corporate banking operations by instituting risk management policies.
- Served as liaison to account officers, clients and bank departments, ensuring quality customer service through problem resolution.
- Supervised personnel; handled salary reviews, performance counseling and training.

GREAT MID-WESTERN BANK, Cleveland, OH, 1998-2001
Management Trainee
Administrative Assistant

- Compiled and calculated statistics for weekly and quarterly reports.
- Prepared human resources reports that included salary and turnover analyses.

UNIVERSITY OF CLEVELAND, Cleveland, OH, 1996-1997
Full-time MBA Student

WHITE MEADOWS CENTER, INC., Cleveland, OH, 1995-1996
Assistant Marketing Manager

- Assisted in development of annual calendar and budget for this large shopping center.
- Collaborated with merchants and management to produce joint promotions.

EDUCATION

MBA, Marketing, 2000, University of Cleveland, Cleveland, OH
BA, Administration and Legal Processes, 1995, Kent State, Kent, OH

Chapter 8

Step Five: Show 'Em You're an Achiever!

In This Chapter

- Why achievement statements are a smart use of your resume real estate
- How to present major headings in your functional resume
- How to make the value of your experience obvious to an employer
- Add power to your sentences with action verbs

Most resumes are dry (so dry you need to drink a couple of glasses of water just to get through them) because they focus on boring job duties. Although your potential employer wants to know what you've done, she is even more concerned with whether you've achieved the desired results on the job. In this chapter, you determine what your relevant achievements are and learn how to put them on your resume, so you can get the most out of every word.

Chronologically Clear

The achievement statements in your chronological resume appear under the company name where you performed the achievements. To understand what section I'm referring to, look at the highlighted areas in the following chronological template.

By the way, Professional Experience is the name of the midsection in the chronological template shown in this chapter (which contains your work history and achievement statements). That section may also be called the following:

- Professional Accomplishments
- Career Achievements
- Achievements
- Selected Accomplishments
- Experience

(Achievement Statements in Chronological Resume)

Name
Street
City, State Zip
Phone, Fax, E-mail

JOB OBJECTIVE

The job you want next

SUMMARY OF QUALIFICATIONS

- How much experience you have in the field of your job objective, in a related field, or using the skills required for your new position.
- An overall career accomplishment that shows you'd be good at this job.
- What someone would say about you as a recommendation.

PROFESSIONAL EXPERIENCE

20xx-pres. **Company Name, City, State**
Job Title

- An accomplishment you are proud of that shows you're good at this profession.
- A problem you solved and the results.
- A time when you positively affected the organization, the bottom line, your boss, your co-workers, your clients.
- Awards, commendations, publications, etc., you achieved that relate to your job objective.

20xx-xx **Company Name, City, State**
Job Title

- A project you are proud of that supports your job objective.
- Another accomplishment that shows you're good at this line of work.
- Quantifiable results that point out your skill.

19xx-xx **Company Name, City, State**
Job Title

- An accomplishment you are proud of that shows you will be valued by your next employer.
- An occasion when someone "sat up and took notice" of your skill.

EDUCATION

Degree, Major (if relevant), 20xx (optional)
University, City, State

If you're a chronological resume writer, skip past the next few sections about the functional resume and jump into "Dynamite Achievements" later in this chapter.

Functionally Sound

You're still reading, so you must be a functional resume writer. Your achievement statements should appear under the appropriate skill headings in the body of your resume. Check out the next functional resume template to see what I mean.

Do you have a feel for where your achievements are going to be listed? Good. Now read on to learn some important things about creating the skill headings for your functional resume.

Functional Help

One of the key advantages to using a functional resume is that you define yourself by your skills, rather than by your former job titles. That's why it's an especially good format for career changers and those with tricky employment histories.

The way to put the spotlight on your skills in the functional resume is to create skill headings, which appear in the body of the resume. The purpose of using the skill headings is to help the potential employer quickly identify you as someone with the talents needed to do the job. (Don't forget you have to make a good impression during an initial eight-second scan!) If you keep your skill headings brief and put them in bold or large print, the employer will quickly define you by your skills, rather than by your previous job titles.

> **Bonus Check**
>
> Be sure that the print of your skill headings appears smaller than your major section headings. You can achieve this by doing one of the following:
>
> - Make the skill heading type one or two font sizes smaller than the major section headings. (To learn about font sizes, see Chapter 14.)
> - Use all uppercase letters in the major heading, and use uppercase and lowercase in the skill headings (see Michael Wong's resume later in this chapter).

One Plus One Is Enough

To figure out what skill headings to put on your functional resume, imagine that you are an employer who is writing an ad for the job mentioned in your Job Objective statement. What skills would you list as requirements?

Let's say you're the manager of a retail store, and you're looking for a Director of Customer Service. Your help wanted ad might read: "Applicant must be skilled in supervision and customer service." Now step back into the shoes of the job seeker. Supervision and Customer Service would be the two skill headings you should use on your resume.

Don't overwhelm your reader by having too many skill headings. Two (at most three) headings are usually plenty to make a good first impression. Also, don't write lengthy skill headings in your resume. Limit them to no more than three words each. Otherwise they become too difficult to read in the employer's typical initial eight-second scan.

(Achievement Statements in Functional Resume)

Name

Street
City, State Zip
Phone, Fax, E-mail

JOB OBJECTIVE

The job you want next

SUMMARY OF QUALIFICATIONS

- How much experience you have in the field of your job objective, in a related field, or using the skills required for your new position.
- An overall career accomplishment that shows you'd be good at this job.
- What someone would say about you as a recommendation.

RELEVANT EXPERIENCE

MAJOR SKILL

- An accomplishment you are proud of that shows you have this skill.
- A problem you solved using this skill, and the results.
- A time when you used your skill to positively affect the organization, the bottom line, your boss, your clients.
- Awards, commendations, publications, etc., you achieved that relate to your job objective.

MAJOR SKILL

- A project you are proud of that supports your job objective.
- Another accomplishment that shows you're good at this line of work.
- Quantifiable results that point out your skill.
- An occasion when someone "sat up and took notice" of your skill.

WORK HISTORY

20xx-present	Job Title	COMPANY NAME and city
20xx-xx	Job Title	COMPANY NAME and city
20xx-xx	Job Title	COMPANY NAME and city
19xx-xx	Job Title	COMPANY NAME and city

EDUCATION

Degree, Major (if relevant), 20xx (optional)
University, City, State

Let's role-play again: As a supervisor in a software development firm looking for a technical supervisor, you might write, "Applicant must be proficient in computer programming and team leadership." As a job seeker, you understand that Programming and Leadership would be good skill headings to use on your resume for this job.

Take a look at the resume for Michael Wong, found at the end of this chapter. Notice how his skill headings define his job objective, which differed from his Work History. This resume is an excellent example of how a resume should be about a job seeker's future, not his past.

Skills for Sale

Some functional resume writers have trouble coming up with skill headings. When selecting the skill headings for your functional resume, be sure to choose ones that define your future (your job objective), not your past (your Work History). If you feel stuck, take a look at the following list of skills. It's also a good idea to visit your industry's websites to learn what skill sets are sought after in your field. Notice that I've categorized this list according to four general occupational areas: business management, education, engineering/technical, and nonprofit management. Although you may want to focus on an area that's close to your job objective, I suggest you read through the entire list. Maybe a word in another category will inspire you to define your skill set in a way that is uniquely yours.

Business Management

Accounting
Accounts Payable
Accounts Receivable
Administration
Advertising
Benefits
Budget Management
Business Development
Client Relations
Community Relations
Conflict Resolution
Consulting
Copy Writing
Corporate Giving
Customer Service
Executive Management
Financial Management
Human Resources
Insurance
International Relations
Inventory Control
Inventory Management
Investor Relations
Leadership
Legal
Management Consulting
Marketing
Media Relations
Mediation
Meeting Planning
Negotiations
Office Management
Operations
Order Fulfillment
Organizational Development
Personnel
Presentation Coaching
Presentations
Product Development
Production
Project Management
Promotions
Public Relations
Purchasing
Quality Assurance
Re-engineering
Recruitment
Retail Management
Sales
Shipping
Speech Writing
Strategic Planning
Supervision
Training
Vendor Relations
Writing

Education

Administration
Admissions Evaluation
Classroom Management
Committee Leadership
Counseling
Curriculum Development
Interdisciplinary Teamwork
Parent Relations
Program Development
Research
Teaching
Tutoring

Engineering/Technical

Analysis
Computer
Customer Support
Data Collection
Database Management
Design
Development
Documentation
Engineering
MIS
Planning
Presentations
Programming
Research
Survey Coordination
System Design
System Evaluation
Systems Analysis
Team Leadership
Teamwork
Technical Support
Technical Writing

Nonprofit Management

Advocacy
Board Relations
Calendar Management
Community Outreach
Consensus Building
Counseling
Development
Event Planning
Financial Management
Fund-Raising
Grant Proposal Writing
Leadership
Major Donor Giving
Media Relations
Needs Assessment
Program Coordination
Program Development
Project Coordination
Public Relations
Public Speaking
Recruiting
Service Delivery
Solicitations
Staff Management
Volunteer Management
Volunteer Recruitment
Writing

Dynamite Achievements

Nab the employer's interest right away with an achievement-oriented resume. By writing about your experience in terms of achievements, not job descriptions, you'll convey three things:

- You have the experience and skills to do the job.
- You're good at this work and at using these skills.
- You like your work. (You must! There's pride in your statements.)

Achievements will impress the reader, make your resume far more interesting to read, and stimulate productive conversation during the interview. Powerful achievement statements that speak to the employer's bottom line also build a strong foundation for your salary negotiations. When you create your achievement statements, be careful not to emphasize any aspect of the experience that you don't enjoy doing. Only stress the parts of the achievement that you would like to repeat. Also, when listing items within an achievement statement, prioritize those items so that the most relevant one comes first. When listing them in a column, list them either according to relevance or alphabetically.

Terms of Employment

Responsible for is a slippery phrase that doesn't clearly describe your level of involvement. Did you think of an idea that others carried out, or did you work overtime to implement every detail of a project? Either way, be sure to give yourself full credit by using action verbs (instead of "responsible for") to indicate exactly what your role was.

Who's Your Audience?

Keep in mind while you write your resume that your audience is the hiring manager for the position mentioned in your Job Objective statement. To sell yourself to this potential employer, talk about yourself in ways that are meaningful to her. In some cases, you may need to do one or more of the following:

- Translate terminology to downplay differences between your past experience and your job objective.
- Select only aspects of your achievements that paint a picture of you at your next job.
- Prioritize your points so that your most relevant achievements are emphasized.

Downplay Differences

Avoid job-specific jargon in order to downplay the differences and emphasize the similarities between your previous position and your job objective. For example, Elizabeth was a nurse who was applying for a customer service position at a department store. She used general terms when referring to her hospital work so the employer would see that her customer service skills were just what was needed in the department store.

> **Instead of writing:** Explained medical procedures and equipment to Hamilton Medical Center patients and their families to enable them to make wise decisions regarding surgery, care, and discharge.
>
> **Elizabeth wrote:** Educated clients about new products and procedures at the medical center and assisted them in making personal decisions based on financial, lifestyle, and timeline concerns.

When Charles's military service ended, he wanted a job in corporate public relations, so he phrased his statements using civilian terminology to de-emphasize his career transition.

> **Instead of writing:** Managed public relations for the U.S. Navy's Fleet Week, a $1.5 million celebration that drew 50,000 civilians.
>
> **Charles wrote:** Managed public relations for a $1.5 million celebration sponsored by the Bay Area's largest employer and attended by some 50,000 people.

Always make it simple for an employer to understand how you fit into her organization. If necessary, translate your experience into terminology that she will identify with easily.

Keep It Relevant

Your achievements consist of several ingredients, some of which may have nothing to do with what you will offer your next employer. Make an impression that you're a good fit by presenting only the aspects of your achievements that relate to your job objective.

For example, Henry was an excellent event planner who wanted to use his organizational skills in a new field: graphic layout for a daily newspaper. He knew he could not assume the employer would conclude that Henry was capable of laying out newspaper copy just because he knew how to plan events, so Henry took extra care to draw the parallels between the two occupations.

> **Instead of writing:** Produced social and business events for up to 2,000 people, managing budgets, catering, entertainment, and logistics.
>
> **Henry wrote:** Maintained a perfect record of on-time delivery of at least 20 projects a month, involving time, budget, and space constraints.

As a horticulturist, Patty realized that the part of her job she liked the most was answering clients' questions. When she wrote her resume for a job as a travel agent, she emphasized her customer service skills and downplayed her scientific expertise.

> **Instead of writing:** Provided scientific information on thousands of plant species as the lead horticulturist of the country's most prestigious botanical garden.
>
> **Patty wrote:** Assisted customers in selecting from more than 2,000 options by patiently answering questions and educating them about costs and benefits.

To have effective achievement statements, refer to the aspects of your experiences that paint the picture of your job objective, and therefore, have meaning to your prospective employer.

First Things First

Prioritize your statements so the achievement most relevant to your job goal is first. For example, as a former office manager, 75 percent of Andrea's time was spent processing administrative paperwork, and less than 25 percent of her time was spent on training and supervision. However, she wanted to get a job as a corporate trainer. So she prioritized her achievement statements to stress the training experience, even though it was not her primary responsibility.

> CAUTION
>
> **Career Casualty**
>
> Most chronological resume writers make a big mistake: because they're creating a history-based resume, they write job descriptions instead of dynamic achievements. Don't fall for that logic! By writing achievement statements, you'll turn a stereotypically boring document into a winning sales piece.

The following order reflects the amount of time Andrea spent on each achievement:

- Supervised administration of firm's largest litigation department with more than 300 cases per week.
- Led office to achieve "#1 Team" award by motivating staff to take a customer service approach to all internal and external interactions.
- Trained 13 employees on new automated accounting system, providing classroom sessions, individual coaching, and written instructions.

This order reflects which achievements are most important to Andrea's job goal:

- Trained 13 employees on new automated accounting system, providing classroom sessions, individual coaching, and written instructions.
- Led office to achieve "#1 Team" award by motivating staff to take a customer service approach to all internal and external interactions.
- Supervised administration of firm's largest litigation department with more than 300 cases per week.

The order in which you list your achievements should indicate what tasks you like best and which ones you wish most to perform on your next job.

Lights, Camera, Action Verbs!

A film crew may have lights and cameras, but there's no movie until there's action. Likewise, your resume needs dynamic language to make it move. To deliver the most punch in your achievement statements, use an action verb at or near the beginning of each line. Action verbs make your resume more powerful by emphasizing how you accomplished your goals.

The following list of verbs is categorized under two headings: Management and Communication. Which verbs most powerfully describe your achievements?

Management

accelerated
accomplished
achieved
activated
added
administered
advanced
allocated
analyzed
anticipated
appointed
appropriated
approved
arranged
assigned
attained
augmented
authorized
bid
boosted
budgeted
built
capitalized on
carried out
caused
centralized
certified
chaired
championed
collaborated
completed
conceived
concentrated
conducted
consolidated
contracted
controlled
converted
coordinated
corrected
cultivated
cut
decided
defined
delegated
delivered
designated
determined
developed
devised
directed
dominated
doubled
downsized
drove
earned
empowered
endorsed
engineered
enhanced
enlarged
enlisted
established
evaluated
exceeded
executed
expanded
expedited
facilitated
financed
focused
forced
forged
fostered
founded
fulfilled
gained
generated
governed
guided
handled
headed
heightened
hired
implemented
improved
incorporated
increased
induced
initiated
installed
instituted
integrated
intensified
introduced
invested
launched
led
lowered

Management (continued)

magnified
maintained
managed
marketed
maximized
merged
met
minimized
mobilized
modernized
modified
monitored
motivated
multiplied
netted
obtained
opened
orchestrated
organized
oversaw
performed
piloted
pioneered
planned
positioned
precipitated
presided
prioritized
processed
produced
promoted
proposed
purchased
ran
ranked
rated
reengineered
reached
realized
recommended
recruited
reduced
regulated
rejuvenated
remedied
renewed
represented
resolved
restored
restructured
revamped
reviewed
revitalized
revived
revolutionized
scheduled
secured
served as
set
shepherded
sold
solved
started
steered
stimulated
streamlined
strengthened
structured
succeeded
supervised
synchronized
systematized
targeted
trained
tripled
triumphed
turned around
underwrote
unified
united
upgraded
upheld
verified
won

Communication

addressed
adjudicated
advertised
advised
advocated
annotated
announced
answered
appeased
arbitrated
argued
articulated
asserted
assuaged
assured
authored
bargained
briefed
campaigned
canvassed
clarified
coached
coined
collaborated
communicated
compelled
compiled
composed
compromised
conversed
converted
convinced
corresponded
counseled
created
defined
delivered
demonstrated
demystified
depicted
described
detailed
developed
dictated
discussed
drafted
edited
educated

elucidated
encouraged
explained
expounded
expressed
facilitated
formulated
guaranteed
guided
illustrated
impressed
influenced
informed
inspired
instigated
instructed
interpreted
intervened
interviewed
intonated
lectured
litigated
lobbied
mediated
moderated
motivated
negotiated
ordered
outlined
persuaded
phrased
pitched
preached
prepared
presented
pressured
proclaimed
promoted
prompted
proofread
proposed
publicized
reassured
recommended
reconciled
remarked
represented
settled (disputes)
specified
spelled out
spoke
stated
stimulated
stipulated
stressed
swayed
taught
trained
translated
urged
verbalized
voiced
won over
wrote

How'd the Other Guys Say It?

A quick look at what others have written might give you the jumpstart you need for writing about your own accomplishments. The following achievement statements were taken from several different resumes:

- Restructured entire Service Department, resulting in more efficient outreach programs.
- Initiated procedures to increase employee productivity while reducing stress levels.
- Successfully explained and demonstrated technical products in lay terminology to prospective buyers.
- Negotiated the sale of $100,000 worth of unprofitable inventory.
- Created sales and marketing programs that increased shopping center profits by 33 percent.
- Won more than 80 percent of cases, delivering persuasive arguments as legal representative for corporate clients in administrative law hearings.
- Increased MediSave's stock value fivefold in nine months by repositioning the product and company.
- Convinced more than 400 commuters to carpool, reducing the number of vehicles on the road by 225 per year.
- Managed a national and international sales force of 32 manufacturers' representative companies for Teekel Press, a publisher.

Bonus Check

A well-crafted functional resume that makes it clear where the job seeker's achievements took place can win over employers, even those who claim not to like functional resumes.

Job Hunt Hint

Name-dropping is the name of the game. Look for opportunities to enhance your image by slipping in names of impressive people, companies, or organizations.

- Exceeded delivery performance by 10 percent, taking it from 85 percent to a record 95 percent in an industry where the norm is 75 percent.
- Managed the sales and Profit & Loss for 20 stores in Northern California region.
- Handled daily news coverage of the San Francisco 49ers and Oakland A's, which involved extensive travel.
- Authored two published pieces on international touring, which demystified the hardships and emphasized the rewards of independent travel.
- Reconciled differences among personnel, creating a more cohesive team spirit.

Brainstorming

The following questions will help you think of relevant achievements for your resume. Not all of the questions will apply to your situation, so answer only the ones that do.

1. What projects are you proud of that relate to your job objective?

   Example: Increased productivity 20 percent as lead engineer on Hewlett-Packard's HMS technical team.

2. What are some quantifiable results that point out your ability?

   Example: Drove profits from $20 million to $34 million by directing a national celebrity marketing campaign.

3. When have you demonstrated PAR (Problem, Action, Result)? What was the problem, what was your action to remedy it, and what was the result?

   Example: Reduced theft 47 percent by instituting Shoppers' Spy, a tight yet discreet security program.

4. When did you positively affect the organization, the bottom line, your boss, your co-workers, or your clients?

   Example: Enhanced staff morale through a six-month incentive program that also prompted a major increase in sales.

5. What awards, commendations, or publications have you achieved that relate to your job objective?

   Example: Awarded "Top Salesperson" for three consecutive years.

6. How is success measured in your field? How do you measure up?

   Example: Selected by the NIH to represent the United States at the International AIDS Conference in Brazil.

7. Are you good at using the skills required for this job? When have you demonstrated that to be true?

   Example: Used advanced CAD tools to create a totally new look in video game modeling.

8. What activities, paid and unpaid, have you performed that used skills you'll be using at your new job?

Example: Offered academic counseling to 40 students at "Make It Happen," a volunteer program at Sanford High School.

9. When did someone sit up and take notice of how skilled you are?

   Example: Commended for achieving 97 percent of production goal in an industry where 85 percent is considered high.

In addition to answering these questions, you might want to browse through the resumes throughout the book, in the "Portfolio of Sample Resumes" at the back of this book, and at my website, www.susanireland.com, to see which phrases trigger ideas for your resume.

Warning! Functional Resume Ahead

Many times functional resume writers make the mistake of writing accomplishment statements without indicating where the achievements took place. This practice makes potential employers uneasy because they have no way of confirming the experience. The solution? Give each accomplishment credibility by saying where it happened. Here are three ways to indicate where your success took place:

1. Incorporate the name of the organization or your position into the sentence:

   Managed Harrington Department Store's $1.5 million budget.

   Collaborated with executives to create a new marketing strategy, as member of the St. Francis Board of Directors.

2. Reference the organization or your position at the end of the statement:

   Managed budget of $1.5 million. (Harrington Department Store)

   Collaborated with executives to create a new marketing strategy. (St. Francis Board of Directors)

3. Group achievements together according to where they happened, still keeping them within skill categories. This kind of organization, in effect, becomes a hybrid resume based on a functional format (explained in Chapter 12).

You'll notice all three of these techniques as you peruse the sample functional resumes in the "Portfolio of Sample Resumes" at the back of this book.

The Least You Need to Know

- In a chronological resume, place your achievement statements under the appropriate job title in the body of your resume.
- In a functional resume, your skill headings become subheadings under the Relevant Experience section in the body of your resume.
- Write powerful achievement statements instead of boring job descriptions.
- Use action verbs at or near the beginning of your achievement statements.
- Prioritize bulleted points within each section so the statement with the most impact comes first.
- Include the information on where an achievement took place in functional resumes.

Michael Wong

123 Adams Street, #1 • Somerville, MA 12345 • (123) 555-1234 • mwong@bamboo.com

JOB OBJECTIVE: A position in Public Relations with an emphasis on Event Planning.

SUMMARY OF QUALIFICATIONS

- Experienced at public relations for a provider of promotional merchandise for national and international concert tours.
- Success in producing events for up to 8,000 people.
- Reputation for achieving goals using a professional yet personable approach.

EDUCATION

MBA, International Marketing, Boston University, Boston, MA, 1997
BA, Marketing, Northeastern University, Boston, MA, 1995

RELEVANT ACCOMPLISHMENTS

Public Relations

- Represented promotional merchandise providers to concert hall managements, bands, and the public. Tours included: Melissa Etheridge, Matchbox 20, Jimmy Buffett, Faith Hill
- Saved as much as 6% of revenues when negotiating venue contracts for promotional merchandise sales of up to $25,000 per night.
- Developed positive rapport between band and merchandise company by creating a team atmosphere rather than a strictly business relationship.
- Commended for establishing strong working relationships with bands and management companies. Consistently requested by bands for repeat and new tours.
- Acted as tour public relations person, handling questions and comments from fans.

Event Planning

- As event planner on the Arts Board, produced sell-out musical and theatrical programs for up to 8,000 attendees.
- As hospitality director for Musical Event Board, negotiated contracts, supervised catering, and managed backstage accommodations for concerts including:

U2	Destiny's Child	Eminem
James Taylor	Brian McKnight	No Doubt

WORK HISTORY

2002-present	**Tour Manager for Merchandise**	DAVIS ENTERTAINMENT, nationwide, 2003-present
		CARMICHAEL GROUP, nationwide, 2003 tour
2003	**Executive Assistant** (contractual)	AXTELL GROUP (advertising/promotions), Boston
2000-2002	**Department Manager**	SHOE SHOPS INC., Cambridge

Chapter 9

Step Six: Give Yourself Credit for Education and More

In This Chapter

- How to create a proper Education section
- Where to put professional affiliations, community service, and other information on your resume
- How to deal with an employer's request for your salary history
- What not to put on your resume

Your resume is looking pretty good, isn't it? You've resolved your work history problems, written dynamite achievement statements, made claims that blow your competition out of the water—you're on a roll! You need to consider only a few more things, and then you'll be ready to drop your resume in the mail. In this chapter, I share some helpful hints on how to make the most of your academic, professional, and vocational training, as well as other activities that support your job objective. I also explain why some information, such as references, salary history, and personal data, may not belong on your resume at all.

Finish Lines

At this point, you may be left with laundry lists of technical, personal, and professional details that don't fit into the primary sections of your resume discussed so far. Lingering lists might include the following information:

- Education
- Professional training
- Community service
- Professional affiliations
- Publications
- Awards
- Computer skills
- Personal pursuits

Even if you feel like just throwing them in a big pile at the bottom of the page, don't! Instead, create one or more logical sections that will spark the employer's interest. Sneak a peek at the following template to see where you might place your extra goodies.

(Extra Resume Sections)

Name
Street
City, State Zip
Phone, Fax, E-mail

JOB OBJECTIVE: The job you want next

SUMMARY OF QUALIFICATIONS

- How much experience you have in the field of your job objective, in a related field, or using the skills required for your new position.
- An overall career accomplishment that shows you'd be good at this job.
- What someone would say about you as a recommendation.

PROFESSIONAL EXPERIENCE

20xx-pres. Job Title **Company Name, City, State**

- An accomplishment you are proud of that shows you're good at this profession.
- A problem you solved and the results.
- A time when you positively affected the organization, the bottom line, your boss, your co-workers, your clients.
- Awards, commendations, publications, etc., you achieved that relate to your job objective.

20xx-xx Job Title **Company Name, City, State**

- A project you are proud of that supports your job objective.
- Another accomplishment that shows you're good at this line of work.
- Quantifiable results that point out your skill.

19xx-xx Job Title **Company Name, City, State**

- An accomplishment you are proud of that shows you will be valued by your next employer.
- An occasion when someone "sat up and took notice" of your skill.

EDUCATION

Degree, Major (if relevant), 20xx (optional), University, City, State

PROFESSIONAL AFFILIATIONS

Association	Position (optional)	Dates (optional)
Association	Position (optional)	Dates (optional)

COMMUNITY SERVICE

Volunteer position	Organization	Dates (optional)
Volunteer position	Organization	Dates (optional)

Education 101

Your education is almost always a point of interest to a prospective employer. The Education section is usually positioned at or near the end of the resume, as noted on the previous template.

In some cases, however, it's better to place the Education section under the Summary of Qualifications section near the beginning of the resume. You might want to put it here if one or more of the following conditions applies:

- Your education is highly relevant to your new position.
- You're a new graduate and you want to show off your degree.
- You have no employment experience in the field you are going into, but you have a degree or training in that field.

What If?

Job Hunt Hint

Instead of listing all the classes and workshops you ever attended, list only the ones that support your job objective.

Education comes in many forms (formal, independent, professional training, and experiential), and there are as many ways to measure its results (degrees, credentials, certifications, equivalencies, years of experience, lists of acquired skills).

You probably fall into one of the following categories:

- You have one or more college degrees.
- You are about to achieve your college degree.
- You have a college degree equivalent.
- You went to college but didn't complete your degree program.
- You just graduated from high school.
- You graduated from high school some time ago and never went to college.

Let's look at how to present each one of these situations and how real job seekers handled the Educations sections on their resumes (found at the end of this chapter).

Hot College Degrees

Perhaps the most common listing for the Education section on a resume is a college degree. So let's begin by talking about degrees and related information. If you have one or more college degrees, keep the following points in mind:

- State where each degree (graduate and undergraduate) was received. You don't have to list all the different schools you attended leading up to achieving your degree, just list the one where you obtained your degree.
- Dates are optional. They sometimes indicate how old you are and how current your knowledge is, so be conscious of that when you decide whether to include dates.

Career Casualty

Don't appear overqualified for the job. For some positions, your Master's or Doctoral degree might scare the pants off an employer because you look too expensive or intimidating. When in doubt, leave the degree off. And if you're tempted to lie about a degree or certification, resist! Getting caught in a lie could put your job in the can.

- Majors, minors, theses, dissertations, internships, projects, papers, and coursework should be listed only if they are relevant to your job objective.
- You can spell out a degree (for example, Bachelor of Arts) or use the representative letters (BA or B.A.).

Phillip Riekels listed his Education section near the top of his resume because his degrees are so important to his job objective.

Getting Credit for Your Pending Degree

If you are currently in a relevant educational or training program but have not yet finished, list the program and name of the institution you are attending, followed by the date you intend to finish or one of the following phrases:

- Currently enrolled
- Anticipated completion: Spring 2004
- In progress
- Six months completed

Robyn Jones's resume demonstrates this point.

Interpreting Degree Equivalents

If you achieved a degree equivalency through a less-traditional or non-American system, state your experience in terms of its equivalency, for example, "B.A. equivalent, St. Paul University, Rome, Italy." Grace Deminier's resume presents her degree equivalent.

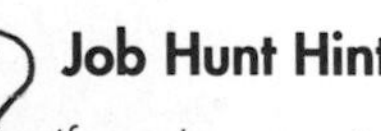

Job Hunt Hint

If you're questioning whether to add another section to your resume, weigh the pros and cons. Does it warrant the extra space it will take, especially if it means the resume will spill onto a second page?

Don't Have a Degree?

If you went to college, but you do not intend to get your degree in the immediate future, write your area of study and the name of the college, for instance: Liberal Arts, Oberlin College. If you attended several schools without completing your degree requirements, list only one or two schools. Listing more than that might make the reader think you tend to move around a lot without finishing things. Leonora Braun's resume shows how you can present a partial college education.

Yahoo! Just Got My High School Diploma

If you're a new high school graduate, write the name of your high school and year of graduation. Frank Jordan's resume lists his high school diploma.

If you've enrolled in a college, you don't have to list your high school, you can simply say that you're enrolled in college. For example, say "Enrolled in Nazareth College, Rochester, NY."

The Not-So-New High School Diploma

If you received your high school diploma more than two years ago and have no additional schooling, you do not need to have an Education section on your resume unless the job you are applying for specifically asks for a high school diploma. If it does, put "Graduate" or "Diploma," followed by the name of your high school. State your graduation date only if it doesn't blow your cover with regard to your age (as explained in Chapter 7). If you have a high school diploma but no formal higher education, one option is to create a section titled Professional Development or Training. In this section, you can list any training, workshops, seminars, or classes you have attended. Another option is to simply omit the Education section on your resume. Rose Manson didn't put an Education section on her resume because she didn't have a college degree, her high school graduation was many years ago, and her professional experience is all that she needs to qualify for her objective.

The Last Word

Your destination is within sight; you don't even need binoculars to see the resume shore anymore! Only a few more sections might appear on your resume, such as professional affiliations, community service, computer skills, and personal interests. Let's talk about them.

Volunteerism That Pays Off

What you do in your unpaid time may say as much about you as what you do for employment. If you feel that your volunteerism makes a statement about your dedication, character, or social awareness, or in any way enhances your qualifications for your next job, a section called Community Service, Civic Leadership, or Volunteerism is the place to list it.

Dates are optional under the Volunteerism section. If you list them, you should present your volunteer work in reverse chronology (your most recent work first). If you don't use dates, list your community service according to impact (the most relevant first).

Professional Schmoozer

Professional associations to which you currently belong or have once belonged can be listed either alphabetically or in order of relevance to your profession under a section called Professional Affiliations. If you currently hold or have held an office, that should also be noted. Listing dates in this section is optional.

Getting Published

Articles, books, chapters in books, and research papers that you have authored or co-authored belong in a section called Publications. Usually, dates accompany this information, requiring presentation in reverse chronology (the most current date first).

Standing Up for Your Award

In the Awards section, list honors, awards, and grants you have received that support your job objective. You can arrange this list according to date received (if you give the date) or by relevance to your next job (if you don't provide the date).

Key Point: Your Computer Skills

If you have computer skills that are important to your next job, you can highlight them under a special section called Computer Skills. Your list might include hardware, software, languages, systems, and networks with which you have experience.

Making a Hobby of It

> **Bonus Check**
>
> After you create your laundry list sections, prioritize them on your resume so that the most important and relevant list comes immediately after your Work History section (on a functional resume) or Professional Experience section (on a chronological resume).

Some job seekers like to have a section called Personal Pursuits, Personal Interests, or Personal Activities in which they can list travel, sports, religious, political, and other personal activities. The Personal Pursuits section is optional and should be included only if you feel your personal activities …

- Add to your qualifications as a candidate for your job objective.
- Say something about your character that might be valued on the job.

Although many employers have said they wouldn't hold it against a job seeker for including that sort of information, consider whether stating your personal activities might create undesired conflict with your employer's views and preferences. A potential conflict of interest could arise over issues such as race, religion, unions, and other controversial topics.

Here are a few assumptions an employer might make from the following listings on resumes:

- An applicant who lists "Board of Trustees, St. Anne's Episcopal Church" is indicating that she is actively involved in her church. Although some employers may welcome this involvement, others may feel uncomfortable with it.
- The owner of a nonunion company might feel threatened by an applicant who lists "Organizer, Teamsters, Local Chapter 47092," because he may be worried the applicant will want to unionize his company.

Anything Missing?

Other headings that might appear on your resume include Exhibitions, Research, Lectures, Licenses, and Certifications. If you have just one or two entries for a section, you might combine two similar sections with a double heading, as in the following examples:

Education and Training

Training and Credentials

Awards and Presentations

Cruise through the many resumes throughout the book, in the "Portfolio of Sample Resumes" at the back of this book, and at my website, www.susanireland.com, to see how various professionals have presented their laundry lists of achievements.

What's Better Left Unsaid

Knowing what to leave off your resume can be just as important as knowing what to include. Do not include the following:

- Salary history or requests
- Reference information
- Personal data

Let's talk about why these items are best left off your resume.

Money Talk

Although some job advertisements ask for a resume and salary history, the two do not go together. Discussion about salary belongs in the interview, not on the resume. It is to your advantage not to make a monetary request before an interview. Indicating salary requirements before the interview may increase your chances of being screened out and decrease your bargaining power during salary negotiations.

If you feel obligated to address salary in order to fulfill the employer's initial application requirements, do so in your cover letter, not on your resume. Turn to Chapter 15 to get ideas for talking about money in your letter.

Referring to References

Addresses and phone numbers of references should not be a part of your resume. They belong on a separate sheet of paper that you bring to the job interview.

Also, a big thumbs-down on writing "References available upon request" at the bottom of your resume. It's unnecessary, because employers will assume that you have references, and they know to ask for them when the time comes.

> **Bonus Check**
>
> When creating your reference sheet to take to the interview, put it on letterhead that matches your resume and cover letter. In addition to looking spiffy, the letterhead will identify whose reference sheet it is if it gets separated from your letter and resume.

Forget the Personal Stuff

Including information about your age, sex, marital status, and health is not appropriate for resumes being used in the United States. If you're applying abroad (in Europe or the United Kingdom), however, it might be expected.

Although personal information doesn't usually appear on a resume, you may want to make an exception if something in your personal life supports your job objective. For instance, if you're applying for a position designing content for a website on diabetes, you might mention in your resume (perhaps in your Summary of Qualifications) that you "have a personal understanding of diabetes" if you think it will increase your chances for an interview.

The Least You Need to Know

- List only the degrees, courses, training sessions, and workshops that are relevant to your job objective.
- If you have a degree or credential that makes you look overqualified for the job, don't put it on your resume.
- If dates within the Education section tell the reader more than you want to reveal, leave them out.
- Take inventory of the relevant information that you still want to include and list that data in appropriate sections such as Community Service, Professional Affiliations, and Awards.
- Do not include salary history, references, or personal data on your resume.

Phillip Riekels, RN, MS, CNA

123 Palmer Avenue • Muskegon, California 12345 • (123) 555-1234 • PhRiekels@bamboo.com

Health Care Administrator with 20 years combined experience:

Project Management

Standards Development/Quality Assessment and Improvement

Staff Training and Development

Client Services

EDUCATION

MS, Nursing Major with dual focus: Administration and Education, 1997
Thesis: Identification of Family Problems During the Treatment Stage of Cancer
University of Oklahoma, Oklahoma City, Oklahoma

BS, Nursing, 1985, University of Arizona, Tucson, Arizona
BA, History of Art, 1979, University of Michigan, Ann Arbor, Michigan

Continuing Education
Numerous courses to maintain **Certified Nurse Administrator** status, 2001-present
Western Network for Nurse Executives, 2000, University of California at Berkeley

PROFESSIONAL EXPERIENCE

1998-present **St. Agnes Medical Center,** Fresno, California
DIRECTOR PATIENT CARE SERVICES, 2003-present
DIRECTOR MEDICAL/SURGICAL, 1998-2003

Managed operating budgets up to $14M, 382 FTEs, and 272 patient beds for this 326-bed accredited, not-for-profit, regional, acute-care facility.

- Revitalized Quality Assurance Program by developing high standards, establishing interdepartmental problem solving, and transitioning to Quality Assessment and Improvement.
- Played primary role in achieving JCAHO accreditation and placement within top 10% of facilities nationwide.
- Improved staff productivity, patient satisfaction, and quality of care.
    - Empowered staff by decentralizing management and decision making within patient-care services. Reorganized, trained, and supported staff.
    - Restructured systems for delivery of care, including staff roles and interdepartmental reporting.
    - Introduced communication and computer technology involving 20 departments.
    - Aligned FTEs with volume and cost variations by introducing staffing by Hours Per Patient Day (HPPD) to replace staffing ratios and static patterns.
    - Improved communication and conflict resolution by providing 20-hour training program, Increasing Personal Effectiveness, for over 500 personnel.

(Continued)

St. Agnes Medical Center (Continued)

- Recruited thirteen British nurses (five of whom have stayed for more than five years) as a result of three trips to London. Worked with advertising agency, State Board of Nursing, and immigration attorney.
- Represented the hospital through newspaper and TV interviews about innovative solutions to health care problems.
- Oversaw remodeling of three major units. Merged intensive and cardiac care into one critical care unit.

1995-1998 **HCA Northwest Hospital,** Tucson, Arizona
MANAGER SURGICAL/ORTHOPEDICS

Played major role in the start-up of this new 150-bed, for-profit, acute-care community hospital.

- Developed and managed a 28-bed surgical unit.
- Managed a 24-bed ortho/neuro unit and hospital-wide messenger service.
- Started the nursing Quality Assurance Program and chaired its committee.
- Implemented the HCA Patient Classification System.
- Established HPPD staffing guidelines for all nursing units.

1994-1995 **University of Oklahoma, College of Nursing,** Tulsa, Oklahoma
TEACHING ASSISTANT

1993-1994 **CSI Productions,** Tulsa, Oklahoma
RESEARCHER AND WRITER

Wrote narratives for this producer of health care training materials on Cardiac Monitoring, Medicating the Patient, and Antiembolism Stockings.

1990-1993 **Gila Pueblo College,** Globe, Arizona
NURSING INSTRUCTOR

- Saved the nursing program by achieving 100% graduate passing rate on State Board Exams, a drastic improvement from previous years' unacceptably low rates.
- Redeveloped entire content of first year associate degree nursing program to update information and improve presentation.

1986-1990 **Hospitals in Arizona and Oklahoma**
CLINICAL PATIENT CARE positions: Charge Nurse, IV Therapist, Staff Nurse

AFFILIATIONS

World Affairs Council

Nursing Administrators Council (NAC) of Central San Joaquin Valley

- As President, established NAC as a voice of influence on nursing and health care in the valley.

Organization of Nurse Executives, California (ONE-C)

Sigma Theta Tau, National Nursing Honorary Society

ROBYN JONES

123 Primavera Ct., Portland, ME 12345 (123) 555-1234 robynjones1@bamboo.com

JOB OBJECTIVE

A position in organizational systems management

PROFILE

- Expertise in developing and managing organizational systems that:
  - Facilitate efficiency
  - Encourage creativity
  - Promote responsible behavior
  - Respond to change
  - Optimize the group's diversity
  - Build team spirit
- Committed to improving the environment through research and education.
- Particular skill in empowering others to acknowledge and articulate their value and role in an organization/society.

EXPERIENCE

1999-present **Facilitator, Navy Program for Personal Responsibility**
The Prevent Office, University of Maine, NAS Biddeford, ME

- Facilitate weekly classes for 20 Navy personnel from diverse cultural backgrounds, promoting personal responsibility through communication and appropriate lifestyle behaviors. Topics include:
  - Decision Making and Problem Solving Strategies
  - Interpersonal Skills
  - Personal and Organizational Values and Conflicts
  - Resistance to Addictions

1995-1999 **Manager, Project Management and Contracts**
Accounting Manager
Loonery & Crosby, Inc., Saco, ME

An international consulting firm specializing in projects that address energy efficiency.

- Facilitated forums for organizational dialogue, encouraging excellent communication among all levels of personnel (president through support staff).
- Improved client relations by establishing procedures and training staff to develop strong consultant-client rapport.
- Worked with staff to provide tools and resources needed to manage projects.

1990-1995 **Independent Bookkeeping Contractor**

1987-1990 **Paralegal**
Raddison, Maloney & Powers, Portland, ME

EDUCATION

Candidate, Master's Program, Social and Cultural Anthropology
Maine Institute of Multicultural Studies, Portland, ME

B.A., Anthropology and Social Studies
Macalester College, St. Paul, MN

Grace Deminier

123 California Street, Fort Wayne, Indiana 12345 (123) 555-1234 graced@bamboo.com

JOB OBJECTIVE: Director of Customer Service

SUMMARY OF QUALIFICATIONS

- 10 years as department manager with experience in internal and external customer service.
- Excellent supervisory skills that enhance employee skills to produce quality work.
- Computer literate in Windows and Macintosh.

PROFESSIONAL ACCOMPLISHMENTS

MANAGEMENT

Paramount Credit Services Corp.

- Monitored $500,000 per month in expenses and compiled data for upper management.
- Decreased expenditures 35% by standardizing purchasing procedures.
- Created and directed all administrative procedures for this 58-person financial firm affiliated with Xerox Corporation.
- Wrote six manuals (70-100 pages each) to clarify responsibilities of accounts payable, telecommunications, records, check processing, and administrative support.

Public Information Group

- As manager of 28 employees, increased productivity, morale, and individual and team initiative by fostering employee career development within the company.
- Improved staff performance evaluations by upgrading job descriptions.
- Created and administered an $850,000 annual budget.

CUSTOMER SERVICE

Public Information Group

- Created system for identifying and notifying past-due accounts, recovering $236,000 of uncollected premiums from previous years.
- Used diplomatic yet firm approach to resolve disputes with customers, agents, and sales staff.
- Encouraged interdepartmental cooperation through excellent internal customer service.

Paramount Credit Services Corp.

- Resolved client issues promptly as liaison to branch offices and attorneys.
- Anticipated and handled hardware and software problems, achieving minimum of downtime for six departments that work with offices in other time zones.

WORK HISTORY

2006	Administrative Assistant	Environmental Review Group, Fort Wayne, IN
2001-05	Supervisor, Administration	Paramount Credit Services, Fort Wayne, IN
1995-01	Manager, Policy Administration	Public Information Group, Toledo, OH
1993-95	Family Management	Les Sables d'Olonne, France

EDUCATION

B.A. equivalent, French, Sorbonne, Paris, France, 1992

Leonora Braun

123 Sea Cliff Drive • San Diego, CA 12345 • (123) 555-1234 • lbraun@bamboo.com

JOB OBJECTIVE

Bookkeeper/Accountant

HIGHLIGHTS OF QUALIFICATIONS

- Experienced Bookkeeper/Accountant for small and medium-size businesses.
- Ability to work independently.
- Strong list of references.

PROFESSIONAL EXPERIENCE

1988-present BOOKKEEPER/ACCOUNTANT

Selected Clients/Projects

Michael Smith, CPA, San Diego, CA
Blue Nile Cafe, San Diego, CA
Star Mountain Texaco, La Jolla, CA
The Walters Marketing Group, San Diego, CA
Paintings '83, La Jolla, CA
Fleur D'Alsace Restaurant, San Diego, CA
Mark-Thomas Corporation, San Diego, CA

Michael Smith, CPA

- Prepared federal and state tax returns for corporations, partnerships, individuals, and estates.
- Maintained general ledgers and prepared financial statements for assigned clients.
- Prepared payrolls, quarterly federal and state payroll tax returns, and state sales tax returns.

Blue Nile Cafe and Star Mountain Texaco

- Set up company books, maintained general ledgers, and prepared Schedule C and partnership returns.

The Walters Marketing Group

- Maintained general ledger, accounts receivable, and accounts payable. Prepared financial statements.
- Prepared payroll, federal and state payroll tax returns, and sales tax returns.
- Assisted in the conversion to computer-generated accounting.

EDUCATION

Accounting: University of California, Berkeley Extension, San Francisco, CA
Healds Business College, San Francisco, CA
San Diego State University Extension, San Diego, CA

Computer: Computer Options, San Diego, CA

Frank Jordan
P.O. Box 123
Bayview Meadow, ND 12345
(123) 555-1234

OBJECTIVE: Bus Driver

SUMMARY OF QUALIFICATIONS

- Dependable, hard worker who can be counted on to "get the job done."
- Excellent driving record; always give first priority to safety.
- Friendly and well liked; good at customer relations.
- Available to relocate.

EXPERIENCE

Driver/Tour Guide **Trolley Tours, Bay Meadows, ND, 2004-2006**

- Drove small tour bus through scenic parts of this resort, pointing out sites, providing friendly service, and assisting senior citizens.
- Did light repair work as needed.
- Recognized as #1 employee within this company of 15.

Sales Representative **Recycled Tractor Parts, Townsend, ND, Summer '04**

- Sold used tractor and equipment parts by phone and over the counter.
- Handled inventory, shipping, and nationwide teletype service.

Driver **Paris Oil Recycling, Paris, ND, Summer '03**

- Picked up and delivered waste oil (until business was sold).

EDUCATION

Diploma, Wells High School, Wells, ND, 2005

ROSE MANSON
123 Fourteenth St., #123
Birmingham, AL 12345
(123) 555-1234
roseman@bamboo.com

OBJECTIVE: To retain insurance company relations as new owner of Highland Insurance Agency

Reliable reputation among Birmingham attorneys.

Proven ability to work profitably with home office.

Currently developing underwriting practice at Highland Insurance Agency.

PROFESSIONAL ACCOMPLISHMENTS

CLIENT RELATIONS

As Branch Manager, Bonding Service, American Insurance:

- Developed and serviced a loyal client base, almost doubling branch premium dollars from $190,000 to $365,000 per year.
    - Gained a reputation among attorneys for providing timely service/markets.
    - Recaptured accounts lost during departure of previous branch manager.
    - Offered additional services to gain accounts.
    - Generated new business through regular court appearances.

As Vice President, Highland Insurance Agency:

- Secured clientele, based upon my established reputation among local attorneys.

UNDERWRITING

As Branch Manager, Bonding Service, American Insurance:

- Authorized to execute under power of attorney in all counties in Alabama, with underwriting authority up to $50,000. Branch bond amounts ranged from $6,000 to $3,000,000.
- Simplified application form to more effectively gather underwriting data.
- Established and implemented more efficient procedures for home office approval, reducing turnaround time from three days to eight hours.
- Dealt directly with surety home office in Springfield, IL.
- Gained extensive knowledge of litigation process as it relates to judicial bonds.
- Negotiated with brokerage firms to perfect surety positions.

MANAGEMENT

As Branch Manager, Bonding Service, American Insurance:

- Developed a user-friendly billing system that increased efficiency of premium collections.
- Managed office relocation, keeping down-time to a minimum.

WORK HISTORY

2005-pres.	**Vice President**	Highland Insurance Agency, Birmingham, AL
2000-2005	**Branch Manager**	Bonding Service, American Insurance, Birmingham, AL
1992-2000	**Operations Manager**	Windows Plus, Inc., Birmingham, AL

Part 3 So You Need a Special Resume

When I go to the grocery store, I like lots of variety, especially when it comes to the cookie aisle. I like to choose from as many different kinds of chocolate chip cookies as possible, just to be sure I'm getting the best. When I get my package home, I examine each cookie and pick the one that has the most chocolate chips. I've been persnickety since I was a kid, and I probably always will be.

That's the kind of discriminating attitude I expect you to have when it comes to deciding which resume format to use. Now that you know all about chronological and functional resumes from Parts 1 and 2, I'm going to tell you about some spin-offs on these two formats. By the end of this part, you'll be able to pick the format that's right for you.

Chapter 10

The Big Winner: An Achievement Resume

In This Chapter

- Why employers like achievement resumes
- When to let your achievement statements do the talking
- Why your achievement resume will make you look like a winner
- How to create your own achievement resume

Of all the resume formats, the achievement resume is the one I find to be most powerful. It doesn't fit all job seekers' situations, but if it fits yours, it can have tremendous impact. The achievement resume is frequently the most effective way to stop potential employers in their tracks and get the salary dollars rolling in an upward direction. I bet you'd like that to happen to you! This chapter explains what an achievement resume is and helps you decide whether it's the right format for you.

This Resume Packs a Punch!

Being brief is more effective than saying a lot, and that's what the achievement resume is all about: brevity and punch! With a few strong accomplishments, an achievement resume can generate more questions and interest than pages of details. This type of resume works well for sales professionals, top-level executives, and those who want to keep the spotlight on just a few successes from their whole career.

Imagine how short and powerful a former U.S. president's resume could be. Take Jimmy Carter. Although he could fill pages and pages with his achievements, he doesn't need multiple pages to make his point. At most, two lines such as the following will get him in the door for any interview he's after:

- Thirty-ninth president of the United States
- Negotiator of 1979 Camp David Accords between Egypt and Israel

> **Bonus Check**
>
> Don't think that a one-page resume makes you look like a lightweight. On the contrary, a heavy-weight professional can make a strong impression with just a few carefully chosen lines of print. Not only that, a confident resume (and a good achievement resume definitely overflows with confidence) places you in an excellent position to negotiate your salary.

Likewise, the late Ronald Reagan's resume might read:

- Fortieth president of the United States
- Known as the "Great Communicator," who drastically improved U.S. relations with the Soviet Union

The achievement resume is also a marvelous way to throw attention onto your strengths while de-emphasizing a weak or complicated employment history. Using this format, I've created dynamite resumes for many a client whose career history was a mess.

Asking the Right Question

When writing your achievement statements for this type of resume, here's the key question to ask yourself: "How does the potential employer define success for the position I'm seeking?" Write four or five achievement statements in the body of your resume to answer that all-important question. When you've done that, you've snagged employers into calling you for an interview to talk about how your new job would impact their bottom line.

Oooh, You're Going to Look Great!

An achievement resume looks like a functional resume except that it doesn't have skill headings (in other words, you aren't going to categorize your statements according to skills) in the body of the resume. Instead it just lists five or six strong, relevant achievements under a main heading such as Professional Accomplishments or Selected Achievements. Look through your old performance evaluations to find references to relevant achievements and quotable quotes for your resume.

The following template represents an achievement resume. It's followed by five achievement resumes by real job seekers. A scan of these resumes will tell you that the job seeker in each case is a winner in his or her field. That's the beauty of this format!

The Perfect One-Pager

Anthony Wright, whose resume is among the sample resumes at the end of this chapter, had an achievement-packed, 20-year career in management, which he distilled down to one page using an achievement format. This concise format did two things:

- It allowed him to state his relevant experience in just five bullet point statements.
- It downplayed his career in the military and government by listing his work history near the end of the resume.

You'll also note that because he had so few statements on the page, he was able to write some pretty hefty ones, sometimes taking three lines each.

(Achievement Resume Template)

Name

Street
City, State Zip
Phone, Fax, E-mail

JOB OBJECTIVE

The job you want next

SUMMARY OF QUALIFICATIONS

- How much experience you have in the field of your job objective, in a related field, or using the skills required for your new position.
- An overall career accomplishment that shows you'd be good at this job.
- What someone would say about you as a recommendation.

SELECTED ACHIEVEMENTS

- An accomplishment you are proud of that shows you'd be a valuable employee.
- Another achievement that demonstrates you have the skills to produce results.
- A project you are proud of that supports your job objective.
- A problem you solved using the skills required for your job objective.
- A time when you used your skill to positively affect the organization, the bottom line, your boss, your clients.
- Awards, commendations, publications, etc., you achieved that relate to your job objective.

WORK HISTORY

20xx-present	Job Title	COMPANY NAME and city
20xx-xx	Job Title	COMPANY NAME and city
20xx-xx	Job Title	COMPANY NAME and city
20xx-xx	Job Title	COMPANY NAME and city
19xx-xx	Job Title	COMPANY NAME and city

EDUCATION

Degree, Major (if relevant)
University, City, State, 20xx (optional)

Quality vs. Quantity

There isn't a lot of quantity on Cliff McMillan's achievement resume, but there's plenty of quality. His achievement resume's impressive statements made him shine. He not only hit the nail on the head when it came to the type of experience and skills the employer was seeking, Cliff also demonstrated his good taste in the layout of his resume. Good idea!

Your achievement resume doesn't have to be only one page; your information can spill onto a second page if necessary. Whether it's a one- or two-pager, be sure it contains only the very best you have to offer a prospective employer.

Professional Titles Count

Thomas Redding cleverly highlighted his professional roles throughout his achievement resume by doing the following:

- He put "P.E." next to his name in the Heading to show that he's a certified civil engineer.
- He stated his professional title immediately below his heading.
- He highlighted his professional roles at the beginning of each achievement statement in the body of his resume.
- He listed his former job titles in his Work History, all of which support his job objective.

One can't help but identify Thomas's expertise in civil engineering from the highlighted titles that pop out all through his resume.

CAUTION

Career Casualty

Saying too much on a resume can be fatal. You want to say enough to entice the employer to ask questions (in an interview) without giving away the juicy details.

Number One in Sales

The achievement resume is often an excellent format for the sales professional. With four or five dashing accomplishment statements, the salesperson can sweep an employer off her feet and close the deal. I've seen many sales professionals win an interview in record time using an achievement resume. Take a look at Wendy Fowler's resume to see how effectively it sold her.

It's Your Turn to Shine

It's time to sit down at your computer (or get out your pencil and paper) and use the template found earlier in this chapter to create your achievement resume. All the principles discussed in Part 2 apply here (using action verbs, writing punchy summary statements, and so on). The only difference is the midsection of the resume, where you're going to write just a few smashing accomplishments that shoot you light-years ahead of your competition. That's right: no boring job descriptions, no skill headings, just the cream from the top of your career. Like I said, you're going to look great!

The Least You Need to Know

- An achievement resume that exudes confidence is hard for any employer to resist.
- Emphasize only selected achievements that say you're the best person for the job.
- De-emphasize a tricky employment history by placing it concisely at the bottom of the page.
- Because your resume presents you as one of the best in your field, you can start salary negotiations at a higher level.

Anthony Wright

123 Whitehall Place • Austin, TX 12345 • (123) 555-1234 • anthony_wright@bamboo.com

ADMINISTRATIVE MANAGER

- 20 years of experience directing complex organizational and technological changes.
- Recognized leadership skills and a natural talent for relating to people of various ethnic, socioeconomic, and educational backgrounds.
- Customer-focused management style.
- Ability to find innovative solutions to resource constraints.

QUALITY MANAGEMENT ACCOMPLISHMENTS

- Implemented two major organizational changes in the U.S. Air Force personnel and human resources management administration. Commended for relocating and retraining personnel while maintaining quality customer service.
- Directed the conversion from hierarchical to relational information systems at the U.S. Air Force Facilities. Recognized by technical team for using effective training and internal marketing to achieve management and staff "buy-in" of this major change.
- Developed a self-directed team to conduct process analysis in preparation for decentralization of 35 Medicare process operations. Trained staff in the practical and theoretical aspects of process improvement.
- Reduced U.S. Air Force Airbase's unreconciled material costs $1.5M by reorganizing administrative procedures, introducing a new information system, and directing the first complete physical inventory certified by the GAO.
- Improved goal tracking at U.S. Air Force Facilities by analyzing the workload evaluation process, assessing its validity, and convincing headquarters to revise the methodology.

WORK HISTORY

2003-present	Medicare, Austin	Program Manager, 2005-present Senior Budget Analyst, 2003-2005
1986-2003	U.S. Airbase, Austin	Director Workload Analysis, 1992-2003 Program Analyst, 1989-1992 Accounting Manager, 1986-1989

EDUCATION

B.S., Organizational Behavior, Austin State College, 1999

Cliff McMillan

123 Ocean Street • Rocky Hill, NC 12345 • (123) 555-1234 • cmcmillan@bamboo.com

JOB OBJECTIVE

Member of Creative Team with emphasis on Graphic Design

SUMMARY OF QUALIFICATIONS

- Skilled fine artist with experience in applied graphics.
- Competent in:
  QuarkXpress
  PageMaker
  Adobe Illustrator
  Design Studio
  Freehand
- Designed promotional pieces for clients including:
  Coffee-O-Rama
  University of North Carolina
  We-R-Juice
  Pack & Ship

GRAPHICS PROJECTS

- Designed several of Coffee-O-Rama's promotional T-shirts, worn by all North Carolina store employees.
- Team-developed promotional materials for Pack & Ship used in 30 stores.
- Combined computer and applied graphics in designing the cover for *The Finnegan Corporation Plans Book* for the University of North Carolina.
- Designed POP standup card for We-R-Juice, displayed in stores throughout the New York metropolitan area.
- Created numerous promotional pieces for university and community events.

WORK HISTORY

2002-pres.	Freelance Graphic Designer	Rocky Hill, NC
1998-2002	Store Manager	Coffee-O-Rama, Rocky Hill, NC
1997-1998	Desk Top Publisher	Copies Ink, Eugene, OR

EDUCATION

B.A., Graphic Design/Fine Arts, University of North Carolina, Rocky Hill, NC, 2002
Internship: Project Coordinator, RRM Marketing, New York, NY

— Portfolio available —

Thomas Redding, P.E.

123 Sylvan Avenue • San Francisco, California 12345 • (123) 555-1234 • tredding@bamboo.com

Civil Engineer

Project Management Construction Estimating

SUMMARY OF QUALIFICATIONS

- Wide variety of construction engineering experience ranging from heavy vessel transportation to commercial interior wall construction.
- Estimator and project manager for some of the most profitable specialty subcontracting jobs in the San Francisco Bay Area.
- Strong communication and analytical skills.

SELECTED ACCOMPLISHMENTS

- **Estimator and Interior/Exterior Wall Design Coordinator** for Highland Hospital, Oakland. Project consisted of 135,000 sq. ft. of EIFS material on built-in-place light-gauge metal framing. Coordinated structural analysis and shop drawing production for integration into project drawings by engineer-of-record.
- **Project Engineer, Scheduler, and Subcontract Administrator** for Exxon Oil refinery modernization in Fremont, CA. Project involved transportation and erection of multiple refinery process vessels up to 600 tons.
- **Project Manager** for highly profitable interior/exterior wall design and construction for the San Francisco Shopping Center. Project included 20,000 sq. ft. of built-in-place EIFS wall and detailed interior atria.
- **Estimator and Project Manager** for the $1.5 million structural fireproofing, load-bearing wall framing, and massive drywall and plaster ceiling construction for the redesign of San Francisco's Warfield Theatre. Maintained strict critical path schedule.

WORK HISTORY

2006-present **Estimator/Engineer**
Phillips Construction Contractors, Inc., Hayward, CA

2002-2005 **Estimator/Project Manager**
Browning and Dunn Contractors, San Mateo, CA, 2004-2005
Calabasas, Inc., San Francisco, CA, 2002-2004

2000-2002 **Estimator/Project Engineer**
Reynolds Construction, Inc., Oakland, CA

1997-2000 **Project Manager/Engineer**
Brendan Walsh Rigging, San Leandro, CA

EDUCATION AND CERTIFICATION

Registered Professional Civil Engineer, certified 1997, State of California

Bachelor of Science, Civil Engineering, 1996, University of California, Santa Cruz

Wendy Fowler

123 Coolidge Road • Santa Monica, CA 12345 • (123) 555-1234 • wfowler@bamboo.com

JOB OBJECTIVE

Sales Consultant/Representative

SUMMARY OF QUALIFICATIONS

- Nine years as a business development manager, using a collaborative approach to build an international clientele.
- Intuitive interpersonal skills. Ability to think on my feet and use humor to mix with people.
- Comfortable working with cross-cultural and multi-functional teams.

RELEVANT ACHIEVEMENTS

- Generated international business by developing TraxNet promotional material that was included in Writeword's developers' package.
- Managed TraxNet's broker relations, which generated accounts with Fortune 500 clients, including:

Bank of America	Cincom
Disney	First Interstate Bank

- Solicited donations within an affluent community for organizations including the Sierra Club, National Organization for Women, and the Los Angeles SPCA.
- Served as active member of fundraising team that doubled contributions for Echo Park School through donor solicitations and event planning.
- Made persuasive presentations before multi-city councils in Los Angeles, which influenced tax funding of public school bussing.

WORK HISTORY

2001-present	Business Development Manager, TraxNet, Inc., Century City, CA
2000-2001	Business Manager, The Shopper's Weekly, Pasadena, CA
1997-2000	Sales Representative, Open Door Travel Agency, Pasadena, CA
1994-1997	Full-time parent/fundraising volunteer

EDUCATION

B.A., Psychology, University of California at Los Angeles, 1993
M.A. Program, Social Work, City College of Los Angeles, 1994-1996

Chapter 11

A Chronological Hybrid That Adds Up

In This Chapter

- When to use a chronological hybrid resume
- Where to add skill subheadings
- How to bring out the dynamism of a lengthy career
- How to create your own chronological hybrid resume

You're stuck! You've considered the chronological and functional resume formats, but neither one is quite right for your situation. Here's an idea: Combine the benefits of both formats to develop a hybrid. Creating a hybrid resume is kind of like borrowing from two recipes to come up with a wonderful new entrée. In this chapter, I explain how to put together a resume that is a chronological hybrid. Then, in Chapter 12, I show you how to create a functional hybrid.

It's Got Structure

Let's say your career transition fits the criteria for using a chronological resume (see Chapter 2), but you want to highlight your transferable skills the way a functional resume would. You could start with the chronological structure and then add skill subheadings under the job titles in your Professional Experience section. To see this hybrid in action, take a look at the following template, which represents a *chronological hybrid* resume.

At first glance, the chronological hybrid looks like the traditional chronological format because the job seeker's achievements are presented as part of the work history in the body of the resume. The difference is that the achievement statements under each job heading are listed under skill subheadings.

Take a look at the following sample Professional Experience section of a resume. The applicant has created the two skill subheadings, Management and Marketing, under which she placed relevant achievement statements.

Terms of Employment

The **chronological hybrid** is a chronological resume with skill subheadings (similar to the skill headings in a functional resume) incorporated into the Professional Experience section.

After you've created two or three skill subheadings under a job title on your chronological hybrid resume, prioritize those subheadings according to how relevant they are to your Job Objective statement.

Now that you have a handle on what the chronological hybrid looks like, let's see whether it's the right format for you.

Are You the Hybrid Type?

When should you consider using a chronological hybrid instead of the regular chronological format? If you fit into one of the following circumstances, a chronological hybrid might be the way to go:

- You're looking for a promotion.
- You're switching industries.
- Your job titles are nondescript.
- Your Work History looks stagnant; that is, you've been in the same position for many years.

Let's see how real job seekers used chronological hybrids (found at the end of this chapter) to handle these situations.

Climbing Higher

If you want to use your resume to get a position that's a rung higher on your career ladder, use the chronological hybrid. Its skill subheadings will help the employer understand right away that you've already acquired and used the skills required for your job objective. Be sure to use skill subheadings that paint the picture of you performing your next job. (Follow the brainstorming techniques in Chapter 8 to come up with skills that support your job objective.) There's no set number of bullet point statements that should follow a skill subheading, but here's my rule of thumb: You can have as many as eight.

For example, Gireesh Vaid had worked her way up to vice president within a prominent nonprofit organization. When the position for president opened up, she decided to go for it. Using a chronological hybrid, she showed off her recent success in the company and used skill subheadings to demonstrate that she had the skills for the new job.

Variations on a Theme

If you want to continue with the same kind of work you've been doing but you want to change industries, the chronological hybrid can be a great promotional tool for you. This format will encourage the employer to identify you by your job titles and skills, even though your work history is from a different industry.

Tyler Zahn had been in management positions in the newspaper business for years. When he decided to transfer his management skills to a new industry, he chose the chronological hybrid format. In a flash, the employer saw that Tyler had honed valuable leadership abilities, even though he had not held typical manager titles.

(Chronological Hybrid Resume Template)

Name

Street
City, State Zip
Phone, Fax, E-mail

JOB OBJECTIVE

The job you want next

SUMMARY OF QUALIFICATIONS

- How much experience you have in the field of your job objective, in a related field, or using the skills required for your new position.
- An overall career accomplishment that shows you'd be good at this job.
- What someone would say about you as a recommendation.

PROFESSIONAL EXPERIENCE

20xx-pres. Company Name, City, State
Job Title

MAJOR SKILL

- An accomplishment you are proud of that shows you're good at this profession.
- A problem you solved and the results.
- A time when you positively affected the organization, the bottom line, your boss, your co-workers, your clients.

MAJOR SKILL

- A project you are proud of that supports your job objective.
- Another accomplishment that shows you're good at this line of work.
- Quantifiable results that point out your skill.

19xx-xx Company Name, City, State
Job Title

MAJOR SKILL

- An accomplishment you are proud of that shows you will be valued by your next employer.
- An occasion when someone "sat up and took notice" of your skill.

EDUCATION

Degree, Major (if relevant), 20xx (optional)
University, City, State

The Hidden Functional Message

You may have job titles in your Work History that don't express the level of responsibility you held. (This is frequently the case for government and university employees, where titles such as Assistant, Level III tell the reader almost nothing about the job.) Inserting skill subheadings into your Professional Experience section will help the employer understand what your responsibilities were and give you the credit you deserve.

A case in point: From some of his job titles (such as "specialist" and "coordinator"), it was hard to understand where Robert MacIntyre stood in the organizational hierarchy where he worked. So he presented his work history in a chronological hybrid format so that he could use skill subheadings to define his previous positions according to the skills needed in his job objective. That way, the employer saw that he had the qualifications for the job.

Standing Still

Longevity at an organization is something to feel proud of. But if you've spent many years in one spot, you might look stagnant in the eyes of a new employer. How can you highlight that you developed new skills, increased your industry knowledge, and took on more responsibility, even though your job title remained the same throughout your many years of dedication to the company? Use the chronological hybrid format. Your loyalty will ring clear in the work history, and the subheadings that categorize your achievements will demonstrate growth.

In Christine Whitley's resume, she divided her accomplishments according to the type of law she was involved with as a legal secretary. Her resume tells the story of diversity and stability—two attributes of an excellent legal secretary.

Putting Words on Paper

If you've decided the chronological hybrid is the right format for you, it's time to put your thoughts on paper. Follow the step-by-step guidelines in Part 2 for creating each section of your resume, using the hybrid template presented earlier in this chapter as your foundation. It's that simple!

Be creative in developing a hybrid resume that promotes you as the best candidate for the job. You can mix and match ideas from this book's guidelines, templates, and sample resumes to create your own special format.

If you still haven't decided which resume format to use, turn to the next chapter and learn all about the functional hybrid resume. It just might be the best format for you.

The Least You Need to Know

- The chronological hybrid emphasizes your career history while highlighting skills that are particularly relevant.
- The chronological hybrid is ideal if you're looking for a promotion within your current place of employment.
- The chronological hybrid is great for a professional who wants to switch industries.
- Skill subheadings help define vague job titles.
- The chronological hybrid gives life to a long work history at one company.

Gireesh Vaid

123 Mark Twain Ave. • St. Louis, MO 12345 • (123) 555-1234 • gvaid@bamboo.com

JOB OBJECTIVE: President, St. Louis Community Health Association

SUMMARY OF QUALIFICATIONS

- Accomplished Assistant Vice President in the St. Louis Community Health Association.
- Doubled donations during the '02 Campaign, achieving stretch goal of $500K.
- Allocated $750K to community service agencies.
- Enjoy motivating and establishing rapport with volunteers, donors, and co-workers.

PROFESSIONAL EXPERIENCE

2003-pres. **ST. LOUIS COMMUNITY FOUNDATION, Saint Louis, MO**
ASSISTANT VICE PRESIDENT
Manage a wide range of activities within the organization, including:

Fundraising • Manage four fundraisers with a $750K goal - 25% over last year. • Manage 110 existing corporate accounts; develop new accounts with high potential for giving. • Speak to community and corporate groups to solicit funds.

Allocations and Agency Relations • Allocated $750K after reviewing fiscal stability, board governance, and program services of 43 St. Louis Community Health-funded agencies. • Serve as liaison to coordinate activities.

Staffing Committees • Staff the Marketing, Agency Relations, Special Events Committees, creating effective teams of volunteers.

Volunteer Management • Recruit, develop, and manage high-level volunteers.

Special Events • Conceive and produce special events throughout year, including public relations events and prestigious fundraising galas.

LOANED EXECUTIVE
- Sponsored by Fossil Fuels Inc. to fundraise for the '02 St. Louis Community Health campaign.
- Personally doubled annual donations, raising more than $250,000 from local businesses, schools, and city officials. • Contributed half of overall stretch goal of $500K.

2002-03 **CROSS & CROWDER CORPORATION, Kansas City, MO**
PUBLIC RELATIONS ASSISTANT
- Assisted in corporate and product public relations during leveraged buy-out.
- Collaborated on PR strategies. • Co-managed sensitive internal issues such as layoffs and restructuring due to buy-out.

1998-02 **Jiffy Business Services, Kansas City, MO**
CONTRACTOR
- Provided sales and administrative assistance to nonprofit and for-profit organizations.

EDUCATION

B.S., Psychology, Rockhurst College, Kansas City, MO

Tyler Zahn

Executive Management Professional

123 Steep Street • Denver, CO 12345 • (123) 555-1234 • tyzahn@bamboo.com

QUALIFICATIONS

- 11 years' progressive leadership experience for a Denver company recognized as the best in its field.
- Success in managing 75% of organization's total revenue and expenditure, affected by multiple markets and fluctuating economy.
- Excellent supervisor who motivates staff by instilling confidence and dedication.

PROFESSIONAL EXPERIENCE

1995-present ***Daily Journal,*** Denver, CO
Associate Publisher, 2003-present
General Manager, 1999-2003
Director of Legal Information Services, 1997-1999
Calendar Manager, 1995-1997

BUSINESS

- Manage a $1.5M annual print budget, requiring creative negotiations with vendors to maintain quality, despite 40% rise in paper costs.
- As director of a $300K legal budget, achieve consistent sales in a declining market.
- Approve all capital acquisitions (approximately $50K per year) for the entire company.

PROJECT INITIATION

- Cut costs 35% by creating a 25-user, in-house editorial and production system.
- Doubled subscriptions by establishing a daily stand-alone supplement that provides crucial legal information to over 25,000 industry professionals.
- Increased sales market 45% by expanding courtroom coverage from one to six counties.

SUPERVISION

- Hired, trained, and supervise 10 art, production, MIS, advertising, and clerical personnel, using a management style of staff empowerment and delegation.
- Motivate an interdepartmental team of 25 to consistently meet two publication deadlines per day (500 per year).
- Maintained excellent retention rate, experiencing turnover only due to employee advancement or education.

1991-1994 **Peace Corps,** Brazil, South America
Volunteer, Medical Services Officer

EDUCATION

B.A., Anthropology, Nebraska Wesleyan University, Lincoln, NE, 1991
Internship, *The Omaha Free Press,* Omaha, NE, 1989

Robert MacIntyre

123 Long Shore Street • Evanston, IL 12345 • (123) 555-1234 • rmacintyre@bamboo.com

JOB OBJECTIVE

Environmental Health & Safety Coordinator

SUMMARY OF QUALIFICATIONS

- 10 years as an Environmental Compliance Professional with recent experience in Environmental Protection and OSHA compliance.
- Demonstrated ability to build rapport and resolve complex issues among multiple entities with conflicting interests.
- Working knowledge of industrial and research settings.

PROFESSIONAL EXPERIENCE

2001-present **Environmental Compliance Specialist**
SIDNEY LABS (SL), Chicago, IL

Leadership

- As Facility Coordinator for a building on the University of Chicago campus, closed out 85% of 1,800 deficiencies, turned around maintenance and custodial standards, implemented a recycling program, and improved security.
- As Chairperson of the Life Sciences Division Safety Committee, revitalized the group, improved productivity, increased recognition within SL, and facilitated a self-assessment inspection program.
- Served as liaison between Principle Investigators and Environmental Health and Safety (EH&S) Division. Developed strategies for EH&S compliance including OSHA and waste management.
- As Manager of the Medical and Biohazardous Waste Program, developed a comprehensive compliance document including a generator's guide and training plan. Program was fully implemented in only five months.

Compliance Enforcement

- Conducted advice visits to hazardous and mixed-waste generators to review procedures, labeling practices, and adherence to accumulation time limits.
- Updated and managed the Underground Storage Tank (UST) Program, which included the creation of four-page Monitoring Plans that were used as models by the Department of Energy (DOE).
- Coordinated certification of tanks and secondary containment for six Permit-by-Rule (PBR) Hazardous Waste Treatment Units. Ensured upgrades were in compliance and directed the permit writing effort.

— Continued —

Robert MacIntyre
Page 2

2000-2001 **Environmental Compliance Consultant**
SafeTech, Springfield, IL
An environmental consulting firm providing support to DOE facilities.

- Developed and wrote the first-ever Quality Control Inspection Plan/Procedure to monitor quality assurance of Pleasant Hills Laboratories' Hazardous Waste Management storage and treatment facilities. Plan was incorporated into their Part B Permit.
- Audited hazardous waste management facilities and Waste Accumulation Areas (WAAs) for compliance with EPA and Cal-EPA regulations, and DOE policies. Waste included: Hazardous
  Radioactive, high and low level
  Mixed

1996-2000 **Environmental Program Manager,** 1999-2000
Environmental Compliance Specialist, 1999
Chemist, Materials Engineering, 1996-1999
U.S. AIR FORCE, Wichita, KS
An aircraft re-work facility comprised of 125 manufacturing shops and a materials engineering laboratory.

- Ensured EH&S compliance in 75 WAAs by performing frequent surveillance and enhancing the training program.
- Co-developed directives for issues including waste minimization, solvent substitution, recycling, chemical storage, fire safety, and OSHA standards.
- Directed preparation of individual shop contingency plans for the Hazardous Material Management Plan.

1993-1995 **Physical and Inorganic Chemistry Advanced High School Teacher**
MARLON RIGGS HIGH SCHOOL, Topeka, KS

1990-1993 **Chemist,** 1993
Lab Technician, 1990-1993
TOXMOX INC., Topeka, CA
A hazardous waste disposal company.

EDUCATION

B.S., Biochemistry, Emporia State University, Emporia, KS, 1988

Seminars:

OSHA/RCRA	Hazardous Materials
Hazardous Waste	Medical Waste
Emergency Preparedness	Radioactive and Mixed Waste
Fire Safety	Underground Storage Tanks

Christine C. Whitley

123 Tall Tree Drive • San Diego, CA 12345 • (123) 555-1234 • cwhitley@bamboo.com

JOB OBJECTIVE: Legal Secretary

SUMMARY OF QUALIFICATIONS

- 13 years as a legal secretary for two prominent law firms.
- Specialization in litigation support.
- Experienced at integrating interpersonal and professional skills to facilitate the objectives of a legal team.

PROFESSIONAL EXPERIENCE

1994-present **Legal Secretary**
VALENCIA & STEIN, San Diego, CA

Litigation, 2001-present

- Provided legal and administrative support for two partners and three associates who specialized in underwriters' insurance and international securities litigation.
- Managed voluminous amounts of paperwork, gaining a reputation for providing information accurately and promptly.
- Frequently asked by co-workers to clarify litigation procedures.

Estate Planning/Administration, 1994-2001

- Played supportive role on legal team comprised of an attorney, a paralegal, and myself.
- Commended for accuracy in preparing and assembling legal documents and correspondence for large complicated estates.

1993-1994 **Legal Secretary**
WILLARD & PORTER, San Diego, CA

Maritime Law

- Handled correspondence and prepared legal documents for two partners specializing in sexual harassment cases.
- Gained basic knowledge of legal procedure including litigation.

EDUCATION

Degree: Legal Secretary
Lane College of Business, Los Angeles, CA

Legal Secretary Procedures
University of California at Riverside, Riverside, CA

Chapter 12

A Functional Hybrid That Makes Sense

In This Chapter

- Turning the employer's questions about a functional resume into a positive exclamation
- Knowing when to use the functional hybrid
- Letting your reader know where your achievements took place
- Creating your own functional hybrid resume

There aren't any limits to how creative you can be with your resume format. Sure, there are guidelines of what to do and what not to do, but it's your marketing piece, and you can be innovative with it!

So far, you've learned about four resume formats: functional, chronological, achievement, and chronological hybrid. Hang on to your marketing hats a little longer—you're about to discover one more: the functional hybrid. In this chapter, you'll see how to design a functional hybrid resume and figure out whether it's the right format for you.

The Skillful Hybrid

You might be the ideal candidate for using the functional resume (based on what you learned in Chapter 3), but you may be worried that the functional resume won't be well received by a conservative employer. In that case, you could start with the basic functional layout and add subheadings composed of the name of the company where your achievements took place. This *functional hybrid* has enough of the characteristics of the traditional chronological resume to please your conservative potential employer.

(Functional Hybrid Resume Template)

Name
Street
City, State Zip
Phone, Fax, E-mail

JOB OBJECTIVE

The job you want next

SUMMARY OF QUALIFICATIONS

- How much experience you have in the field of your job objective, in a related field, or using the skills required for your new position.
- An overall career accomplishment that shows you'd be good at this job.
- What someone would say about you as a recommendation.

PROFESSIONAL EXPERIENCE

MAJOR SKILL

Company where the following achievements took place
- An accomplishment you are proud of that shows you have this skill.
- A problem you solved using this skill, and the results.

Company where the following achievements took place
- A time when you used your skill to positively affect the organization, the bottom line, your boss, your clients.
- Awards or commendations you achieved that relate to your job objective.

MAJOR SKILL

Company where the following achievements took place
- A project you are proud of that supports your job objective.
- Another accomplishment that shows you're good at this line of work.

Company where the following achievements took place
- Quantifiable results that point out your skill.
- An occasion when someone "sat up and took notice" of your skill.

WORK HISTORY

20xx-present	Job Title	COMPANY NAME and city
20xx-xx	Job Title	COMPANY NAME and city
19xx-xx	Job Title	COMPANY NAME and city

EDUCATION

Degree, Major (if relevant), 20xx (optional)
University, City, State

The functional hybrid looks very much like a straight functional format. Its Work History section is concise and placed at the bottom of the page; achievement statements are categorized according to skill headings in the body of the resume. What makes it a hybrid is that under the skill headings there are subheadings that indicate where the achievements took place. These subheadings can be either the names of the organizations where your accomplishments took place or the job titles that you held when you completed your achievements. Take a peek at the template on the preceding page to get a picture of how a functional hybrid is structured.

Now let's look at reasons to use the functional hybrid format and some case studies of three job seekers and their resumes (found at the end of this chapter).

Terms of Employment

The **functional hybrid** is a functional resume with company subheadings included in the Relevant Achievements section to indicate where the achievements took place.

Looking the Part

As I mentioned in Chapter 3, one of the biggest objections employers have about functional resumes is that most of them unwittingly fail to say where each achievement took place. The functional hybrid identifies this information loud and clear through subheadings in the body of the resume (similar to the job subheadings in the chronological format). That's the advantage—the hybrid resembles the chronological resume (and therefore feels familiar to the employer), yet it has the structural advantage of the functional resume. The functional hybrid is a great format for job seekers who fit the criteria for the functional format and who have several achievements from one place of employment.

Conservative Employer Alert!

Let's imagine you're applying to a conservative company (such as insurance or banking) where you assume that the hiring manager will expect a traditional chronological resume. But for reasons discussed in Chapter 3, you're leaning toward using the straight functional format. The problem is that your prospective employer may think you don't fit in if you send a functional resume, because it's an atypical format for the field. What should you do? Try the functional hybrid. By adding subheadings that indicate where your achievements took place, the hybrid format will look enough like the chronological resume to ease the employer into trusting that you're a stable worker with valuable skills.

Check out Dennis Beauregard's resume. He wanted to use the functional format because he was transferring his skills from the legal field to the public service arena. Because he was applying to a conservative organization (the Chicago Police Department), he created a functional hybrid resume. By using company names as subheadings under his skill headings, his resume looked enough like a chronological resume to gain his potential employer's respect.

Red Flags Down

Some employers don't like functional resumes. They worry that a job seeker who uses one is trying to hide something, and if they're not careful, they'll end up with a problem employee on their hands. Red flags on a resume—anything that looks fishy to employers and might cause them to discard a resume—might include the following:

- Unexplained gaps in employment, which could indicate instability due to personal problems
- A hard-to-follow presentation, which could be an attempt to hide something in the applicant's past
- An inappropriately long resume, which could mean the job seeker is unorganized

To relieve the fears of the employer and still use the functional format, categorize the achievement statements under your skill headings according to where they happened. That way the employer can easily reference your subheadings with your Work History at the bottom of the page.

Carmen Bishop's functional hybrid took advantage of the functional format and put the reader's mind at rest by organizing her achievements under job title subheadings. Her resume clearly shows that she has the sales and project management skills to fulfill the employer's expectations.

Giving Order to Chaos

Having a complicated work history (one that has concurrent employment, short-term jobs, or gaps) is one reason to use a functional resume, because it downplays the sequence of events and throws the spotlight on the important stuff: your transferable skills.

But eventually the reader is going to notice that your Work History is complex. By using the functional hybrid with company subheadings (which don't have dates in them), you can help the employer easily make sense of an otherwise confusing presentation. For example, Todd Grey used subheadings under his skill headings to clarify what took place where and to gather several projects under one logical subheading (Public Relations for Political Figures). Nice touch!

Getting Down to It

Now that you've learned the ins and outs of the functional hybrid, you're ready to create yours. Follow the steps for creating the sections of a resume in Part 2 and use the hybrid template that appears earlier in this chapter, and you'll be all set!

The Least You Need to Know

- By using the functional hybrid format, you can de-emphasize your work history and spotlight your transferable skills in a structure that resembles a chronological resume.
- Create subheadings in the Relevant Experience section to indicate where groups of achievements took place.
- You can use organization names or job titles as subheadings in your functional hybrid resume.
- Within a skill heading, prioritize the subheadings so the most relevant one comes first.

Dennis Beauregard

123 Quincy Street • Chicago, IL 12345 • (123) 555-1234 • denbeau@bamboo.com

JOB OBJECTIVE: President of Civilian Oversight Board, Chicago Police Department

SUMMARY OF QUALIFICATIONS

- More than 20 years as an executive manager in the legal and business fields.
- Excellent researcher with ability to manage a heavy caseload.
- Skilled supervisor who knows how to build consensus among personnel.
- Strength in public relations. Experienced public speaker and spokesperson.

RELEVANT ACCOMPLISHMENTS

MANAGEMENT / SUPERVISION

Get Down Music

- Served as one of five members on the Executive Management Committee, which resolved harassment, discrimination, labor relations, and public relations issues.
- Enhanced departmental and interdepartmental teamwork by fostering strong company-wide communication.
- Managed Business Affairs and Legal Department comprised of attorneys, paralegals, secretaries, and contract administrators from diverse cultural backgrounds.

LEGAL

Leder & Porzio, Esqs.

- Conferred with and advised clients with respect to claims against them or their organizations.
- Researched and evaluated validity of claims.
- Conducted conciliation meetings and made concrete recommendations for disposition of claims.
- Scheduled and participated in hearings.

Get Down Music

- Served as legal advisor to management regarding claims by artists, distributors, and employees.
- Conducted and supervised research of claims and prepared evaluations and recommendations.
- Provided statistical reports with respect to departmental operations.

WORK HISTORY

2005-pres. Legal Consultant, Chicago, IL
1992-05 Attorney (private practice), Brooklyn, NY
1989-92 Vice President, Business Affairs and Legal Dept., Get Down Music, Inc., New York, NY
1980-89 Associate, 1986-89; Paralegal, 1984-86; Director, International Music Dept., 1980-84
Leder & Porzio, Esqs., New York, NY

EDUCATION

J.D., Columbia University, New York, NY, 1986
B.A., Columbia University, New York, NY, 1979

Carmen Bishop

123 Fairmount Street • Santa Barbara, CA 12345 • (123) 555-1234 • cbishop@bamboo.com

JOB OBJECTIVE: A sales position

SUMMARY OF QUALIFICATIONS

- Enthusiastic and motivated; sincerely enjoy developing and maintaining excellent customer relations.
- Outstanding ability to understand others' needs and offer solutions.
- Resourceful and innovative; proven talent to adapt quickly to challenges.
- Commended for top-notch organizational skills.

RELEVANT ACCOMPLISHMENTS

SALES/INTERPERSONAL RELATIONS

Word Processing Contractor:

- Consistently developed new business despite slow economy through prospecting, persuasive presentations, and persistent follow-up.
- Easily developed rapport with clients, quickly assessing needs and responding effectively to pressure and deadlines.

Assistant to Executive VP of Production, Magic Movies:

- Handled phones for this successful VP working with celebrities and politicians. Used diplomacy to accommodate demanding schedules and powerful personalities.
- Negotiated terms with vendors for special events.

Inside Sales Representative, Vermont Makes It Special:

- Resolved customer service problems; i.e., deliveries, quality control.

PROJECT MANAGEMENT

Assistant to Executive VP of Production, Magic Movies:

- Planned private screenings for 50-100 VIPs. Evaluated needs for the event, personally invited guests and handled on-site logistics.
- Maintained an extremely high-profile appointment schedule with prominent directors, producers and actors. Managed correspondence, film proposals and expenses.
- Supervised immediate support staff.

WORK HISTORY

2001-present	Word Processing Contractor	West Hollywood
1999-2000	Assistant to Executive VP of Production	Magic Movies, Inc., Los Angeles
1997-1998	Booking Assistant	Actors-Plus Agency, Los Angeles
1995-1997	Inside Sales Representative	Vermont Makes It Special, Santa Monica

EDUCATION

B.A., Political Economics, St. Francis College, Mosswood, CA
Culinary Program, Fine Foods Institute, San Luis Obispo, CA

Todd C. Grey

123 Coolbrith Street • Berkeley, CA 12345 • (123) 555-1234 • tgrey@bamboo.com

JOB OBJECTIVE: A position in Fundraising

SUMMARY OF QUALIFICATIONS

- Experienced at fundraising work for nonprofit organizations and political leaders.
- Talent for generating support for causes that increase community involvement.
- Skilled at fostering relationships with people from diverse backgrounds.

EXPERIENCE

FUNDRAISING / PUBLIC RELATIONS

Fundraiser for Access Education, a nonprofit organization dedicated to getting and keeping disabled youth on the college track.

- Played key role in focusing the fundraising committee. Clarified goals, set priorities, and created action plans.
- Organized a pubic relations/fundraising event that attracted 250 disability rights supporters/donors who saw the need to "make a difference" through education.

Public Relations for Political Figures

- Represented Congressman Hanley to the public, explaining his platform, answering questions, and responding to complaints by phone and through correspondence.
- Prepared packets for public appearances, debates, and press conferences for Governor Kunin during her presidential campaign, frequently responding to public controversies.
- Served as front-end person for Senator Dooley, handling hundreds of phone calls per day from a diverse constituency of 20 million.

ADMINISTRATION

- Created and maintained donor database for Access Education, which has recently experienced a dramatic expansion.
- As assistant to political figures, managed extremely busy calendars that juggled numerous meetings, press conferences, and media events.
- Wrote commemorative announcements and letters on behalf of Senator Dooley.

RELEVANT WORK HISTORY

2003-present	Fundraiser	Access Education, Berkeley, CA
2002-2005	Financial Aid Advisor	San Francisco State College, San Francisco, CA
(Mostly concurrent with education)		
1994-1998	Assistant to political figures:	Congressional Office of Andrew Hanley Kunin/Sanders Campaign Office of Senator Stanley Dooley

EDUCATION:

B.A., San Francisco State, San Francisco, CA, anticipated 2006
Grant Proposal Writing, The Support Center, San Francisco, 2006

Chapter 13

When You Really *Are* a Brain Surgeon: The Curriculum Vitae

In This Chapter

- How a curriculum vitae differs from a resume
- Who needs a curriculum vitae?
- How to write an interesting and dynamic curriculum vitae
- Why more is more on a curriculum vitae
- How to create your own curriculum vitae

Curriculum vitae have been called the brainy resumes because they're used by scholars, scientists, and, yes, brain surgeons. But you don't have to have a degree in brain surgery to write one. In fact, now that you understand the principles behind good resume writing, you're almost ready to write your curriculum vitae.

A quick run through this chapter will teach you a few tricks of the curriculum vitae trade and will get you on track. Pretty soon you'll have a curriculum vitae you can present with pride.

Curriculum Vitae vs. Resume

When seeking a faculty, research, or leadership position at an academic or scientific organization, you need a special resume called a *curriculum vitae* (vita or CV for short). If you think a curriculum vitae sounds like a formal document, you can relax; there's no need to put on your evening gown or tuxedo to write your CV! Writing one will be a casual event for you because you've already learned the principles behind an effective resume. (Take another look at The Resume Commandments in Chapter 1.)

Terms of Employment

Curriculum vitae is Latin for "life's course." In the academic and scientific worlds, it's a document used as a resume. A curriculum vitae is also referred to as **vita** or **CV**.

To create a CV, there are four exceptions to the resume guidelines you read about in Parts 1 and 2:

1. Most CVs are more than two pages long.
2. The information on a CV tends to be detailed, providing extensive data about your publications, presentations, and other academic activities.
3. A CV doesn't necessarily contain a Job Objective statement, although it's perfectly okay to include one.
4. Most CVs don't have Summary of Qualifications sections; however, if you have a special need for one (perhaps you're making a career change and a Summary of Qualifications section would introduce that change), it's acceptable to have one on your CV.

Let's look at each of these exceptions more closely.

When More Is More

The length of a CV may vary. A CV for a recent Ph.D. graduate would normally range from three to eight pages. For someone with extensive professional experience, a CV could run as long as 20 pages. That's a lot of paper, but in the academic world, that's a good thing. The people reading CVs seem to live by the slogan "more is more." (That's the CV twist on the "less is more" theme I've been espousing all along for resumes.)

Just the Facts

Your CV audience is more interested in the facts and details of your career than it is in hype (that is, language that sounds exaggerated in order to impress). Data such as reference information, dates, and exact titles are important, because they give a means for verifying information. Providing technical descriptions also gives you a chance to show that you know what you're talking about without sounding like a braggart.

Here's an example of what I mean. Instead of saying

> Prominent scientist who has been honored at universities around the world for groundbreaking discoveries.

Use a more modest tone:

> Organic chemist who has presented discoveries and research at universities in Russia, Mexico, Canada, and the United States.

No Objections

Many CVs don't include Job Objective statements, especially if the applicant intends to stay in the same field. Between the college degree and the work history, it's usually obvious what type of position is being sought. However, if you're planning to change careers (for example, from research to teaching), a Job Objective statement at the top of your CV would be helpful to the potential employer.

No Need to Summarize

Most CVs target employers who are more interested in facts (found in the Professional Experience, Publications, and other laundry list sections) than in the interpretation of facts (typically found in a Summary of Qualifications section). For this reason, the Summary of Qualifications section is not necessary on most CVs. If your job objective is in line with your education and career achievements, do not place a Summary of Qualifications section on your CV. However, if you're making a career change, it's fine to create a Summary of Qualifications section that helps the reader understand how your education and background will apply to your new job objective.

Freedom of Format

Because the CV usually addresses a conservative reader, many people assume that it needs to follow a standard, rigid format. Not so! You can be creative in presenting your strengths while respecting the expectations of the academic, scientific, or institutional employer. That means you can consider using any one of the five formats I've suggested so far:

- Chronological (see Chapter 2)
- Functional (see Chapter 3)
- Achievement (see Chapter 10)
- Chronological hybrid (see Chapter 11)
- Functional hybrid (see Chapter 12)

Use the guidelines in each respective chapter to determine which format is best for your CV.

CAUTION

Career Casualty

Some employers will want to see that you know how to follow strict guidelines for academic writing. Be sure to list your published work properly. To learn the appropriate style for your industry, consult the bibliography section of a style guide that's commonly used in your field, or look at how bibliographies are presented in your trade publications.

Hanging Out Your Laundry

Following are headings of laundry list sections commonly found on CVs:

- Education
- Publications
- Presentations
- Committees and Appointments
- Affiliations

The following sections cover what should be listed under each of these headings. If a heading isn't applicable to you, disregard it. If you have only one or two items to list in a section, combine two similar sections. Then create a section heading to reflect your combination, such as Publications and Presentations.

Good Schooling

The Education section almost always appears near the top of the first page. It should provide information about each degree you have acquired:

- Your major
- The date you received your degree
- The institution where you received it
- The city and state of the institution
- Titles of your thesis and dissertation

You might also list course titles if they demonstrate relevant knowledge and aren't obvious from the major you declared. You can place internships under the Education heading, in a section of their own (called Internships), or under Experience, depending on which strategy makes the most sense for your situation.

Are You Published?

You need a Publications section if you've authored or co-authored material such as articles, books, or chapters in books. When listing publications, mention the following:

- The author (that's you!) or co-authors (you and your colleague)
- The title of your article or chapter (if one of these applies)
- The title of your book or the publication in which your article or chapter appeared
- The date of publication
- The publisher
- The ISBN (if it applies)

Job Hunt Hint

To indicate that a laundry list on your CV does not include every single item in that category, add *Selected* or *Relevant* in the heading; for instance, Selected Presentations or Relevant Presentations.

This information appears in sentence format with commas placed between each element. There are a few standards for order in which you place the elements within the sentences, so check a style manual such as *The Chicago Manual of Style* or *The Gregg Reference Manual* to find one that's right for you.

Putting On a Show

You may have presented papers at conferences. If so, you could have a section called Presentations, Lectures, Symposia, Conferences, or Seminars. In this section, state the following information:

- Titles of papers you presented
- Names of conferences
- Locations
- Dates

It's a good idea to elaborate on other roles you played at the conferences (such as serving on panels) if doing so will add to your qualifications.

Joining the Team

If you've been selected to serve on one or more committees, consider creating a section entitled Committees, Appointments, Boards, or the like. Under your heading, list the following:

- Your titles
- Names of committees
- The city and state of each committee
- Dates you served on the committees

If appropriate, you could include bullet point statements that say what results were achieved during your tenure. For instance:

President, University of Colorado Alumni Association, 2000–02

- Designed the organization's first website, which enabled online member giving.
- Collaborated with Board to develop the Annual Alumni Scholarship Award.

Hangin' with the Right Folks

The associations that you belong to can be listed alphabetically, chronologically, or in order of relevance to your profession. You could call this section something like Professional Affiliations, Professional Associations, or Professional Memberships. If you held or currently hold an office, also note that in this section.

Forget Anything?

Here are some other headings that might appear on your CV:

- Exhibitions
- Awards and Honors
- Research
- Studies
- Grants
- Lectures
- Teaching
- Licenses
- Media Appearances

Remember, more is more when it comes to your CV, so think hard about all that you can include.

High Marks for a University Instructor

Ruth Schwartz used the curriculum vitae at the end of this chapter to apply for college-level positions teaching Creative Writing. She realized that her main strength lay in her numerous publications and awards, rather than her experience at the university level. Therefore, she highlighted her list of publications by putting it on the first page of her CV. That way readers would already be impressed by the time they reached her teaching section, which began on page four.

Create Your CV

Now that you have your feet wet, it's time to jump in. Create strong sections in your CV by using the concepts presented in Part 2. With the additional sections mentioned in this chapter, your CV is likely to run several pages, all of which should have the following information:

- Your name at the top of each page
- The page number (placed on either the top or bottom of each page)
- *Continued* at the bottom of each page (except the last one)

When you've done all of this, sit back, read through your CV, and admire how accomplished you are!

The Least You Need to Know

- Curriculum vitae is the term used in academic and scientific communities for resume.
- CVs are usually longer than two pages (and may be as long as 20 pages) and typically don't include Job Objective and Summary of Qualifications sections.
- You can use a chronological, functional, achievement, chronological hybrid, or functional hybrid format, but keep it conservative in presentation and language for most uses.
- A large part of your CV should be laundry list sections such as Publications, Awards and Honors, and Presentations.
- Be sure to number all pages and include "Continued" at the bottom of all but the last page.

Ruth L. Schwartz
6035 Majestic Avenue • Oakland, CA 94605
510/333-3572 • Ruthpoet@aol.com

Education

M.F.A. in Creative Writing, 1985 - University of Michigan, Ann Arbor, MI

B.A. in Writing and Women's Studies, 1983 - Wesleyan University, Middletown, CT

Selected Honors & Awards

- **Winner,** National Poetry Series (Book Competition), 2001 *(Judge: Jane Hirshfield)*
- **Winner,** Anhinga Prize in Poetry (Book Competition), 2000 *(Judge: Allison Joseph)*
- **Winner,** Associated Writing Programs Poetry Book Competition, 1994 *(Judge: William Matthews)*
- **Fellowship,** Ohio Arts Council, 2000
- **Fellowship,** National Endowment for the Arts, 1992
- **Fellowship,** Astraea Foundation, 1992
- **Fellowship,** Wisconsin Institute for Creative Writing, 1992
- **Fellowship** to attend M.F.A. Program at the University of Michigan, 1983-85
- **First Prize,** Chelsea Magazine Poetry Competition, 2000
- **First Prize,** Hardman/Pablo Neruda Award (Nimrod Magazine), 1999 *(Judge: Mark Doty)*
- **First Prize,** Sue Saniel Elkind Poetry Contest (Kalliope), 1998 *(Judge: Maxine Kumin)*
- **First Prize,** Chelsea Magazine Poetry Competition, 1995
- **First Prize,** Randall Jarrell Poetry Contest (North Carolina Writers Network), 1993 *(Judge: Maxine Kumin)*
- **First Prize,** Americas Review Poetry Contest, 1992
- **First Prize,** New Letters Literary Award for Poetry, 1991 *(Judge: Charles Simic)*
- **First Prize,** Hardman/Pablo Neruda Award (Nimrod Magazine), 1991 *(Judge: James Ragan)*
- **First Prize,** S.F. Bay Guardian Poetry Contest, 1991
- **International Merit Award Winner,** Atlanta Review International Poetry Competition, 2000, 1999
- **Reader's Choice Award,** Prairie Schooner Magazine, 1998
- **Second Prize,** George Bogin Memorial Award (Poetry Society of America), 1998 (*Judge: Marvin Bell)*
- **Second Prize,** Eclectic National Poetry Prize, 1998 (*Judge: Eavan Boland)*
- **Second Prize,** Ann Stanford Award (So. California Literary Anthology), 1993 (*Judge: Diane Wakoski)*
- **Third Prize,** South Coast Poetry Journal Contest, 1989 *(Judge: Mark Strand)*
- **Fourth Prize,** Marlboro Review Poetry Contest, 1997 *(Judge: Ellen Bryant Voigt)*
- **Honorable Mentions,** National Poetry Competition (Chester H. Jones Foundation), 1999, 1998, 1990

Poetry Publications

Books:

Harper-Collins, 2002	Edgewater
Anhinga Press, 2001	Singular Bodies
University of Pittsburgh Press, 1996	Accordion Breathing and Dancing

- continued -

Ruth L. Schwartz

Page Two

Poetry Publications: Anthologies

Pending

Henry Holt – The Body Beautiful: An Anthology (One poem)
Partisan Press – Clockpunchers: Poems about Work (One poem)

2002 **University of Akron Press** – Modern Poems About Ohio (Three poems)

2000 **Southern Illinois University Press** – New Young American Poets (Four poems)
St. Martin's Press – The World in Us: Lesbian and Gay Poetry (Four poems)
Carnegie Mellon Press – American Poetry: Next Generation (Three poems)
Poets' League of Greater Cleveland – Imagining an Inland Sea (One poem)

1999 **National Poetry Competition Winners 1999** "Proof"
Ashland Poetry Press – And What Rough Beast: Poems at the End of the Century – "The City"

1998 **National Poetry Competition Winners 1998** "Why You Listen"

1997 **W.W. Norton** – The Poet's Companion "Bath"

1996 **Crown Press** – The Zenith of Desire "January Vineyards"
Ballantine Books – My Lover is a Woman "Midnight Supper," "January Vineyards"

1995 **St. Martin's Press** – The Key To Everything "The Offering"

1992 **Sidewalk Revolution Press** – Sister/Stranger "The Same Moon"

1990 **National Poetry Competition Winners 1990** "By Asking"

Poetry Publications: Journals

2002	**Paterson Literary Review**	"This Monkey"
	Sow's Ear Poetry Review	"Oakland Sky After a Week of Rain"
2001	**The Sun**	"Still Life"
	Crab Orchard Review	"Failure," "The Swan at Edgewater…," "Aliens…"
	Mudfish	"All-Night Crisis Line"
	Prairie Schooner	"Figs," "Morning in Our One and Only World," "Letter from God"
2000	**The Sun**	"Cleveland, March," "Dog on the Floor…"
	Chelsea	"Edgewater Park," "September, Edgewater Park," "Now," "Fetch," "Sunday," "After you held me..."
1999	**Nimrod**	"Millennium Love Poems," "Shrine," "Belief"
	Atlanta Review	"Important Thing"
	Cleveland Plain Dealer Sunday Magazine	"Cirque du Soleil" (reprint)
	Eckerd College Review	"Land," "Rafting the Illinois," "Landing"
1998	**Prairie Schooner**	"The Roses," "Flood Winter"
	Marlboro Review	"Albuquerque B&B," "Can Pigeons Be Heroes?"
	Sow's Ear Poetry Review	"Turkey Vulture, Cove Beach"
	Kalliope	"Gravity"
1997	**Poetry Flash**	"The Work of Morning"

- continued -

Ruth L. Schwartz
Page Three

Poetry Publications: Journals *(continued)*

1995	**Chelsea**	"The Greatest Show...," "Why I Forgive...," "Golden Gate," "Flamenco Guitar," "Hayward Shoreline," "Because Summer"
	N.W. Poets & Artists Calendar	"Late Summer"
1994	**Chelsea**	"The City at Sunset"
	Southern California Anthology	"AIDS Education: 7th Grade"
	Artful Dodge	"Scene with Pelicans," "Letter from Anywhere"
1993	**Parnassus: Poetry in Review**	"History"
	Provincetown Arts	"And the light"
	Americas Review	"The City," "In Guatemala" (reprints)
	Southwest	"The Offering," "Late Monologue for a Traveler"
1992	**Zone Three**	"After the Killed Bird"
	Sow's Ear	"Almolonga"
	San Francisco Bay Guardian	"The City"
	New Letters	"In Guatemala," "Possible," "Near us, a new house"
1991	**Yellow Silk**	"Homecoming," "Fear of Sex"
	Visions, International	"Mother and Child"
	Primavera	"How We Might"
	Nimrod	"Poems of the Body" (six-poem sequence)
	Outlook	"The Same Moon"
	Confrontations	"Life in the Forest"
1990	**Birmingham Poetry Review**	"Future Tense"
	S.F. Bay Guardian	"It is National Poetry Week and Navy Fleet Week ..."
	Madison Review	"When They Know"
	Taos Review	"Here Among Mountains Without You," "By Asking"
	Pudding Magazine	"At Eight"
	American Writing	"The Snake," "The Juggler...," "September...," "17 Aliens"
1989	**Hayden's Ferry Review**	"Father, After the Divorce"
	South Coast Poetry Journal	"The Burglars"
	Moving Out	"The Seamstress"
1988	**Evergreen Chronicles**	"Making it Last"
1987	**Berkeley Poetry Review**	"A Neighbor Remembers Invention"
	South Coast Poetry Journal	"The Secret"
	Evergreen Chronicles	"Taking Leave," "Grapefruit Ice"
	San Francisco Sentinel	"The Surface Break," "Next Time"
1985	**Widener Review**	"Choices"
	Blue Ox Review	"Contours"

Creative Non-Fiction Publications

Book *(scheduled):*

2004	**Michigan State University Press**	**Death in Reverse: A Memoir**

Anthologies:

1996	**Anchor Press** - The Wild Good	*from* "The Kidney Transplant Chronicles"
1996	**Dutton Press** - Sisters, Sexperts, Queers	"New Alliances: Lesbians, Gay Men & AIDS"
1988	**Cleis Press** - AIDS: The Women	"Many a Long Month"

-continued-

Ruth L. Schwartz
Page Four

Journals:

2000	**The Sun**	"Giving Thanks"
1998	**The Sun**	"Acts of Love"
	Utne Reader	"My Fat Lover" (reprint)
1997	**The Sun**	"Pills," "Roommates," "My Fat Lover"
1996	**The Sun**	"We Don't Know What It Is"

Teaching Experience

Recent Courses Taught:

- **Poetry Writing** (introductory, advanced and graduate workshops)
- **Poetry Editing and Publishing** (graduate level)
- **Introduction to Creative Writing** (undergraduate, multi-genre)
- **Sexuality in Literature** (crosslisted graduate/undergraduate)

Teaching Positions

Assistant Professor, California State University, Fresno, CA, 2000-present

- Develop and teach courses in Poetry Writing and Literature, for both undergraduate and M.F.A. Program students.

Associate Professor of Creative Writing, Goddard College, Plainfield, VT, 1999-2000

- Teach, mentor and advise low-residency M.F.A. students, including preparation of individualized study plans and supervision of creative theses.
- Initiate, develop and lead specialized workshops during M.F.A. program residency.

Assistant Professor, Cleveland State University, Cleveland, OH, 1998-2000

Co-Director, Poetry Center, Cleveland State University, Cleveland, OH, 1998-2000

- Develop and teach courses in Poetry Writing, Creative Writing, Creative Non-Fiction, Literature, and related topics, for both undergraduate and graduate students.
- Advise M.A. students on creative and scholarly thesis projects.
- Participate in planning and development of Cleveland State's M.F.A. Creative Writing Program.
- Facilitate monthly community Poetry Forum and co-coordinate community reading series.
- Coordinate Poetry Center contests, publication and editing projects, including annual poetry book competition.

Poetry Instructor, Antioch Writer's Workshop, Yellow Springs, OH, 2000, 1999, 1998

- Delivered craft-related lectures to large audiences, facilitating stimulating, productive discussions among participant writers at all levels of expertise; provided individual conferences on student work.
- Led week-long small-group Poetry Intensive, combining reading, writing and craft exercises.

Poetry Instructor, Oklahoma Summer Arts Institute, Tahlequah, OK, 1998, 1997

- Conceived and taught two intensive poetry courses, combining a variety of activities -- including craft lectures, free-writing, and writer's-eye-view analysis of contemporary poetry -- to provide the academic equivalent of a semester-long college seminar over two weeks of all-day classes.

Guest Poet/Workshop Leader, *Nimrod Magazine* Writing Seminar, Tulsa, OK, 1999, 1991

Graduate Teaching Assistant, University of Michigan, Ann Arbor, MI, 1983-85

- continued -

Ruth L. Schwartz
Page Five

Recent Readings & Presentations

Featured Reader / Presenter (Selected appearances, 1997-2000)

Antioch University, Yellow Springs, OH ◆ Antioch University, Los Angeles, CA

WCPN Public Radio, Cleveland, OH ◆ Cody's Books, Berkeley, CA ◆ Albany Public Library, Albany, CA

Fresno Poets' Association, Fresno, CA ◆ Wright State University, Dayton, OH

WRITE ON! Cleveland, Cleveland, OH ◆ Oklahoma Summer Arts Institute, Lone Wolf, OK

Little Tiger Bookstore, Willoughby, OH ◆ Oklahoma Summer Arts Institute, Norman, OK

San Francisco State University, San Francisco, CA ◆ A Different Light Bookstore, San Francisco, CA

Panelist:

"Writing the Body" -- Summer Salon, Antioch University, Yellow Springs, OH, 2000
"Poetry and the Erotic" -- Associated Writing Programs Annual Meeting, Kansas City, MO, 2000
"When the Pen Is the Sword: Writing About Violence" -- Antioch Writer's Workshop, 1999
"Going Naked on the Page: Writing About Sex and Sexuality" -- Antioch Writer's Workshop, 1998

Editorial Experience

Co-Director, Editorial Committee, Cleveland State University Poetry Center, 1998-2000

- Participate in selection of finalists from among the approximately 1,000 book-length poetry manuscripts submitted to the Poetry Center's annual contest.

Poetry Reader (Editorial Committee), *FEMSPEC* Journal, Cleveland, OH, 1999-2000

Editorial / Administrative Volunteer, *Poetry Flash*, Berkeley, CA, 1997-98

Screening Judge, *The Loft* Annual Poetry Contest, 1996

Screening Judge, *San Francisco Bay Guardian* Poetry Contest, 1996

Co-Editor, *Five Fingers Review*, San Francisco, CA, 1989-91

- Initiated chapbook contest; co-edited and produced nationally renowned literary magazine.

Editor, *The Singing Bridge: An Anthology of Poetry About AIDS*, 1989-92

Additional Work Experience

Professional Writer / Editor, Oakland, CA, 1990-99

- Wrote and edited a wide variety of technical and professional documents, including health education materials, brochures, resumes, and marketing copy, both independently and as a partner in Susan Ireland's Resume Service.

Health Educator, San Francisco, San Mateo and Union City, CA, 1986-97

- Coordinated AIDS education programs in schools (San Mateo County AIDS Program, 1992-94), the Northern CA AIDS Hotline and AIDS Speaker's Bureau (San Francisco AIDS Foundation, 1986-92).
- Served as overseas AIDS education consultant, helping to establish AIDS Hotlines in St. Lucia, West Indies and Swaziland, Africa (AIDSCOM/U.S.A.I.D., 1989-92).
- Provided detailed medical information, advocacy, counseling and referrals to callers to a federally funded Cancer Information Service (1994-97).

- continued -

Ruth L. Schwartz
Page Six

Languages

Verbal and written fluency in Spanish, with special interest in literary translation.

Sample Comments from Recent Student Evaluations

(Original evaluations available upon request)

- *"Professor's attitude was very helpful to novice writers."*
- *"She knew her content, and made the course fun by having structured and enriching classes."*
- *"The course was inspiring and constructive."*
- *"(She was) able to be honest and candid in her comments and instruction, while remaining respectful."*
- *"Gave good constructive criticism ... very personable, easy to talk to, and open to suggestions."*
- *"(The course) definitely improved my writing ... and the instructor successfully interested me in poetry."*

Part 4

Wrapping It Up

With the exception of junk mail, a letter is welcomed by almost everyone, and your prospective employer is no exception. In fact, your cover and thank you letters might be the elements of your application that send the message that you're the one for the job. Whether it's the way you sell yourself in writing or the personality that comes through in your words, your letter holds the power to make a personal connection between you and the manager.

"Easy for you to say," you mumble. "You're a writer. I freeze at the thought of putting my pen to paper." Relax! Part 4 gives some easy-to-follow advice that will make your fingers fly across your keyboard to create letters that work.

Chapter 14

The Big Production

In This Chapter

- Making sure your resume is in order
- Design tricks to help you look spiffy on paper
- Using the right type
- Sending it out the door

See, it wasn't all that bad writing your resume. I knew you could do it. But before you start stuffing envelopes and announcing your career move to the world, take one more minute to review the following tips on printing and circulating your resume, as well as the sample resumes at the end of this chapter. Then you'll be armed with a winning strategy for getting your resume out to the job market.

Designer Resumes

These few design tricks will help to ensure that your resume looks spiffy once it gets into the hands of the employer:

- Use an appropriate typeface.
- Use the right size of type.
- Use bullet points for your achievement statements.
- Add vertical or horizontal lines. (This is completely optional and should only be used if the lines increase ease of reading or the aesthetics of the resume.)
- Make sure you have enough white space.
- Keep a clean master copy.
- Make sure your reproductions are clean.
- Use good paper.

Following are instructions for how to take advantage of some of these design concepts using Microsoft Word (MS Word). If you're working in an application other than MS Word, consult your manual to learn how to get the job done.

Job Hunt Hint

When lining up text in a column, always use tabs instead of the space bar. Then your words will align perfectly every time.

Fancy Fonts and Practical Print

Choosing the style of type for your resume can be fun. You have several choices, and each one has a slightly different look and feel. To help you pick one for your resume, let me explain the ABCs of type styles. Fonts are typefaces, which come in two styles: serif (with the little feet on the characters) and sans serif (without the feet).

There are two categories of type (or *font*, as it's called in the business):

- Serif
- Sans serif

Either a serif or sans serif font is okay for your resume, but most graphic designers say that serif type is easier to read.

Serif's Up!

Serif type has little "feet" on its characters (see examples following). There are many serif fonts, ranging from super-fancy scripts to basic typewriter print. For your resume, stay away from the two extremes and pick one that's mid-range so that your resume is easy to read and pleasing to the eye.

The following serif fonts are found on most word processing programs and are suitable for the job. As you can see from the resume samples in this book, serif fonts are what I use most of the time. Notice that I've printed each of the following names in the font it represents so that you can compare them:

New Century Schoolbook

Garamond

Palatino

Times

Simply Sans Serif

Sans serif characters don't have little feet on them. Following are some sans serif fonts that I like:

Helvetica

Univers

Arial

Bonus Check

If you're going crazy dealing with fonts, bullet points, indents, and spacing, take a shortcut and use the Ready-Made Resumes program mentioned at the very end of this book. The program offers MS Word templates with all the formatting done for you!

To change the font in your MS Word document, follow these steps:

1. Select the particular text you want to change, or click Select All from the Edit menu.
2. Choose Format in your pull-down toolbar at the top of your screen, and select Font.
3. Highlight the font you want.

After you get the hang of changing fonts, you'll be able to do it in the blink of an eye.

Does Size Matter?

Font sizes are measured by points, and with a few exceptions, those measurements are standard among the various fonts. Use either 11 or 12 point for the text of your resume. Don't be tempted to use 10 point or smaller to make it all fit on one page; it'll be too hard to read.

The type size for your major headings (Job Objective, Summary of Qualifications, Professional Experience, and Education) should all be equal to each other and may be as small as 11 point and as large as 13 point. Choose the point size to please your taste, staying within the 11- to 13-point limit.

Although there is no standard size of type for your name on your resume, a good rule of thumb is that it should be no larger than 18 points and no smaller than 12 points.

You can adjust a font's point size by pulling down the Format menu from the toolbar. Then click Font and choose a size from the Size box.

Sharp-Shooting Bullets

Bullet points are little dots placed at the beginning of a statement, which help the reader move swiftly through your resume. They let you present your information in bite-size pieces and avoid unwanted paragraphs (as I mentioned in Chapter 1). Here's how to create the bullet point in MS Word:

1. With your cursor, highlight the line you want to place a bullet in front of.
2. Select the bullet icon on your toolbar or go to the Format menu and click Bullets and Numbering.

There are symbols other than bullet points that can be used to separate statements on your resume. Here are others available on MS Word that I like:

■ The square

□ The check box

◆ The diamond

→ The arrow

You can elaborate on a bullet point statement by adding sub-bullet statements. Sub-bullet statements should be indented and should start with a symbol other than the bullet point, perhaps a dash, plus sign, or one of the untraditional symbols mentioned above.

The resume by Joanne Rainey demonstrates the use of dashes to create indented sub-bullet point statements under her achievements.

Shady Bars

You may like the look of lines, double lines, bars, or shaded bars running across or up and down your resume. Here's how to do those nifty extras if you're working in MS Word:

1. Put your cursor where you want to insert a line or bar into your resume.
2. In your toolbar, access the Format pull-down menu.
3. Click Borders and Shading.
4. Under Setting, choose Borders.
5. Under Style, choose the type of line or bar you want.
6. Under Preview, click the icon representing the bottom of the box.

It's that simple, and the results will make you look like a desktop publishing pro!

Horizontal lines and shaded bars can help an employer immediately identify the different sections of the resume allowing him to move through your document quickly. Too many lines, however, can make a resume look cluttered. So use your judgment or consult a friend who has an artistic eye to create the right balance.

Check out the lines Sean Goodridge used on his resume, and flip through the "Portfolio of Sample Resumes" at the end of this book to see how others have incorporated shaded bars and lines into their documents.

Spacing Out

Think of your resume as a valuable piece of Manhattan real estate where every increment of space must be used. As land is used for buildings, signs, and pathways, use your resume real estate for headings, phrases, and lists. And just as landscaping and parks are appreciated in congested urban areas, white space gives relief to the resume reader's eye.

One way to create white space on your resume is to set generous margins. Here's how:

1. In your MS Word toolbar, select the File pull-down menu.
2. Click Page Setup.
3. Click Margins.
4. Set the left and right margins to no less than 1 inch each.
5. Set the top and bottom margins to no less than .5 inch each.

Adjusting the leading (the space between your lines) is another clever way to add white space without eating up too much real estate. For example, you may want to have just a little space (but not a full line space) between each bullet point statement to set them apart. Customizing space before or after lines (which are considered paragraphs for formatting purposes) is easy:

1. Highlight the paragraph (or bullet point statement) you want to add space before or after.
2. In your MS Word toolbar, select the Format pull-down menu.
3. Click Paragraph.
4. Click Indents and Spacing.

CAUTION

Career Casualty

Don't staple your cover letter and resume together. Clip them together with a paper clip instead so the recipient can easily separate them for copying and filing.

5. Under the heading Spacing, you'll see boxes next to Before and After. Insert a number, such as 6, in either the Before or After box to add space before or after a paragraph. (The smaller the number, the smaller the space will be.)
6. Click OK to see the results of your work.

A third white-space technique is to use the Tab key to indent text to create columns or sub-bullet point statements, as demonstrated in the Job Objective statement in the resume by Joanne Rainey.

Resume Reality

Now that you've learned what good resume design and type style are, it's time to get your resume printed and out in the real world where it's going to work wonders for you. Let's move on to the nuts and bolts of getting your resume out of the printer and into the hands of your next employer!

Mastering Your Resume

After the content of your resume is written and laid out in either the chronological or functional format, you need to print and copy it. Print your master resume on a laser or inkjet printer. Your master printouts should be on white paper of any weight.

In the Mood to Reproduce

After you have printed your master, it's off to a copy center, unless you have access to a high-quality copier elsewhere. Don't order a whole slew of copies; start with the number you think you'll need for one or two weeks of your job search.

By copying your resume in short runs, you'll be more inclined to adjust your marketing approach as you pursue your ideal job. That's important because you need to be prepared to change your Job Objective statement and tweak your resume, if necessary, as you get feedback from employers along the way.

Looking Classy on Paper

Your next step is to select paper that's appropriate for the type of work you're after. It makes sense that someone going for a CEO position is going to have higher-end paper than someone seeking a clerical position.

Personally, I don't like fancy textured or parchment sheets—to me they look pretentious. I like plain white that has just a little more weight than the standard 20-pound paper used for copying. That extra weight sends a subconscious message of quality to the reader without screaming out, "This is expensive paper!"

Job Hunt Hint

Your resume needs to be ready to survive a long process of faxing and photocopying. That means you should use black print on white paper.

But don't go overboard on the weight. As one administrative assistant pointed out to me, "When the paper is too thick, it jams up the copier. That makes me mad, and I'm apt to throw the resume away." Oops! You better not get on the wrong side of an administrative assistant who, at that moment, wields the fate of your career. Solution: choose something a little heavier than 20-pound but not as thick as card stock.

I can just see you now—your chin lifted high and chest puffed out as you walk out of the copy center with your stack of fresh resumes. You're ready to conquer the world!

Getting It Out the Door

Just a few more steps and your resume will be in your new boss's hands. Here's what's left to do:

- Wrap it up.
- Send it out.

Although sending out a resume isn't rocket science, it's worth taking a few minutes to look at the following hints to ensure a smooth send-off and landing.

Stuffing Envelopes

First of all, don't staple your cover letter and resume together. Clip them together with a paper clip instead so the recipient can easily separate them for copying and filing.

Instead of stuffing your cover letter and resume into the standard 4 × 9-inch business envelope, mail your marketing duo in a large 9 × 12-inch envelope (white, manila, or gray will do). In the larger envelope, your documents will lie flat, allowing them to arrive without creases that can crack the print. (Imagine how badly cracked print will look after the resume is photocopied and faxed a few times—a common paper trail in corporate America.)

If your printer doesn't accept a 9 × 12-inch envelope (and most don't), it's perfectly fine to hand-address your envelope. Or you could type or print out the address on a plain white label, if you have sticky labels for a typewriter or computer printer.

Snail Mail

If you have plenty of time before the application deadline, the U.S. Postal Service (fondly referred to as snail mail) is a great and fairly reliable way to send your resume and cover letter. There's no need to send your packet certified or registered; simply put a stamp for first-class delivery on that big envelope I suggested and head for a mailbox.

Special Delivery

If you're in a hurry to get your resume and cover letter to an employer, use one of the overnight or two-day courier services such as FedEx, UPS, or the U.S. Postal Service's Express Mail. Most of these services will pick up your packet at your address, or you can take it to their dispatch center and have it sent from there.

Job Hunt Hint

Figure out when your resume and cover letter are likely to land on the employer's desk (depending on whether you send it via U.S. mail, courier, fax, or e-mail). Then make a note to follow up by phone one day after you think your packet has arrived.

Fax Magic

When you're up against a tight deadline or the job posting says to fax the resume, go straight to a fax machine and start pushing those buttons. Your faxable cover letter and resume should be created exactly like the ones you would send via the U.S. mail. But they need one more ingredient—a fax cover sheet, which simply states the following information:

- The date
- The recipient (to whom the fax is being sent)
- Who is sending the fax (that's you!)
- The total number of pages being faxed and the general contents of those sheets (for example: Cover sheet and resume)

If you fax your cover letter and resume, call the employer and ask whether you should also send your resume by mail. Some companies are so inundated with paperwork that they prefer not to receive duplicate resumes. Others appreciate having the real thing sent on nice paper, especially if they don't have high-quality fax machines or copiers.

E-Mail Flash

If your potential employer is expecting your resume and cover letter to arrive by e-mail, check out Chapter 17, where I explain how to format a resume that will survive and thrive in the world of e-mail.

The Least You Need to Know

- Limit your resume to one or two pages.
- Instead of paragraphs, use bullet point statements to make your material quick and easy to read.
- Choose an appropriate font, set wide margins, adjust line spaces, and indent text to make the body of your resume inviting to read.
- Print your resume on a laser or inkjet printer.
- Reproduce your resume on a high-quality copier using appropriate paper.
- Send your cover letter and resume via U.S. Postal Service, express/courier service, fax, or e-mail, depending on how quickly it must arrive and which way the employer would like it to be delivered.

JOANNE RAINEY

123 Essex Street • Healdsburg, CA 12345 • (123) 555-1234 • jorainey@bamboo.com

OBJECTIVE: A position in the alternative health field with a focus on communication, administration, and client relations

HIGHLIGHTS OF QUALIFICATIONS

- A clear and straightforward communicator, skilled in establishing strong, long-term client relationships and cultivating productive teams.
- Highly organized, directed, and detail-oriented; able to juggle multiple responsibilities simultaneously and maintain calm in fast-paced environments.
- Committed to a healthy and balanced lifestyle; passion for conveying the wisdom of alternative healing.

RELEVANT ACCOMPLISHMENTS

COMMUNICATION & CLIENT RELATIONS

- Provided comprehensive in-person and telephone assistance to clients and prospects at Fast Forward:
  - Acted as initial contact for new and prospective members.
  - Advised clients regarding individual counseling and workshop options specific to their career goals.
  - Responded to client concerns with directness, and used diplomacy to resolve problems equitably.
- Coordinated with other Fast Forward Client Services Representatives to ensure smooth scheduling transitions and effectiveness in daily operations and client satisfaction.
- Answered phones and scheduled acupuncture appointments for Sung Lee, L.Ac.

ADMINISTRATION

- Registered new clients for membership, counseling sessions, seminars, and workshops at Fast Forward.
- Updated records and maintained efficient office organization for Sung Lee's active acupuncture practice.
- Researched, synthesized, and edited relevant articles for publication in 20th Century Publishing's weekly international newsletters, with circulation of over 2,000.

PROFESSIONAL EXPERIENCE

1999-pres.	**Client Service Representative**	Fast Forward, Sebastopol, CA
1997-99	**Office Manager**	Sung Lee, L.Ac., Occidental, CA
1994-97	**Office Manager**	20th Century Publishing, Novato, CA

EDUCATION

B.A., Psychology and English Literature, Mills College, Oakland, CA
Counseling Internship with Family Service Agency of Sonoma County
Ongoing independent research into numerous alternative health modalities

Sean Goodridge

123 La Cage Ave.
Miami Beach, FL 12345
(123) 555-1234
sgoodridge@bamboo.com

PROFILE

- Aspiring Interior Designer with experience in design development and drafting.
- Produced preliminary drawings and construction documents for commercial and residential projects.
- Creative approach to problem solving.

EDUCATION

BS, Interior Design, Rhode Island School of Design, Providence, RI

Conceptual Design	Architectural Lighting Design
Creative Problem Solving	Model Making
Space Planning	Computer Design: MiniCAD, Adobe Illustrator

RELEVANT ACCOMPLISHMENTS

INTERIOR DESIGN

- Designed residential addition. Drafted preliminary drawings and construction documents. Worked with architect who followed plans through to completion.
- Completed drafting for projects:
  - Water treatment plant
  - Housing developments
  - Apartment complexes
- Developed floor plans and elevations for commercial and residential projects.
- Conceptualized and created design for a cafe. Completed a specification book and made material selections for presentation boards.

CLIENT RELATIONS

- As part of space planning class, met with business owners to discuss their ideas and needs for developing conceptual plans.
- Built a clientele at Hayward's by providing personal attention to customer needs and comprehensive product knowledge.

WORK HISTORY

2005-present	Salesperson	Hayward's, Miami Beach, FL
2004-2005	Junior Designer	Burton & Duncan Architects, Tallahassee, FL
2001-2004	Assistant to Interior Designer	Brown & Walton Associates, Johnston, RI

– Portfolio available –

Francine M. Ling

123 Frontier Avenue, #2 • Madison, Wisconsin 12345 • (123) 555-1234 • fmling@bamboo.com

ADMINISTRATIVE PROFESSIONAL
with strengths in:

Project Management	Executive Support
Office Management	Team Building

PROFESSIONAL EXPERIENCE

1997-present **XEROX CORPORATION - MADISON RESEARCH CENTER**
Executive Secretary/Member Support Staff, Madison, WI, 2000-present
Office Manager/Member Support Staff, Milwaukee, WI, 1997-2000

- One of first five members of research team that consults with corporate and institutional clients regarding their document creation and publishing problems.
- Logistics manager of research team awarded for completion of educational project for Harvard Business School.
    - Honorary MBA from Harvard Business School.
- Excellence in Science and Technology Award plus $1,000, Xerox's second-highest employee award.
- Co-planned "Vision & Values" and "Milestones & Goals" statements for the team.
- One of five originators of "Office of the Future," a successful pilot project involving two sites connected by audio/visual communications through a gateway.
- Supervised construction/remodeling and furnishing of offices in Milwaukee and Madison. Set up administrative operations for both 10-person sites.
- Managed the physical facilities including compliance with corporate requirements.
- Office manager for 10 research and marketing professionals. This included customer contact, consultant contracts, accounting, budgets, purchasing, travel, and conferences. Commended for best record keeping in the corporation.

1993-1997 **PELLEY & CO.,** Milwaukee, WI
Executive Secretary

- Provided office management and administrative assistance to President and Vice President of this lumber equipment manufacturer.

EDUCATION

Honorary MBA, Harvard Business School, Cambridge, MA
Business and Business Law, Milwaukee State College, Milwaukee, WI
Xerox Training: Leadership Through Quality

WINDOWS AND MACINTOSH SKILLS

MS Word	Excel
PowerPoint	FrameMaker

Chapter 15

The Cover Letter Connection

In This Chapter

- Your secret weapon: a cover letter that lets your personality shine through
- The issue of including salary information in your cover letter
- An effective cover letter, part by part
- Four easy steps to creating multiple cover letters
- How to write an effective thank you note after an interview

You have a great-looking resume, and you're eager to send it off to Mr. or Ms. Employer. But wait! You need one more thing: a cover letter. And not just any old cover letter—you want a terrific letter that makes a great first impression. In this chapter, you'll learn how to write a cover letter that's quick and easy to compose, sounds personable, and gets you the results you want!

The Secret to Success

Here's my secret for writing an outstanding cover letter: Think of your letter as the basis of the ideal script for the job interview you'll have with the person to whom you're writing. Let your letter indicate the following things to the reader:

- What topic could break the ice at the beginning of the interview
- What kind of personality you have
- What types of things you have to talk about in your meeting
- What you hope to get from the interview

If your cover letter can say these four things, it will make an employer start imagining that you and she are having a conversation. When she does that, she'll be more apt to read your resume and then reach for the phone to call you for an interview!

Salary Small Talk

You may run into a job posting that asks for your *salary* expectations. Most job seekers don't feel comfortable talking about these details before the interview. If you feel compelled to do so in your cover letter (maybe you worry that you'll be disqualified if you don't comply with the ad's request), however, do so gingerly.

I suggest that you first find out what the position typically pays. You can do this by asking a job counselor or employment agency or by reading ads for similar jobs in the newspaper. Then do one of the following:

- Mention your salary expectations in your cover letter, using language that gives you room for negotiations, such as, "I am looking for a position in the $X to $Y salary range."
- Indicate that you would prefer to discuss salary during the interview.

In either case, you've addressed the issue, and you'll likely stand a chance at winning an interview where you can discuss the full compensation package, not just the take-home pay (which is what a salary range implies).

The Template of Zoom

CAUTION

Career Casualty

Use bold and italic sparingly in your letter. An overdose of these features can make your letter hard to read.

Here's how to zoom through your letter-writing process: As I go through each step of writing a cover letter, follow the template in this chapter. That will help you understand what goes where.

A Head Start

Your heading should contain the same info as the one on your resume.

- Name
- Address
- Telephone number(s)
- E-mail address (optional)
- Fax number (optional)

For help figuring out how to create a tasteful heading, see Chapter 4. In fact, you could just duplicate the heading from your resume and use it for letterhead of your cover letter.

Set the Date and the Place

Immediately under the heading, place the date and inside address. The inside address is your recipient's name and mailing address. (There's no need to include the recipient's phone, e-mail, or fax numbers.)

Your Name
Street address
City, state, and zip
Contact number(s)
E-mail address (optional)

Today's date

Your addressee's name
Professional title
Organization name
Mailing address
City, state, and zip

Dear Mr. (or Ms.) last name,

Start your letter with a grabber — a statement that establishes a connection with your reader, a probing question or a quotable quote. Briefly name the job you are applying for.

The mid-section of your letter should be one or two short paragraphs that make relevant points about your qualifications. You should *not* summarize your resume! You may incorporate a column or bullet point format here.

Your last paragraph should initiate action by explaining what *you* will do next (e.g., call the employer), or asking the reader to take a specific step (e.g., contact you to set up an interview). This is also a good place to thank the reader for his or her attention.

Sincerely yours,

Your name (signed)

Your name (typed)

Enclosure: resume

Hello, Hello!

The salutation is very simple: Dear so-and-so. Hopefully you know the person's name and can use it in the salutation. If not, a quick call to the company's Human Resources department can give you that information. If you know the person on a first-name basis, use just her first name (for example, Dear Jane). If you've never met her or you have a formal rapport with her, use her last name (for example, Dear Ms. Graham).

If you don't know the manager's name and have no way of finding it out, start your letter with a job title that makes sense for your letter, as shown in the following examples:

- Dear Manager
- Dear Director
- Dear Recruiter

Don't write "To whom it may concern" or "Dear Sir or Madam" as a salutation in your cover letter. It's far too formal and impersonal. Instead, use one of the suggestions above.

Jumping In

The opening line is one of the most important parts of your letter. It has to be a good one, or you could lose the employer before you even begin. Think of a grabber that will make the employer want to keep reading. (For ideas, see the sample letters later in this chapter and on my website, www.susanireland.com.)

Be creative in how you start your letter. Avoid openings with the ho-hum phrases so many job seekers use, such as these:

Enclosed please find my resume for …

I'm responding to your ad in the …

I'm applying for the position as …

Job Hunt Hint

Think of your letter as the bridge between your resume (which is a monologue) and your interview (which is a dialogue).

These overused openers are boring and show no personality or originality. They sound like a form letter, which is the very thing you want to avoid.

Here are some ideas for how you could kick off your letter:

- Lead in with the name of someone you both know.
- Briefly explain how you learned about the job opening you're applying for.
- Begin with a question that piques the reader's interest.
- Start out with a quote that applies to the type of business the employer is involved with.

For details on each of these ideas and lots of sample letters that use these techniques, refer to my website, www.susanireland.com.

The Meat of the Matter

The middle of your letter is your opportunity to paint the picture of what you'll be able to contribute to the interview. Use this section to point out …

- Topics you want to discuss that relate to the organization's issues.
- Your understanding of what it takes to fill the specific position and be a good employee.
- That you've done your homework and therefore have a hunch as to what the company's up to and how you would fit in.

Getting What You Want

Near the end of your letter, do two things:

1. Ask for what you want (probably a job interview).
2. Thank the person.

Try to keep the ball in your court by saying something to the effect of "I'll call you to see when we can meet" instead of a more passive approach such as "I hope to hear from you."

If you don't have contact information for the employer and therefore can't call her, or if the ad specifies no phone calls, try an assertive close that nudges the employer to call you for an interview, such as the following:

- I'll be interviewing in Florida during the last week of this month. Please call me to schedule an appointment.
- With the end of the second quarter approaching, you may need to do some catch-up in sales. The sooner I get to work, the more I can contribute to reaching your annual goals. Let's talk!

You can thank the employer very simply:

- Thank you for reviewing this resume in advance of our meeting.
- I appreciate the time you've spent considering my request.
- I'm looking forward to our meeting. Thank you.

Don't be afraid to use demonstrative language in your letter—after all, you really want a job from this employer, don't you? As long as your phrases are natural and appropriate, say them with confidence. What would you say in person to thank a prospective employer for considering you for a job? What you would say verbally is a hint as to what to write at the end of your cover letter.

Ten-Four

It's time to sign off with a complimentary close such as the following:

- Sincerely,
- Sincerely yours,

- Very sincerely,
- With regards,
- Regards,
- Thank you!

Skip a few lines after your complimentary close, and type your name. After you've printed out your letter, sign the letter in the space between your close and your typed name.

Flush left on the next line, type "Enclosure: resume." In the grand scheme of corporate paper shuffling, your resume and cover letter may get separated. This way, the recipient of your package knows that you've included your resume, without your having to take up valuable space in your letter saying so.

By Example

Following are three sample cover letters that demonstrate the points I've been talking about. They should give you some ideas for formulating your one-of-a-kind cover letter.

Name-Dropping

A great way to start your letter is with the name of someone both you and your reader know. This person could be any of the following:

- A mutual friend ("Your cousin Larry suggested I contact you about ….")
- A respected professional associate ("When Linda Standall mentioned your name at the dental convention ….")
- A well-known person, even if neither of you knows him personally ("In the words of our industry's guru, Bill Gates ….")

A familiar name is apt to make the employer sit up and take notice. It'll also make the employer realize that you already have something in common and that a conversation with you will feel natural. Check out Bill Steinberger's introductory sentence in his cover letter. See how it grabs you and draws you into the rest of the letter?

Getting Personal

Your cover letter should not summarize your resume. After all, you worked hard to write about your qualifications in concise statements on your resume. Why would you do it again in the cover letter? Instead, the cover letter should add a personal message that your resume doesn't convey.

In her letter, Kelly Brown introduces the fact that she has multiple sclerosis, a point that will help her identify with the employer's clients. Although such a personal statement did not appear in her resume, it's perfectly appropriate in her cover letter.

Take My Hint, Please!

Sometimes it pays to give an idea away. By proposing a solution to the manager, you take the risk of having it stolen, but more than likely you'll be perceived as a bright individual the employer wants on his team.

In her cover letter, notice how Carla Smith hints at what she thinks is a great idea for her prospective employer's Marketing department. Without giving away the details of her program, she indicates that she knows what she's talking about and can pull it off—to the employer's benefit!

Getting the Hang of It

If you need to write cover letters to more than one potential employer, follow these steps:

1. Make a list of all the cover letters you need to write.
2. Prioritize the list so that your most preferred potential employer is first, second most preferred is second, and so on.
3. Write your first letter, concentrating on your number-one employer.
4. When your first letter is completed, make a copy of it on your computer to use as a guide to create cover letters to your other prospects.

This technique for writing several letters will bring some magical results. By starting with your number-one choice, you'll bring the most juice to your creative process of writing. And by concentrating on just one employer at a time, your letter will be customized for your recipient and therefore won't sound like a form letter. That's an important aspect of good cover letter writing: Your letter must sound personalized to the specific employer.

Now you have some good strategies for creating a winning cover letter. With your smashing resume and cover letter, you're bound to hit a home run!

After a Job Interview

As soon as you walk away from a good job interview, ask yourself how it went:

- Were you pleased with your performance?
- What things in particular did you appreciate about the way the manager conducted the interview?
- What did you learn about the company that especially interested you?
- What thoughts have come to mind about your conversation that you'd like to share with the employer?

The answers to these questions are grist for the mill for your thank you letter. Your letter should be short, to the point, and essentially say "thank you." This letter is also your opportunity to continue the conversation from your interview with one or two follow-up thoughts.

> CAUTION
>
> **Career Casualty**
>
> Don't worry that sending a thank you letter will pester the employer. Keep your note short and to the point. It will take the employer just a minute to read and will send the right message: You sincerely want the job.

In her letter, Jane Harbinger thanked Ms. Gomez for her interview and added a hint of things to come at their next meeting. Jane's letter showed that she was very interested in this job.

The Least You Need to Know

- Make your cover letter personable and targeted to the employer. Don't let it sound like a form letter.
- Create an opening sentence that grabs your potential employer's attention.
- Paint the picture of you and the employer conversing about the company through the body of your letter.
- End your letter with a word of thanks and a request for an interview.
- After you've written a strong cover letter for your number-one choice of employment, tailor it toward other employers.
- Following up with a short thank-you letter after an interview increases your chances of winning the job.

Bill Steinberger

123 Terrace Street
El Sobrante, CA 12345
123-555-1234
bsteinberger@bamboo.com

January 3, 2006

Mr. Ron Gratchet, Owner
Tools, Etc.
123 Greystone Road
Portland, OR 12345

Dear Mr. Gratchet,

Linda Zeffer has often spoken highly of you, usually in reference to the likelihood of our meeting someday.

In fact, that's what this letter and resume are about. I'd like to speak with you about the opening for General Manager at Tools, Etc.

I grew up in the hardware business — my parents owned and ran an Ace Hardware store in a small town for 25 years before they sold it to me. As much as I love managing the store, it's time to move on to bigger things ... such as Tools, Etc.

Could we talk soon? I'd like to be the first candidate you consider. I'll call your office to see when you are free to meet with me. Thank you!

Sincerely,

Bill Steinberger

Enclosure: resume

Carla Smith
Marketing Professional
123 Halstead Rd.
Rochester, NY 12345
123-555-1234
carlasmith@bamboo.com

November 3, 2005

Mr. James Callahan
General Manager
Household Paints, Inc.
123 Grand Blvd.
White Plains, NY 12345

Dear Mr. Callahan:

Research shows that women have a greater sensitivity to color than men. For that reason, I propose that I create a marketing program for Household Paints that targets women.

As your Marketing Director, I can design programs that keep down production costs by generating "umbrella" collateral to be used for multiple niches. My enclosed resume demonstrates how I've used this technique to save thousands of dollars and bring in significant revenue for former employers.

Let's talk in person about your new "Colors for Women" program. I'll call you in a few days to arrange an appointment.

Thank you!

Carla Smith

Enclosure: resume

Kelly Brown

123 Alameny Ave.
Sheridan, WY 12345
(123) 555-1234
kbrown@bamboo.com

December 10, 2005

Ms. Alice Foremost
Director of Job Placement
Agency for the Disabled
123 Congress Rd.
Sheridan, WY 12345

Dear Ms. Foremost:

Do you believe in fate? I didn't until I opened the *Sheridan Bee* this morning and saw your ad for Job Placement Officer. It sounded like the job I've been searching for.

In a flash, you'll see from my resume that my qualifications line up perfectly with your announcement. But here's how I *really* fit into your agency: I have a deep commitment to working with people with disabilities.

As a person with MS, I have a solid comprehension of the American Disabilities Act, as well as a full understanding of career development issues experienced by your job candidates.

I would very much like to speak with you in person. I'm eager to learn more about the agency and, specifically, the job placement position. I'll call you in a few days to see when we can talk.

In the meantime, thank you for reviewing my application.

Sincerely,

Kelly Brown

Enclosure: resume

Jane Harbinger
123 Coolidge Lane
Cranston, NY 12345
123-555-1234
jharbinger@bamboo.com

March 23, 2006

Ms. Francine Gomez
President and CEO
Highcrest Divisions Management Group
123 23rd Ave.
Albany, NY 12345

Dear Ms. Gomez:

My interview with you this morning was all that I had hoped for and more. Not only are we on the same page regarding consumer education, we share a similar view on management training. I agree that distance learning is a must if we're to keep our management abreast of our industry's trends.

I plan to research the points we discussed and bring you more concrete ideas at our next meeting on Monday.

Thank you for a truly exhilarating meeting.

Sincerely,

Jane Harbinger

The Electronic Job Search

E-mail. The World Wide Web. Cyberspace. If you haven't had lots of experience with the Internet, you may worry that you're not techno-savvy enough to use it, or that somehow you might endanger the world if you click that little mouse on the wrong icon.

The surprising thing is how easy it is. Conducting an online job search is, without a doubt, simpler than programming your VCR. So sit down at your computer and let your cyberfingers do the walking through the career sections of online directories.

In Part 5, you'll learn how to prepare a resume for your cyberspace job search. You'll also learn about the scanning technology that your resume may encounter when it reaches the employer's desk.

Ready? Set? Click!

Chapter 16

The ABCs of E-Resumes

In This Chapter

- What an e-resume is
- How resume databases work
- What it means to have your resume searched
- How to get your resume into a resume bank

Electronic resumes, or e-resumes, are no longer a thing of the future: They're here now, and they're here to stay. They come in a variety of formats, and employers can process them in different ways. The challenge is to keep up with the techniques and opportunities in the quickly changing world of e-resumes. In this chapter, you'll learn what's behind the e-resume trend and how this technology can benefit your job search.

What Is an Electronic Resume?

An electronic resume is a nonpaper resume, meaning it's a computer document that can be …

- Viewed on a screen.
- Stored on a hard drive.
- Sent over the Internet.
- Searched for keywords.
- Manipulated into other types of documents.
- Printed for review as a hard copy.

E-resumes are used for e-mailing, depositing into Internet resume banks, posting on personal websites, and sending through scanners to be entered into resume banks. A resume bank is a database that holds lots of resumes. Most resume banks have search capabilities to select resumes according to job objective and keywords specified by the employer or headhunter.

The E-Resume Appeal

Job Hunt Hint

The content of your electronic resume should employ the same marketing principles used in your hardcopy resume:

- Write about experiences that support your job objective.
- List achievements, not job descriptions.
- Disclose only information that promotes you as a qualified job candidate.
- Avoid mentioning things you don't want to do again.
- Tell the truth; don't exaggerate or lie.

Who benefits from e-resumes? Everyone: you, employers, and recruiting agencies. That's because e-resumes make the job hunt/hiring process more efficient for all concerned.

Here are the three major benefits to employers:

1. **Money.** Employers can save tremendous amounts in recruiting costs through the use of e-resumes.
2. **Speed.** E-resumes can be processed much faster than hardcopy resumes.
3. **Organization.** Resume databases can store, sort, and search thousands of e-resumes according to a variety of criteria.

The same three major benefits apply to you, the job seeker:

1. **Money.** Aside from saving money in postage, an electronic job search may help you get a job sooner (which means you'll be collecting a paycheck sooner) because it's usually more efficient than the nonelectronic job search.
2. **Speed.** An e-resume's capability to get in front of a hiring manager quickly could give you an edge over your competition.
3. **Organization.** E-resumes are easy for you to keep organized on your computer, and you can rest assured that your resume is in good hands once it's in the employer's computer system.

Sounds like a win-win situation, doesn't it? The crux of these winning points is the electronic backbone of the e-resume system: the database. Let's look at why a resume database can be a hiring manager's best friend and how it can take you to the top of the candidate lineup.

Data in the Database

Bonus Check

Unlike a filing system for hardcopy documents (the standard filing cabinet), a resume database allows several people to access the same resume at the same time. For example, three managers in three different locations could each pull up your resume for review at the same time. In the old-fashioned filing cabinet, only one manager at a time could access the resume.

Resume databases (also referred to as resume banks) are systems for storing information about applicants. Resume databases vary in their complexity. A high-end system will hold the following information:

- A Summary of Qualifications form for each applicant; this information is extracted from the job seeker's resume and placed in a database file according to predetermined fields such as education, work history, or job objective.
- A list of each job seeker's keywords (see the "Key Placement" section later in this chapter for a sample list) compiled by the database's search engine.
- Each job seeker's resume, either the electronic version or an image of the paper resume if it was scanned into the system. (See Chapter 19 to learn more about the scanning process.)

Low-end systems have an abbreviated version of the preceding information, or they have the same set of information but require manual inputting, which inevitably increases the chance of errors.

The value in a resume database lies in its ability to store, search, and display resumes in a matter of minutes. Let's look at how this process works.

The Inner Workings

When your resume is in a database, it can be accessed in a few ways. A manager or human resources clerk might:

- Browse through resumes at random.
- Sort resumes so they can be seen in groups according to job objective, industry, or other logical categories.
- Conduct keyword searches to select and prioritize resumes by how many of those words appear in each resume.

The beauty of this system is that even if your resume doesn't make the cut for one hiring manager's search, it remains in the database for others to consider. With this collective storage system, your resume is potentially visible to anyone who has access to the database.

Keyword: Search

Most searches rely on two things: a search engine and keywords for the engine to search for. The search engine is built in to the system (and works similarly to Google, Yahoo!, and other engines you use to search the Internet for a topic). The keywords are usually subjective, because they're created by the person who is operating the search engine. For that reason, there may be no set list of keywords for your profession because it depends entirely on who is generating the list on the hiring side.

A keyword search might examine each resume for up to 60 keywords. Keywords could indicate the following information:

- Technical expertise
- Management skills
- Industry knowledge
- Education
- Geographic location
- Employment history

After the keywords are entered into the search engine, the engine goes through its database, matches resumes with the designated keywords, and even ranks the selected candidates against each other according to how many keywords appear in each resume. The most sophisticated systems have synonym-search capabilities that find not only the exact word listed for the search (such as *management*), but also related words (such as *supervision*, *administration*, and *leadership*).

The E-Creation

An e-resume isn't all that different from your hardcopy resume. With just a few alterations to that hardcopy version, your resume will sail through e-mail systems, online resume banks, and resume scanners.

Here are a few guidelines:

- Use formatting that's acceptable for the type of e-resume you're creating. In addition to the general principles for e-resumes in this chapter, see details for specific types in Chapters 17, 18, and 19.
- Include keywords in your resume that an employer would use to search for a top candidate in your field.

Let's go over some tips for good e-resume construction.

Electronic Headings

Your name should be the only thing that appears on the first line at the top of your e-resume. Here's why: When your resume is entered into a resume database file, the first line of your resume (no matter what's written on the line) will likely be entered into the Name field of the database file. Because everything in the first line may be interpreted as your name, be sure you put your professional title (if you include it in your heading) on the second line.

Also, place each piece of your contact information on a separate line, as in this example:

Kerrie Oslow
Medical Technologist
123 Perkins Cove Lane
Brentwood, CA 12345
123-555-1234
OslowK@bamboo.com

In today's electronic job search world, it makes sense to include your e-mail address in your heading because it's a tool the employer is likely to use to contact you.

Bonus Check

Consider signing up with Hotmail (www.hotmail.com) or Yahoo! (www.yahoo.com) for an e-mail account. Your personal Hotmail or Yahoo! account can be accessed from anywhere in the world as long as you are at a computer that's hooked up to the Internet. This type of e-mail service is ideal if you travel a lot or if your access to the Internet doesn't offer you a personal e-mail account (for instance, if you use your company's ISP account, it would be inappropriate for you to use it to send and receive personal e-mail). And to top it off, Hotmail and Yahoo! e-mail accounts are free!

Key Placement

Make a list of 20 to 60 keywords you think the hiring manager will use to search for the position mentioned in your Job Objective. Keywords can be technical, such as *MIS analysis*, or nontechnical, such as *Conflict resolution.*

For example, a resume for an accountant might have a Keyword section that looks like the following:

C.P.A.	Lotus	Cost control
CPA	Quattro Pro	Audit
Certified Public Accountant	Microsoft Word	Compliance
Accounting	MS Word	Policies
Controller	Conversion	Procedures
Great Plains	Internal accounting system	Administration
MAS 90	Job costing	Communication
Peachtree	Strategic planning	Team relations
QuickBooks	Supervision	
Excel	Management	

If you list an acronym (such as C.P.A.) in your list of keywords, also include the acronym's spelled-out version (Certified Public Accountant). You want the term to be noticed whether the hiring manager keys in the acronym or the spelled-out term of that job qualification. Also, if a keyword has different forms (such as *accountant* and *accounting*), list both forms in your resume so you're sure to match the exact word the manager enters into the search engine.

After you've compiled your list, incorporate those keywords into the text of your resume.

Career Casualty

It's easy for a poorly created e-resume to fall through the cracks. If an employer can't open or read the version you submit, she can delete it with a click of her mouse. For that reason, it's well worth your time to learn the technical aspects of creating the particular type of e-resume you plan to use.

Breaking Into the Banks

By now, you're dying to get your resume into a resume database, right? It's a simple task. Basically, there are three ways to do it:

1. Submit your resume to a company via e-mail.
2. Post your resume on an online resume bank.
3. Send your hardcopy resume to an employer who uses resume scanning.

To get the lowdown on how to prepare and deliver your resume for each of these methods, turn to the following three chapters. You'll find out that it's all within a few clicks of your mouse!

Electronic to Paper

A manager may print an electronic resume so that he can read it in its hardcopy form. Here's what might happen:

- After receiving your resume as an e-mail, the manager may print it to read before sending the electronic version to the company's resume database.
- The manager might download your resume from an online resume bank and print it to review.

You see, your e-resume will probably be viewed by a human being at some point. So as you go through the following chapters, pay attention to tips on how to make your resume look good as well as be technically sound.

The Least You Need to Know

- An e-resume can be e-mailed, posted online in resume banks, and sent to employers to be scanned into their resume databases.
- Electronic resumes may be printed out by an employer or entered into a resume database for automated candidate selection.
- Keywords are essential in order for a resume to be spotted by a resume database search engine.
- E-resumes have different formatting requirements depending on how they will be used (e-mailed, posted to an online database, or scanned).

Chapter 17

E-Mail Express

In This Chapter

- ◆ The advantages of e-mailing your resume to an employer
- ◆ Why you shouldn't send your resume as an attached file
- ◆ Preparing your document for its trip through cyberspace
- ◆ Launching your cover letter and resume

"Please e-mail me your resume." If an employer or headhunter hasn't already said that to you, one probably will in the near future. It's important for you to know how to e-mail your resume successfully so that when you get an e-mail request, you'll respond with a confident "Yes!"

In this chapter, I explain the details of how to transform your hardcopy resume into an e-mailable one. Then I tell you how to launch it into cyberspace so that it'll land in an employer's electronic inbox in terrific shape.

By the way, as you're following the step-by-step instructions in this chapter, don't be dismayed if your version of MS Word uses slightly different terminology for its commands than what I've listed here for Windows XP. If the translation is hard to figure out, consult your MS Word manual or the Help menu near the top of your screen.

Easy E-Mail Resumes

E-mailing your resume isn't complicated at all. With an understanding of the process, you'll be zipping your resume through cyberspace in minutes. In a nutshell, here's what to do:

1. Go online, open a new e-mail message, and address it to your prospective employer.
2. Copy and paste your cover letter and resume into the e-mail document.
3. Click Send.

To do these three simple steps, you need a version of your resume specially prepared for e-mail transmission. Let's look at how to create your e-mailable resume so you can send it on its way quickly.

Career Casualty

Never send your resume in Plain Text format as an attachment. A Plain Text attachment will disappear into cyberspace without any indication to the recipient that a document was ever attached to your e-mail.

Staying Out of Trouble

You can e-mail your resume in one of two ways:

1. Send it as an attached file. This is not recommended unless the employer tells you specifically what type of file (such as MS Word for Windows or Macintosh) your resume should be.
2. Insert it directly into the e-mail message (recommended).

Here are my thoughts on these two options.

Getting Attached to Files

You may be tempted to send your resume as an attached file—a document that accompanies an e-mail message—thinking that the employer will then receive your nicely formatted document. But here are some reasons why you shouldn't do that:

- Many employers won't open an e-mail that has an attachment for fear of getting a computer virus.
- It's possible that the employer's e-mail system won't be compatible with yours and will refuse to accept the attachment.
- If you and the employer aren't both using the same computer system (whether Windows, UNIX, or Macintosh), the employer's system might not be able to accept your attachment.
- Your resume might have been prepared in a word processing application or version that the employer can't read.

Job Hunt Hint

If a job posting specifically says to send your resume as an attached file, rest assured it's okay to do so. The ad's request indicates that the employer has what it takes to open your attached document.

If any of these are the case, your resume will not be read unless the recipient jumps through some technical hoops. Trust me, most employers won't bother; they'll just throw it away.

Direct Message

Sending your resume in the body of an e-mail message (rather than sending it as an attached file) is a much surer way of delivering it to the employer. Granted, it's not going to look like a fancy document, but that's okay because the employer won't expect it to. Besides, I'm going to show you how to make it look pretty darn good, considering the layout limitations of e-mail.

Getting the Job Done

Prepare your cover letter and resume as one e-mailable document. Here are the steps for doing that:

1. Put your cover letter and resume into one MS Word document.
2. Save that document as Plain Text. (Plain Text is very simple formatting—no bold, indents, italics, or varied type sizes—and is ideal for e-mailing and online distribution.)
3. Use all CAPS for words that need special emphasis.
4. Replace each bullet point with a standard keyboard symbol (such as a dash, plus sign, asterisk, or double asterisk).
5. Make sure to use straight ("stupid") quotes in place of curly ("smart") quotes. (I show you the difference a little later in this chapter.)
6. Limit line lengths to 65 characters and spaces.
7. Save the document again, this time as Plain Text with Line Breaks.
8. Close the document and reopen it in Notepad.

Read on to find out more about these steps.

Doubling Up

Ultimately you'll want both your cover letter and resume to appear in your e-mail message to the employer. Because there are a few steps to preparing MS Word documents for e-mailing, it makes sense to combine your letter and resume into one MS Word document so that you can make the adjustments to both at the same time. That should cut your work in half.

Follow these steps for an efficient way to combine your cover letter and resume:

1. Open the document that contains a short cover letter you've composed for your prospective employer.
2. Go to the File menu in your toolbar and click Save As. Create a logical name for your new document (such as "let_res" or the name of the company you're applying to). Choose where on your computer you want your new document to reside. Click Save or OK.
3. Delete the heading, date, and inside address of the cover letter in your new document.
4. Close the gap between the complimentary close and your name.
5. Delete "Enclosure: resume."
6. Open the MS Word document containing the resume you want to send to this employer.
7. Copy and paste your resume into your new "let_res" document so that your resume follows your cover letter one space after the complimentary close and your name.
8. Make sure that each element of your resume Heading (your name, address, and contact information) appears on a separate line. (See Chapter 16 for an example of how your Heading should look.)
9. Check that your resume is loaded with appropriate keywords if you think your resume will be put into a resume database. (See Chapter 16.)

Job Hunt Hint

Stay up-to-date on new versions of your e-mail software. File transfers are bound to keep improving and a day will come when e-mailing your resume as an attached file will be as reliable as Mom's apple pie. Until then, follow the step-by-step instructions in this section for a safe e-mail resume transfer.

> **Bonus Check**
>
> Here's a crash course in how to copy and paste in MS Word:
>
> 1. Using your cursor, highlight the text of the document that you want to copy and place elsewhere (either within that document or in a different one).
> 2. Go to Edit in your toolbar and click Copy. (Doing so puts the text into your computer's memory.)
> 3. Place your cursor where you would like to place the text you just copied.
> 4. Go to Edit in the toolbar and click Paste.
>
> You did it!

10. If your resume is more than one page, eliminate "Continued" at the bottom of page one and your name and "page two" at the top of page two. You won't need these when your resume is in an e-mail message.

Take a look at the original cover letter and resume for Vern Grundy and then check out how they looked when combined into one MS Word document (all at the end of this chapter).

Don't worry if the formatting of your resume changes when you combine the two documents; you'll be adjusting that.

Better Save Than Sorry

Now it's time to adjust the formatting of your cover letter and resume document so that it'll slip into your e-mail message easily. Brace yourself: This two-step process will transform your handsome cover letter and resume into a very blandly formatted document. Here's how to do it:

1. Open the MS Word document that contains both your cover letter and resume (the "let_res" document you just created).
2. Go to File in the toolbar and click Save As.
3. When you have the Save As window open, rename your document using a name that will identify it accurately (such as "res_txt_only").
4. Still within the Save As window, go to the pull-down menu for Save As Type and click Plain Text.
5. Click Save or OK.
6. Close the document (no need to exit MS Word).
7. From within MS Word, reopen the document you just closed, which you've named res_text_only. (With your MS Word application open, go to File in the toolbar and click Open, find the file named res_text_only.txt, and open it.) There's your document, completely stripped of fancy formatting!

You've now converted your document into Plain Text, and you're ready to make just a few more adjustments before sending it off to the employer.

Saving your document as a Plain Text file removes all the formatting, which is perfect for e-mailing. Plain Text documents are by nature no-frills: no italics, bolds, underlines, tabs, or tables. And typically the font size of all text will be the same. Rest assured, your resume is still going to make a good impression if you compensate with the limited e-mail formatting mentioned in this section.

Capitalizing on Headings

In your hardcopy resume, you may have used bold, underline, and italic to highlight particular words. If you've used a lot of bold, italic, and underlines in your resume, you may be floored when you save it as Plain Text because those extras will disappear.

Because Plain Text stripped your document of those special effects, use all CAPS for those words that were previously emphasized on your original. That'll draw attention to important words, and it's perfect for e-mailing!

Bite the Bullet

Bullet points in your original resume were used to break your text into bite-size pieces. But because some e-mail applications won't allow bullet points in their e-mail messages, you need to come up with an alternative that will transfer well. To make sure your e-mail resume still has the punch of your original, replace bullet points with one of the following:

- Dashes (-)
- Plus symbols (+)
- Asterisks (*)
- Double asterisks (**)

Use the spacebar to place a single space immediately after the symbol and before the first word of the statement. (Don't use a tab as you would in creating a hardcopy resume.)

Career Casualty

Keeping organized as you make multiple versions of your resume can be a challenge. Develop a plan to name your files logically and place them in folders that keep things straight.

Straight Quotes

There are two types of quotation marks: straight and curly.

- Curly quotes look like “this” and are known as *smart quotes*.
- Straight quotes look like "this" and are called *stupid quotes*.

Don't use curly quotes in an e-mail message because they sometimes translate as unreadable symbols (shaded rectangles) on the recipient's end. So if you have quotes in your resume, be sure that they are straight quotes. Check your MS Word manual or go to Help in your toolbar to learn how to change curly quotes to straight ones.

Characters That Count

Most e-mail messages have a limit to the number of characters and spaces they will allow per line. This limit is determined by the particular e-mail software being used. The tricky part is that the recipient's e-mail software may have a different character-per-line limit than your e-mail software. If the receiving e-mail software allows fewer characters and spaces per line than your e-mail software, your recipient may see some illogical line wraps when he or she opens your e-mail message.

It's best to cut this problem off at the pass by using very conservative line lengths in your message. My rule of thumb is to limit line lengths to no more than 65 characters and spaces. Here's how:

1. Select the entire document and change the font to Courier, 12 point.

2. Go to File in your toolbar and click Page Setup. Set the left margin at 1 inch and the right margin at 1.75 inches (Yahoo! e-mail users, set your right margin at 2.5 inches).

With the font, size of font, and side margins set, each line of your document will be no more than 65 characters and spaces. Don't worry about whether you want the employer to see your resume in Courier font—eventually your document will be converted to Notepad, which will not require Courier font.

After setting the margins, you may want to do a little adjusting of the text to make sure things look right. For instance, delete extra line spaces that may have been created in the conversion or insert commas into the Work History where tabs once divided information.

Sample of weird e-mail line wraps.

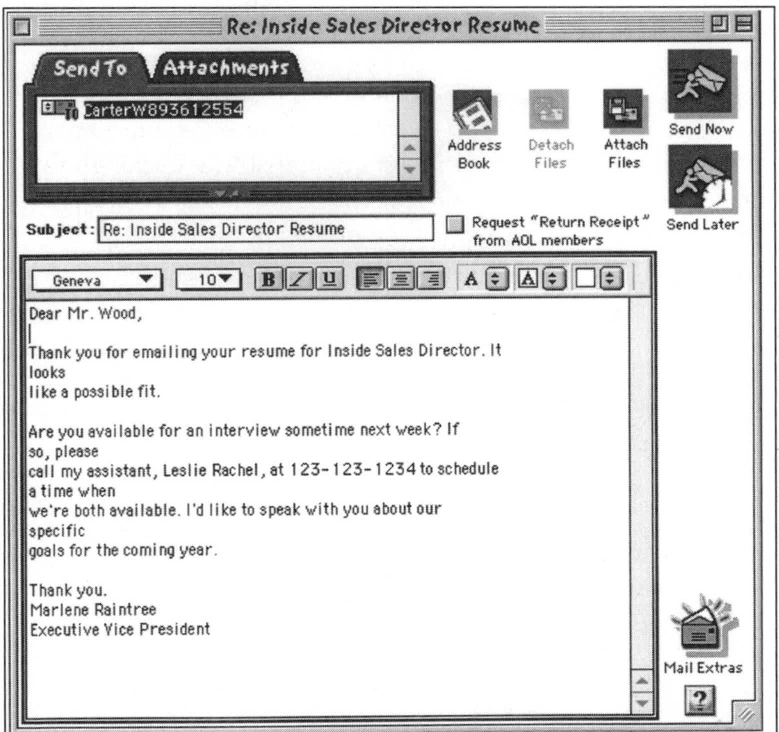

Give Me a Break

You need to save your MS Word document (res_text_only.txt) one more time to preserve the short line lengths you created in the previous section. Here's how:

1. Follow the same steps you did to save the document as Plain Text, only this time name the new document something like "res_txt_brk." When you click Save, a window will open on your screen. Within that pop-up window select the Option for "Insert line breaks."
2. Close your document and exit your MS Word application.

After saving your document as Plain Text With Line Breaks, check that your line breaks were preserved:

1. Go to the Tools menu.
2. Choose Preferences or Options.
3. Click the View tab.
4. Select Paragraph Marks under Nonprinting Characters.
5. Click OK.

When you return to your document, you should see a paragraph symbol (¶) at the end of each line. That symbol ensures that your lines will end at that point when transferred into your e-mail document.

You're doing great—you're just a few tortilla chips away from the big enchilada! Let's keep going.

Using Your Notepad

Some e-mail software inserts a space after every line of a Plain Text with Line Breaks document. To avoid wasting space with those extra lines, you need to open the document as a Notepad document. To do that, exit MS Word, go to Windows Explorer (your C: or hard drive) and open the res_txt_brk document by clicking its Notepad icon. Don't open the document from MS Word.

If you print out your Notepad res_txt_brk document, you may see that a header and footer have been added (which weren't visible onscreen). Don't be concerned—the header and footer won't show when you copy and paste the document into an e-mail message.

3-2-1, Take-Off!

You've done a great job of preparing your cover letter and resume in one Notepad document. Now you're ready to drop them into an e-mail message and send it on its way. The following steps will get the job done:

1. Within your e-mail program, open a window to write a new e-mail message.
2. Fill in the e-mail address in the Send To box by typing the recipient's e-mail address exactly as you see it, right down to the capital and lowercase letters. (Some e-mail programs are case sensitive when it comes to addresses, so this accuracy may be important to ensure that your e-mail actually arrives in your recipient's mailbox.)
3. Put a title in the Subject line, and make it a good one such as "Resume: Marketing Position."
4. Without closing your e-mail message, open the Notepad document (res_txt_brk version) that contains your cover letter and resume.
5. Copy the entire text of your cover letter and resume, and paste it into the e-mail window, where the body of the message goes.
6. Now that your cover letter and resume are in the e-mail message window, check that they look the way you want the employer to see them.
7. Take a deep breath and click Send.

Congratulations—you're now an e-mail resume pro!

Bonus Check

Give yourself the three-word test when it comes to writing a good subject line for your e-mail. Because most e-mail systems show only a few words of a subject line, make the first three words of your subject line strong enough to make the employer open your e-mail.

The Least You Need to Know

- When delivering your resume and cover letter via e-mail, insert them both into the e-mail message window instead of sending them as attached files.
- Use all CAPS instead of bold, underline, or italic to give emphasis to important words.
- Limit the number of characters and spaces per line in your e-mailable resume to ensure that your resume will fit into the employer's e-mail window perfectly.
- Open your e-mailable resume in Notepad to avoid unnecessary spaces being inserted into the text of your document.

(Cover Letter in MS Word)

Vern Grundy

123 Main Street, Chicago, IL 12345, (123) 555-1234, vgrundy@bamboo.com

January 3, 2003

Ms. Janelle Dombrosky
Hastings Bank and Trust
123 Forest Banks Avenue
Chicago, IL 12345

Dear Ms. Dombrosky,

The following resume is in response to the job posting for Project Manager, which I saw posted on www.hastingsbank.com. I have a personal interest in working with professionals who have high business values, and would consider this opportunity a merging of my professional and personal abilities.

Please call me at 123-555-1234 or e-mail me to discuss a time when we can speak in person.

Thank you!

Vern Grundy

Enclosure: resume

(Resume in MS Word)

Vern Grundy

123 Main Street, Chicago, IL 12345, (123) 555-1234, vgrundy@bamboo.com

Project Manager

Business Development • Business Analysis • Client Relations • Marketing

HIGHLIGHTS OF QUALIFICATIONS

- More than five years' high-tech project management experience. Skills include:

Strategic Analysis	Marketing	Proposal Development	Process Improvement
Communications	Business Plans	Team Leadership	Client Relations

- Track record of developing systems that build business and client satisfaction.
- Consistently meet or exceed project goals by deadline.

PROFESSIONAL EXPERIENCE

PROJECT MANAGER 1998-present Clients include: First Chicago Bank, Chicago, IL (2000–present)
MicroAge Corporation, Chicago, IL (1998–1999)

- Implemented a First Chicago Bank Mileage Plus (MP) marketing strategy that positioned member businesses to build customer loyalty in a competitive market.
    - Collaborated with MP team to execute a direct-mail research pilot.
    - Devised analytical tools that accurately measured response rates and product effectiveness.
    - Created and delivered a technical presentation in a style understandable to members.
- Conceived and implemented a system of reporting performance results that increased satisfaction among key MP members.
    - Convinced management to pursue new reporting methods.
    - Redesigned reports and explanation documents into a user-friendly format.
    - Guided team to take ownership and produce high quality reporting documents.
- Key member of a team that earned a competitive First Chicago Bank Employee Involvement Award for a strategic business development plan to strengthen customer relations.
    - Led team to choose a strategic initiative with high business value and potential.
    - Conducted a cost-recovery analysis to support a fiscally sound proposal for a public website.
- Worked closely with client contracts team to write proposals that won accounts from high revenue MicroAge prospects.

MARKETING COMMUNICATIONS ASSOCIATE 1993–1994, Trinity Systems Corporation, Salt Lake City, UT

- Created, wrote and managed an innovative newsletter that combined marketing new products and services with feature articles on the latest business trends. Commended by management.
- Developed marketing packages for new service lines that established recurring revenue for Trinity.

EDUCATION

MBA – Finance & International Business Options, Utah State University, Orem, UT
BA – Liberal Arts, California State University, Orem, UT

PROFESSIONAL AFFILIATION

Advisor, The Entrepreneur Network, Chicago, IL

(Resume and Cover Letter in MS Word)

Dear Ms. Dombrosky,

The following resume is in response to the job posting for Project Manager, which I saw posted on www.hastingsbank.com. I have a personal interest in working with professionals who have high business values, and would consider this opportunity a merging of my professional and personal abilities.

Please call me at 123-555-1234 or e-mail me to discuss a time when we can speak in person.

Thank you!
Vern Grundy

Vern Grundy

123 Main Street, Chicago, IL 12345, (123) 555-1234, vgrundy@bamboo.com

Project Manager

Business Development • Business Analysis • Client Relations • Marketing

HIGHLIGHTS OF QUALIFICATIONS

- More than five years' high-tech project management experience. Skills include:

Strategic Analysis	Marketing	Proposal Development	Process Improvement
Communications	Business Plans	Team Leadership	Client Relations

- Track record of developing systems that build business and client satisfaction.
- Consistently meet or exceed project goals by deadline.

PROFESSIONAL EXPERIENCE

PROJECT MANAGER 1998-present Clients include: First Chicago Bank, Chicago, IL (2000–present)
MicroAge Corporation, Chicago, IL (1998–1999)

- Implemented a First Chicago Bank Mileage Plus (MP) marketing strategy that positioned member businesses to build customer loyalty in a competitive market.
  - Collaborated with MP team to execute a direct-mail research pilot.
  - Devised analytical tools that accurately measured response rates and product effectiveness.
  - Created and delivered a technical presentation in a style understandable to members.
- Conceived and implemented a system of reporting performance results that increased satisfaction among key MP members.
  - Convinced management to pursue new reporting methods.
  - Redesigned reports and explanation documents into a user-friendly format.
  - Guided team to take ownership and produce high quality reporting documents.
- Key member of a team that earned a competitive First Chicago Bank Employee Involvement Award for a strategic business development plan to strengthen customer relations.
  - Led team to choose a strategic initiative with high business value and potential.
  - Conducted a cost-recovery analysis to support a fiscally sound proposal for a public website.

[Resume continues on second page, not shown here]

(Plain-Text Document with Text Adjusted)

```
Dear Ms. Dombrosky,

The following resume is in response to the job posting for Project Manager,
which I saw posted on www.hastingsbank.com. I have a personal interest in
working with professionals who have high business values, and would consider
this opportunity a merging of my professional and personal abilities.

Please call me at 123-555-1234 or email me to discuss a time when we can speak
in person.

Thank you!
Vern Grundy

VERN GRUNDY
123 Main Street
Chicago, IL  12345
(123) 555-1234
vgrundy@bamboo.com

PROJECT MANAGER
Business Development
Business Analysis
Client Relations
Marketing

HIGHLIGHTS OF QUALIFICATIONS
** More than five years' high-tech project management experience. Skills
include: strategic analysis, marketing, proposal development, process
improvement, communications, business plans, team leadership, and client
relations.
** Track record of developing systems that build business and client
satisfaction.
** Consistently meet or exceed project goals by deadline.

PROFESSIONAL EXPERIENCE
PROJECT MANAGER 1998-present
Clients include:
First Chicago Bank, Chicago, IL (2000-present)
MicroAge Corporation, Chicago, IL (1998-1999)
** Implemented a First Chicago Bank Mileage Plus (MP) marketing strategy that
positioned member businesses to build customer loyalty in a competitive market.
- Collaborated with MP team to execute a direct-mail research pilot.
- Devised analytical tools that accurately measured response rates and product
effectiveness.
- Created and delivered a technical presentation in a style understandable to
members.
** Conceived and implemented a system of reporting performance results that
increased satisfaction among key MP members.
- Convinced management to pursue new reporting methods.
- Redesigned reports and explanation documents into a user-friendly format.
- Guided team to take ownership and produce high quality reporting documents.

              [Resume continues on second page, not shown here]
```

(Plain-Text-with-Line-Breaks Document opened in Notepad)

```
Dear Ms. Dombrosky,

The following resume is in response to the job posting
for Project Manager, which I saw posted on
www.hastingsbank.com. I have a personal interest in
working with professionals who have high business values,
and would consider this opportunity a merging of my
professional and personal abilities.

Please call me at 123-555-1234 or email me to discuss a
time when we can speak in person.

Thank you!
Vern Grundy

VERN GRUNDY
123 Main Street
Chicago, IL  12345
(123) 555-1234
vgrundy@bamboo.com

PROJECT MANAGER
Business Development
Business Analysis
Client Relations
Marketing

HIGHLIGHTS OF QUALIFICATIONS
** More than five years' high-tech project management
experience. Skills include: strategic analysis,
marketing, proposal development, process improvement,
communications, business plans, team leadership, and
client relations.
** Track record of developing systems that build business
and client satisfaction.
** Consistently meet or exceed project goals by deadline.

PROFESSIONAL EXPERIENCE
PROJECT MANAGER 1998-present
Clients include:
First Chicago Bank, Chicago, IL (2000-present)
MicroAge Corporation, Chicago, IL (1998-1999)
** Implemented a First Chicago Bank Mileage Plus (MP)
marketing strategy that positioned member businesses to
build customer loyalty in a competitive market.
- Collaborated with MP team to execute a direct-mail
```

research pilot.
- Devised analytical tools that accurately measured response rates and product effectiveness.
- Created and delivered a technical presentation in a style understandable to members.
** Conceived and implemented a system of reporting performance results that increased satisfaction among key MP members.
- Convinced management to pursue new reporting methods.
- Redesigned reports and explanation documents into a user-friendly format.
- Guided team to take ownership and produce high quality reporting documents.
** Key member of a team that earned a competitive First Chicago Bank Employee Involvement Award for a strategic business development plan to strengthen customer relations.
- Led team to choose a strategic initiative with high business value and potential.
- Conducted a cost-recovery analysis to support a fiscally sound proposal for a public Web site.
** Worked closely with client contracts team to write proposals that won accounts from high revenue MicroAge prospects.

MARKETING COMMUNICATIONS ASSOCIATE 1993-1994
Trinity Systems Corporation, Salt Lake City, UT
** Created, wrote and managed an innovative newsletter that combined marketing new products and services with feature articles on the latest business trends. Commended by management.
** Developed marketing packages for new service lines that established recurring revenue for Trinity.

EDUCATION
MBA-Finance & International Business Options, Utah State University, Orem, UT
BA-Liberal Arts, California State University, Orem, UT

PROFESSIONAL AFFILIATION
Advisor, The Entrepreneur Network, Chicago, IL

Chapter 18

Banking on Success: Online Resume Banking

In This Chapter

- What's online resume banking?
- Who benefits from online resume databases?
- What industries use online recruiting sources?
- Where to find the best resume banks for you
- What to watch out for when posting online
- How to deposit your resume into an online bank

Now that you've mastered the e-mail resume, you're ready to take advantage of one of the handiest developments since employment centers discovered the 3 × 5 card and push pin: online resume banks. By posting your resume in an online database, your qualifications can be seen by thousands of employers and headhunters—think of the potential that holds! In this chapter, you'll learn how to find online resume banks, how to post your resume on one, and how to steer clear of pitfalls.

Resumes in a Bank?

Online resume banks appear on job search websites. They're sort of like regular banks, only resume banks deal in their own currency: resumes. Job seekers deposit (*upload*) their resumes into online databases, and employers withdraw (*download*) them from the databases.

Who Pays the Bill

Make no mistake about it, there's money being saved and earned through recruitment websites. Most of the commercial resume bank websites offer their services free to job seekers and charge employers and headhunters to access the

> **Terms of Employment**
>
> To **upload** a document means to transfer it from your computer to a remote computer or to an Internet site. To **download** a document means to transfer it from a remote computer or Internet site onto your computer.

resumes in their databases. A few sites charge the job seeker and give free access to employers and recruiters. Still others charge all parties involved. Then again, some nonprofit and government employment sites are free to job seekers and employers.

Let's look at why employers and recruiters like using online resume banking to find job applicants.

The Employer's Dream

As you can imagine, employers are happy to use online resume banks because they can …

- Greatly augment the talent pool available to them.
- Cut in-house recruiting costs by outsourcing the initial screening process to the online service.
- Eliminate the need to contract a headhunter, potentially saving significant amounts in commission fees.

It's no wonder that many employers love this efficient system for discovering terrific job candidates.

Headhunting on the Web

Headhunters find resume banks an efficient way to search through hundreds of job seekers' qualifications by just a click of the mouse. This system, of course, cuts their time dramatically because they don't have to make a zillion phone calls to find likely candidates for jobs they're trying to fill. And they can do their scouting any time of the day or night.

Who's Looking for Whom?

When online resume banks first came on the scene, they were used primarily by high-tech companies to find technical applicants. Gradually, the range of industries that use online resume banks for recruiting has grown. Today almost all industries use online recruiting to fill most levels and types of employment. It's very likely that your profession is represented somewhere online—your job is to track down where.

Resume banks can fall under one or more of the following categories. They might …

- Specialize strictly in one industry (such as high tech or health care).
- Focus on a particular profession (such as human resources or sales).
- Provide recruiting services to special interest groups (such as women, the disabled, or other minorities).
- Cater to a geographic region (such as a state or metropolitan area).
- Cover a wide range of industries and professions so applicants are considered for lots of job titles.

Let's look at how to find resume banks in these categories.

The Professional Approach

Many websites specialize according to industry, profession, or both. Here are ways to learn of those that apply to your job search:

- Use your Internet search engine (such as Google), inserting keywords that indicate your area of expertise or industry (such as *jobs*, *e-commerce*, and *marketing* for a marketing position in online business).
- Read professional magazines in your field or visit their websites to see what online recruiting services they suggest.
- Ask your colleagues what resume banks they recommend (assuming you can speak freely with them about your job search).

You could also do a search for specific companies in your field and go to their websites, where you might be able to submit your resume.

Job Hunt Hint

If your resume is in an employer's resume bank you could be considered for a fantastic job you didn't know you were qualified for. The search engine might select your resume based on the keywords an employer has used to find the perfect candidate for a job you haven't even thought of.

Specializing in Special Interests

Many resume websites focus on special interests, such as a social cause or an ethnic population. These sites have a couple of advantages over the large generic sites in that they may …

- Offer current employment information that's specific to that interest group.
- Provide job search support through articles, chat rooms, and member profiles to enable individual networking.

Good ways to find your special interest websites include asking friends in your special interest group, using your search engine, and looking for website addresses in literature from your interest group.

It's a Regional Thing

A website that represents regional recruiting efforts is highly valuable, whether you live in that geographic area or are planning to relocate to it. Such sites are often sponsored by the following organizations:

- Career centers
- Local media (TV, radio, or newspapers)
- Special interest groups for the area
- Recruiting agencies
- Specific companies

In addition to supplying their resume databases to local employers, the sites frequently announce (and sometimes sponsor) career fairs, lectures, workshops, and other networking events that you might attend online or in person.

The Big Guys

You've probably heard of online career sites such as Monster Jobs (www.monster.com), Career Builder (www.careerbuilder.com), and others advertised on the radio, TV, and in print. This type of megasite is well managed and usually features a resume bank that offers the following:

- A large client base of employers
- A wide range of industry job categories
- National and international job openings
- A job agent (a service that e-mails you job listings that fit your criteria)
- Online job search advice (for instance, how to write a resume)
- E-newsletters sent to you via e-mail
- The option to keep your resume anonymous to all or particular employers
- The ability to update your resume after it's been posted

These large resume sites have a high volume of companies and headhunters that search their databases regularly. This means that you could get a response within hours of submitting your resume.

The Downside of Uploading

> CAUTION
>
> **Career Casualty**
>
> If confidentiality is a major concern for you, don't post your resume online. There's no guarantee that your employer won't hear about your job search from another employer in your field or from a headhunter who picks up your resume and tries to sell you to your current boss.

Not surprisingly, there are some possible downsides to posting your resume online. Here are some of them:

- Your current employer could find out about your job search.
- You could be shopped around by several recruiters without your knowledge.
- Your personal and professional information becomes public knowledge.

These points are worth examining, because they'll help you weigh the pros and cons of posting online.

The Invisible Job Seeker

Your employer may be using an online database to search for future employees, and she could run across your resume in the process. Yikes! The cat would be out of the bag about your job search.

To spare you from such an embarrassing and potentially job-threatening situation, many of the banks have one or more "anonymous" options:

- You can have your resume made invisible to employers you specify.
- You can have your name, address, and even the companies you've worked for blocked out on your resume so that no employers can see that info.

In the last option, the job bank site's system acts as your agent, notifying you of each employer's request for information about you. Then you can decide which opportunities to pursue.

Headhunter Overkill

Because resume banks are accessed by lots of headhunters, your resume could easily be picked up by several recruiters and shopped around in your field. Here's why that's not to your advantage: many headhunters work on a commission basis with employers. If more than one recruiter presents the same candidate, the employer may disregard the candidate rather than sort out which recruiter wins the commission, should the candidate accept the job offer.

This multiple-submission problem can be eliminated by carefully selecting which resume banks you use. For instance, some sites are run by reputable recruiting agencies (such as Korn/Ferry International at www.futurestep.com) that maintain strict confidentiality and carry exclusive job openings. Posting on such a site essentially gives you many of the advantages of working personally with a recruiter who has a huge database of employment opportunities.

Telemarketing Alert

In most situations, once your resume is deposited into a resume bank, your personal and professional information may no longer be kept confidential. With little effort, a telemarketer, direct-mail solicitor, or scam artist can access the files and download your info.

Here's how data such as your name, contact info, place of employment, and salary history could be misused: Someone could pose as an employer or headhunter, access the database, discover your resume, and use it for their own purposes. For instance, a stockbroker could find your resume, speculate that you're a good client prospect for the type of investments he brokers, and contact you to solicit his services. If the resume website's managers aren't screening their clients for your protection, almost anyone could get access to your files.

CAUTION

Career Casualty

It's so easy to make a typo when typing in familiar information such as your address or job title. To prevent that from happening when you fill in the blanks for your e-form, first type the info in an MS Word document, proofread it carefully and run your spell checker, and then copy and paste the info into your online resume form.

Go to the Bank and Fill Out the Forms

Online resume banks are constantly changing the layouts of their websites and fine-tuning their procedures as they become more sophisticated.

At most resume banks, you'll be presented with a two-step process:

1. Fill in the blanks at the top of an online form (also called an e-form).
2. Copy and paste your resume into a large window.

Both steps are straightforward, but let's look at a few tricks that will ensure your success.

Blankety-Blank

Here are the items you will most probably be asked to type in:

- Your name, address, phone/fax, and e-mail address
- The location where you'd like to work
- Your job objective or professional title (sometimes referred to as the "headline")

Filling in your name and contact information should be no problem. (If you have questions, review Chapter 4 for advice on what to put in the Heading section of your resume. The same concepts apply to the e-form.) Selecting the geographic area where you'd like to find employment is usually done through a pull-down menu where you choose from what's listed.

The headline is a very important part of your e-form. It's likely to be the first thing the employer sees, so this isn't the place for that story about your fishing trip. Keep it simple: tell the employer something about yourself as concisely as possible, with the most important words at the beginning of the line, as in the following examples:

- Sports Industry Marketer
- Energetic Sales Trainee
- Resume: Medical Librarian

What three words describe who you are and what job you're looking for?

The Heart of the Matter

The next step is to fill in the "Your Resume" section. The directions on the site will tell you what type of text format that particular e-form accepts. Usually it will ask for a Plain Text document.

Here's how to prepare your hardcopy resume for posting online (refer to Chapter 17 for detailed instructions on each of these steps):

1. Save your hardcopy resume as Plain Text (without including a cover letter at the beginning of the document).
2. Use all CAPS for words that need special emphasis.
3. Replace each bullet point with a standard keyboard symbol (such as a dash, plus sign, asterisk, or double asterisk).
4. Make sure to use straight quotes in place of smart quotes.
5. Close the document and reopen it in Notepad.

Copy and paste this Notepad version of your resume into the Your Resume window on the website where you would like to post your resume.

Before you click the website's Submit button, click the site's Preview button. Doing so will bring up a window that shows you how your resume will look to the employer. If there's anything you want to change in your document, click the Back button and make your edit. Unfortunately, you may not find a Preview button on all resume websites or sometimes the Preview button is hard to find— you have to do a little searching to find it. It's worth your time to hunt for this button so that you get a last chance to proofread your masterpiece before the employer sees it.

Keeping Up-to-Date

Most online resume banks offer you the capability to edit your resume. This is an important feature for several reasons:

- You can keep the info on your document up-to-date.
- You can improve your resume if it's not drawing the response you want.
- You can correct typos should you detect them after submitting your resume.
- You can extend the life of your resume in the bank if you need to. Some banks will list your resume for a limited number of days (typically 60 to 90). By editing your resume, you essentially reset the clock.
- In some systems, new resumes are listed at the top of the entire list of resumes or may be categorized under a section such as "New Listings," which employers are apt to look at first. By editing your document, you can re-enter the New Listings category.

Update your online resume by following the instructions on the resume website. If your edits are extensive (let's say you want to rewrite your Summary of Qualifications section), compose your points in MS Word, run your spell checker, and proofread carefully. Then copy and paste it into your online resume.

Bonus Check

Some resume bank e-forms will ask for your salary expectations. Before inputting an amount, think carefully about whether you want to disclose that figure online. You may choose to leave that box blank for two reasons:

- You don't want your financial information floating around in cyberspace.
- You want to wait until an in-person interview to discuss the whole compensation package with your potential employer.

Remember, you don't have to answer all the questions on an e-form unless the program specifically requires you to do so.

Getting Out While You're Ahead

As soon as you land a job, be sure to delete your resume from the resume banks where you've posted it (check with the site for instructions). You don't want your resume in circulation after you're happily employed (unless you do contract work, in which case you may always want to have your resume on the market). After all, you don't want your new boss to find your resume floating around in the job market and think that you're already looking elsewhere.

The Least You Need to Know

- Online resume banks can be a very efficient way for you to find a fulfilling job and for employers to recruit great job candidates.
- Some resume banks specialize according to profession, industry, special interest, or location. Others offer a wide range of criteria that can be narrowed to fit your search.
- You can find online resume databases by using your Internet search engine, asking friends for recommendations, and reading professional journals.
- To post your resume online, fill out an e-form, which includes pasting your resume into the form.
- Before uploading your resume onto a site, click the Preview button to see how your resume will appear on the employer's computer screen.

Chapter 19

It's All a Scan: Scannable Resumes

In This Chapter

- ◆ What resume scanning is
- ◆ Which organizations electronically scan resumes
- ◆ What the employer's side of scanning technology is like
- ◆ The pros and cons of resume scanning
- ◆ How to create your own scannable resume

You may be assuming that a person will read your hardcopy resume when it arrives at a potential employer's address. Instead, your resume could encounter a nonhuman "reader": the resume scanner.

Resume scanning, although not widespread, is something you might run into, in which case you'll need to know how to create a resume that passes the scanning test. This chapter tells you when and how to submit a resume that's specially prepared for the almighty scanner.

Who or What's Reading Your Resume?

A resume *scanning* system is a computerized tool used by some Human Resources departments and agencies to manage the flood of hardcopy resumes. Resume scanning software does the following:

1. It creates an electronic image of the hardcopy resume.
2. It uses *Optical Character Recognition* (*OCR*) software to turn the image into an electronic text file.

Terms of Employment

Scanning is the process of turning a hardcopy document into an electronic image. **Optical Character Recognition (OCR)** software is the computer's tool for converting an electronic image into electronic text, which can then be searched for keywords and manipulated into new formats such as database files.

Bonus Check

Not all resume-scanning programs run by the same rules. For example, some accept bullet points, and others don't. Make an effort to get the guidelines from the company you're applying to. If you can't get them, follow the advice in this chapter, because I adopt a better-safe-than-sorry approach that should work for all scanning systems.

Here's how it works on the employer's end: When your hardcopy resume arrives in the mail, it won't be read by human eyes. Instead, it'll be placed face down in a scanner (which looks sort of like a photocopier). The scanner creates an electronic image of your document (sort of the way a camera snaps a picture of a person). The OCR software then goes through the image file to recognize characters and convert the file into a text document, otherwise known as an electronic resume.

From there, the text of the document is stored in a database system. (In sophisticated systems, the snapshot of the original resume is also stored in the database so that the hiring manager can view that as well.) Once in the database, the information from your resume is accessible to hiring managers who use keywords to select qualified job candidates (as discussed in Chapter 16).

Get With the Program

How can you know for sure if you need to adjust your resume for a scanning encounter? Call the Human Resources department of the company where you'd like to work and ask whether it uses resume scanning. If the answer is "no," the paper resume you've created using Parts 1, 2, and 3 of this book is all you need. If the answer is "yes," ask if the department can mail, fax, or e-mail you a set of guidelines so you can create your resume for their system.

Scanning Woes

No matter how hard you try to create the perfect scannable resume (I explain how to do that in the next section), there are no guarantees that it will be read accurately by the scanner. OCR software isn't perfect. It has a rate of error that almost guarantees that there will be a few mistakes in the way it interprets the print on your resume. For this reason, companies are moving away from scanning and encouraging job seekers to submit their resumes electronically (via e-mail or through resume banks) to avoid the scanning process all together. If an employer says "E-mail your resume or send a paper resume for scanning," take the first option. That way you'll bypass the error-ridden scanner and go directly into the resume database. However, many companies still have their scanners at work deciphering resumes, and you may need to produce one for such a system.

Formatting at Its Finest

If you find you need to create a scannable resume, first follow the instructions in Parts 2 and 3 of this book for developing a chronological, functional, achievement, chronological hybrid, or functional hybrid resume. Then make the following changes to adjust your resume for resume scanning:

- Put your name, address, and contact information on separate lines.
- Check that your resume contains all the appropriate keywords.
- Use scannable fonts.

- Don't use fancy formatting.
- Print your resume on white paper.

Let's take a closer look at some of these points.

Career Casualty

Don't worry about resume scanning if you're applying for a senior management position. Resumes for executive-level jobs are rarely subjected to resume scanning because they aren't put into resume databases. Instead, these high-level resumes are usually reviewed in their hardcopy forms by top executives, owners, or boards of directors.

The Skinny on Scannable Fonts

An important factor in passing a resume scanning test is to make sure the OCR can read your text. The following guidelines will help you produce a resume an OCR will love:

1. Stick to scanner-friendly fonts such as Palatino, Helvetica, and the other fonts listed in Chapter 14.
2. Don't use italic.
3. Don't underline words. A scanner can't interpret a word if any letter in that word intersects a line. For example, in "profit," notice how the letter *p* touches the underline. If that happens on your resume, you lose because the computer won't decipher the *p* character and therefore won't acknowledge your "profit."
4. Limit the size of your text to no smaller than 10 point and no larger than 14 point.
5. Don't use bold unless you know that the scanner you're sending your resume to accepts bold.

Use all CAPS to emphasize a word that you would otherwise have italicized, underlined, made bold, or put in extra-large type.

Nothing Fancy-Schmancy

Keep the formatting of your resume simple and straightforward. Follow these tips:

- Don't incorporate horizontal or vertical lines into your layout.
- Don't use shaded bars.
- Change bullet points to dashes, asterisks, or plus signs, because some scanners can't read bullets.

To create a sense of separation between two sections on your scannable resume, insert an extra space instead of a solid line and shaded bar. OCRs interpret white spaces as dividers between blocks of material.

Rest assured that indents, columns, and centered text are also perfectly fine, so use those techniques if you wish.

Printing Protocol

High contrast between the type and background is the name of the game when it comes to easy scanning. Follow these two guidelines for achieving the highest contrast possible:

- Use black ink.
- Print on white paper—I mean real white, not gray or buff.

Job Hunt Hint

When applying to an organization that uses resume scanning, avoid sending your resume via fax. Faxes sometimes blur the print, which could gum up the works when the OCR reads the resume.

By printing black ink on white paper (no colored paper or ink), you stand a good chance of passing the OCR test.

If your resume is more than one page, be sure "continued" is at the bottom of the first page, and your name and "Page Two" is at the top of your second page. This will help the Human Resources clerk keep track of your pages while entering them into the scanning system.

Also, don't print your resume on two sides of the same piece of paper. If you do, it's very likely that the second page won't get scanned into the computer because the scanner operator probably won't notice the second side.

Into the Database

After the scanning and character recognition process is completed, the applicant's files are entered into the resume database. As mentioned in Chapter 16, depending on the sophistication of the system, the entry may include a text file of the resume that's ready for a keyword search by any hiring manager in the organization, and an electronic image file of the original resume.

Ever Ready

Douglas Cruikshank thought it was unlikely that his prospective employer used resume scanning, but he didn't know for sure. So he produced a resume (at the end of this chapter) that was pleasing to the human eye and would also pass through a scanner and keyword search successfully:

- On a separate sheet of paper, he jotted down the following list of keywords that he assumed the employer would program into the database search engine.
- He incorporated those words appropriately into his resume.

Here's the list of keywords he came up with:

Management	Insurance	Policy
Safety	Benefits administration	Human Resources
Employee relations	Personnel	Management Certificate
Health education	Childcare	Insurance claims and appeals
Health-risk assessment	Wellness program	Maternity leave
Employee communications	Communications	Newsletter
Assessment	Health coverage	Training
	Human resources	

Can you find each of these words in his resume, as a search engine would?

The Least You Need to Know

- Before assuming you need a scannable resume, call your potential employer's Human Resources department to ask whether they use resume scanning in their applicant review process.
- If the company uses resume scanning, ask what its guidelines are so that you can produce a resume for the company's particular system.
- You can create a resume that is both scannable and pleasing to the human eye.
- Never use italic, underlines, or fancy fonts on your scannable resume.
- Employ simple formatting in your scannable resume; do not include vertical or horizontal lines.
- Use black ink on white paper; it's the easiest combination for the scanner to read.

Douglas T. Cruikshank
123 Peavy Road
Dallas, Texas 12345
(123) 555-1234
dtcruikshank@bamboo.com

JOB OBJECTIVE: A position in Human Resources with a focus on Benefits Administration.

SUMMARY OF QUALIFICATIONS

- Eight years of experience in human resources-related positions.
- Two years in benefits administration.
- Designer and director of highly successful corporate wellness program.
- Currently enrolled in UTD Human Resources Management Certificate Program.

PROFESSIONAL ACCOMPLISHMENTS

EMPLOYEE BENEFITS

Brown & Brown

- Produced firm-wide Wellness Program including a 20-vendor Health Fair, health education newsletters, and health risk assessments. Chaired 15-member Wellness Committee.
- Played key role in restructuring insurance benefits, as member of Insurance Advisory Committee. Co-developed employee communications regarding program changes.
- Wrote and produced quarterly benefits newsletter, which increased employee awareness of preventive medicine and cost-effective utilization of health coverage.
- Analyzed childcare needs and presented findings that led to firm's pilot childcare program.

Singer Services

- Successfully handled complex insurance claims and appeals.

PERSONNEL ADMINISTRATION

Brown & Brown

- Co-developed new maternity leave policy and introduced options through large staff presentations and written communications.
- Served on Quality Progress Committee and developed telephone skills training series.
- Assisted in organizing safety awareness programs and staff CPR/first-aid training.

Singer Services, Orwell Associates, and The Teachers School

- Supervised teams of 30+, involving performance evaluations and employee relations.

WORK HISTORY

1998-present Wellness Program Administrator/Legal Secretary, Brown & Brown, Newberg, TX
1996-1998 Staffing and Insurance Claims Manager, Singer Services, Houston, TX
1994-1995 Executive Secretary, National Oil, Austin, TX
1990-1994 Personnel and Sales Manager, Orwell Associates, Austin, TX

EDUCATION AND AFFILIATION

B.A., Sociology, 1986, University of Texas at Austin
Human Resources Management Certificate Program, University of Texas at Dallas
Member, Texas Human Resources Council

Portfolio of Sample Resumes

Following is a collection of resumes written or critiqued by professional writers on Susan Ireland's Resume Team. As with the other sample resumes in this book, they have been made anonymous, with the exception of the resumes for Roberta Rosen, Beth Brown, and Joel Garfinkle, all of whom are career consultants.

According to the Job Objective statement or professional title on each resume, it was placed in an occupational category, labeled by the shaded tab on the side margin of each resume. There is also a category for college students and new grads. Turn the page for an itemized list of the resumes within each category.

Administrative Support

Jan Mercedes—Administrative Assistant

Kenneth Baker—Project Manager with focus on administrative support

Rosemary Watson—Administrative Assistant

LaDonna Davis—Office Manager

Counseling

Roberta J. Rosen—Career Consultant

Joel Garfinkle—Career Transition Coach

Regina Andrews—Enrollment Counselor, Rangeley College of the Law, University of Texas

Grant Frost—Psychotherapist

Customer Service

Eduardo Ortiz—Customer Service Representative

Leanne Sayer—Customer Service Representative

Kate Washburn—Customer Service Specialist

Finance/Accounting

Joyce Favor—A position in the accounting department

John Blitzer—Position in accounting in the insurance industry

Lilly Carver—Position as Office Manager/Bookkeeper within the construction industry

Dave J. Ross—Staff Accountant in a public accounting firm

Harry Conduttori—Senior-level financial risk management position

Human Resources

Lee Chin—Human Resources Specialist

Brent Castleton—Position in Human Resources with emphasis on recruitment management

Susan Bleeker—An administrative/management position in Human Resources focusing on project/database management

Sandra Cole—A supervisory position in human resources administration

Law

Nora Jones—Paralegal position

Sofia A. Giovanni—Position as Legal Counsel in workers' compensation focusing on litigation and legislative change

Darrell J. Kramer—Environmental Attorney

Charles C. Gilroy—Civil Litigation Attorney

Marketing

Jared Burke—Marketing Communications Manager in the construction industry

Sally Romerez—Marketing professional

Sandra O'Malley—A marketing communications position within the high-tech industry

Roxy Jean Kennedy—A position in marketing and promotions with an emphasis on sales

Sandi Patterson—Marketing Manager

Nonprofit Management

Shawn Larkin—Arts Administrator

Eunice Graves—Director of a Nonprofit Organization serving the homeless and disadvantaged

Sylvia E. Farlow—A management position within a nonprofit organization, with a focus on team building and community relations

Lionel Lamberdini—An administrative management position in a nonprofit organization

Pearl Sanchez—Arts Program Associate focusing on youth outreach and program development

Loretta King—Career Center Director

Public Relations

James Carpenter—Public relations professional

Taylor Dawkins—A position in a public relations agency

Louise Turner—A position in public relations/marketing

Fred Herrington—Public relations professional

Sales

Lettie Perkins—Sales professional

Tina R. Gelb—A sales position within the high-tech industry

Cynthia Lau—Sales professional

Frank Getty—Sales/marketing professional

Senior Management

Melissa Vasquez—Chief Executive Officer

Joseph Thurgood—A senior-level position in management in the wood products industry

Maria Sedgewick—Information Technology Executive

Henry Hauser—A management position in operations

Lorene Lincoln—Executive Manager or Director of major business projects/initiatives

Gary T. Wilson—Management position in the health-care field

Brenda R. Lincoln—Senior Business Analyst position within a regulated environment with a focus on the health-care and pharmaceutical industries

Frank Ford—Senior Management Consultant

Student/New Graduate

Kate Warren—A research position with a biotechnology or pharmaceutical company in the research and development division

Paul Herkimer—A position in visual merchandising

Janine Borelli—Data-entry work

Luis M. Riskala—A strategic planning position in multimedia and Internet business

Charlotte E. Williams—An audit position

Teaching/Training

George Benicio—Corporate Trainer

G. Vijayalakshmi—Accent Trainer for international call center

Enrique Murillo—Business Trainer

Jason Manriquez—Elementary School Teacher

Mathew Crosby—Elementary School Music Educator

Walter Crumb—Basketball officiating for high school playoff games

Technical

Kerry Wainwright—Software Programmer

Ryan Seymour—Multimedia Developer and Web Designer

Graham Phelps—A senior IT project management position

Patricia Gonzalez—E-Commerce Project Manager

Thomas Perkins—Sr. Research Associate in the environmental energy technology division

Writing/Editing

Beth Brown—Professional Resume Writer

Tawny Hall—Technical Writer

Suzanne Briarly—Copy Editor

Maggie McCullough—Classical Music Journalist

JAN MERCEDES

123 Friendship Avenue • Charlotte, NC 12345 • (123) 555-5555 • janmercedes@bamboo.com

JOB OBJECTIVE

Administrative Assistant

HIGHLIGHTS OF QUALIFICATIONS

- A motivated and personable worker with experience providing superior administrative support.
- Put 100% into every project.
- Highly organized, analytical thinker with strong communication skills.

PROFESSIONAL ACCOMPLISHMENTS

Administrative Assistant, Quest Manufacturing Company, Charlotte, NC, 2003-present

- Developed data-entry process that reduced the number of lost documents by 12%.
- Work closely with senior and middle managers to ensure overall project coordination and completion.
- Prepare written communications for variety of audiences, from corporate clients to maintenance staff.
- Named Employee of the Year, 2005.

Full-time Parent, 2001-03

Receptionist, Franks and Associates, Columbia, SC, 1999-01

- Provided initial contact to clients, responding quickly and diplomatically to concerns to ensure superior service and satisfaction.
- Answered a high volume of calls and in-person inquiries; treated each person with respect and provided information and referrals.
- Used PCs with the latest software.

EDUCATION

Business and Computer Coursework
Columbia University, Columbia, SC

COMMUNITY SERVICE

Bookkeeper, Charlotte Animal Friends, 2002-present
Childcare Volunteer, ParentNet, 2004-04

Kenneth Baker

123 Bay Street • Brookline, MA 12345 • (123) 555-5555 • kenbaker123@bamboo.com

OBJECTIVE

Project Manager with focus on administrative support

PROFILE

- A self-motivated and organized professional; skilled in orchestrating tasks and details to achieve project goals.
- Strong background in project management.
- Excellent communication skills that have led to productive working relationships with clients and staff.

EXPERIENCE

HOMEPORT REALTY, Brookline, MA 2004-present

A real estate development firm with five regional offices and headquarters in New York City

Project Team Leader and Administrative Assistant

- Direct sales campaigns that involve coordinating salespeople from all five offices in the use of marketing collateral and sales incentive programs.
- Create exceptional support and training systems to maximize sales team effectiveness and allow quick rollout of campaigns.
- Supervise administrative staff and facilitate orientation for new hires and independent contractors.
- Respond to numerous questions from sales team on a daily basis, referring them to appropriate resources and offering administrative support.

LANSKY CORPORATION, INC., Boston, MA 2000-04

A clerical outsourcing company with more than 12 large corporate clients

Clerical Supervisor

- Successfully managed projects such as mass mailings, database management, audio transcriptions, and correspondence.
- Supervised team of up to 20 clerical staff, interacting daily with team members to synchronize completion of projects.
- As team leader, resolved power struggles among team members, using a positive approach to conflict resolution and staff development.

X-TRA HARDWARE, Plymouth, MA 2000

A hardware manufacturer that sells directly to consumers through the Internet

Customer Support

- Resolved customer complaints using a persuasive yet nonconfrontational style through phone and e-mail.

EDUCATION

BA, 1999
Boston College, Boston, MA

Rosemary Watson

123 Pole Street • Andronico, MI 12345 • 123-555-5555 • rmwatson@bamboo.com

JOB OBJECTIVE: Administrative Assistant

SUMMARY

- Five years of experience as an administrative assistant to senior corporate managers.
- Skilled at using all Microsoft Office applications, including Excel.
- Exceptional interpersonal skills that contribute to a friendly and efficient working environment for clients, co-workers, and supervisors.

RELATED EXPERIENCE

Administrative

- Re-organized office system that serviced three managers, involving the upgrade of two computers and several hardcopy filing systems. (Unscramble, Inc.)
- Managed travel and accommodation reservations and appointment schedules for two managers and three salespeople who traveled extensively throughout the year. (Hyde Company)
- Quickly adapted to new office systems, using my talent for learning new computer skills and understanding technical manuals. (as Administrative Contractor)
- Won "Employee of the Year" two years in a row. (Unscramble, Inc.)

Interpersonal

- Resolved workplace conflict between two workers by initiating a weekly meeting to discuss project assignments. (Unscramble, Inc.)
- Developed telephone rapport with clients, often using empathy and friendly humor to "smooth feathers" during technical downtime. (Hyde Company)

WORK HISTORY

Administrative Assistant (contractual), Andronico, MI, 2004-present

Selected assignments at:	Windham Heights Newspaper
	St. Paul's Hospital
	Thelma's Beauty Shop
Administrative Assistant	Unscramble, Inc., Andronico, MI, 2002-2004
Administrative Assistant	Hyde Company, Andronico, MI, 2001-2002

EDUCATION

AA, Business Administration, 2001
Andronico Community College, Andronico, MI

COMMUNITY SERVICE

Andronico Business Women's Association, 2001-present
Fundraiser, Mt. George Soccer Team, 2003-present

LADONNA DAVIS
123-6 Highpoint Street, Phoenix, AZ 12345
(123) 555-5555
ladonnadavis@bamboo.com

OBJECTIVE

Office Manager

PROFILE

- Experienced leader; successful in streamlining systems to maximize productivity.
- Impressive reputation for building cohesion among disparate groups and individuals.
- A talent for finding innovative solutions and developing or improving procedures.

EXPERIENCE

2001-06

Buckhead Middle School, Phoenix, AZ
Teacher
ADMINISTRATION
- Initiated electronic filing of class evaluations by teachers to reduce workload of the school's administrative staff.
- Established a parent volunteer sign-up system that significantly increased the quality of classroom management.
- Utilized MS Office Suite including PowerPoint for curriculum development.
- Served on several committees and acted as resource to administrators and staff.

PROJECT MANAGEMENT
- Coordinated and set up after-school field trips for gifted students seeking to improve their computer skills.
- Worked dependably on projects within budgets and timetables.

1997-01

BrightStar Preschool, Phoenix, AZ
Head Teacher
- Oversaw curriculum development for three classrooms, often involving first-time teachers from diverse cultural backgrounds.

EDUCATION

B.A., Education, 1996
University of Tempe, Tempe, AZ

COMMUNITY SERVICE

Telethon Volunteer, ABC Public Television, 1996-pres.
Donation Team Leader, United Way, 2002

Page 1 of 1

ROBERTA J. ROSEN

415-885-4804 roberta_careers@yahoo.com

Career Consultant

Executive Coaching **Career Counseling** **Personal Coaching**

HIGHLIGHTS OF QUALIFICATIONS

- More than 15 years of experience providing career consulting and mentorship to individuals and groups at all organizational levels.
- Adept at quickly engaging each client, establishing rapport, and assessing needs and goals.
- Expertise in combining creativity, humor, intuition, and an in-depth understanding of the job market to assist clients in developing a strategy for personal growth and professional success.

PROFESSIONAL EXPERIENCE

2000-pres. **ROBERTA J. ROSEN CONSULTING,** San Francisco, CA
Career Consultant

- Developed thriving career consulting practice through referrals, an extensive network of contacts, and client satisfaction.
- Provided coaching to individuals and groups, utilizing in-depth assessments to identify career objectives, role-playing to prepare for interviews, and tools for successful cold-calling and follow-through.
- Conceived, designed, and implemented pilot program on Group Coaching with Marin Coaches Alliance.
- Facilitated Group Coaching sessions, providing coaching and mentoring to help groups of diverse individuals achieve personal and professional goals.
- Presented outplacement workshops and other individualized outplacement services for small organizations.
- Trained IBM Sales Executives in sales and communication strategies.

1986-2000 **ALUMNAE RESOURCES,** San Francisco, CA
Career Advisor

- Guided 100+ clients through the informational interviewing process, provided assistance with goal-setting and identifying career opportunities, and suggested methods for navigating the ever-changing job market.

1985-2000 (concurrent) **HEWLETT PACKARD COMPANY,** San Francisco, CA
Account Manager

Leadership & Coaching

- Selected to mentor new sales reps with presentations and meeting facilitation, utilizing shadowing, debriefing, and role-playing techniques to quickly bring them up to speed as productive team members.
- Coordinated and led teams in developing business solutions for customers to reduce costs and increase revenues.

-continued-

ROBERTA J. ROSEN
PAGE TWO

- Member of task forces on increasing effectiveness of sales managers and improving job satisfaction for technical and sales staff. Invited by company executives to present results to 600 field employees.

Sales & Account Management

- Established and cultivated strong relationships with CEOs and CIOs of $500M+ accounts, and developed successful strategic partnerships.
- Negotiated bids for highly competitive contracts.
- Consistently exceeded sales quota for 15 years.
- Wrote and presented proposals to executive committees of target accounts to ensure Hewlett Packard's place as partner of choice for technology decisions.
- Facilitated communication between in-house and customer executives to ensure establishment of ongoing, mutually beneficial relationships.

Previous experience includes:

Teacher Trainer, Upper Valley Regional Center for Education for New Hampshire and Vermont schools, co-sponsored by Dartmouth College and the Office of Education in Washington, DC.

Sales Manager, Control Data Corporation, San Francisco, CA. Directed the 12-member team responsible for the sale and marketing of the Plato Learning System.

Regional Director of Admissions and East Bay Coordinator, Interstudy, San Francisco, CA. Hired and trained 120+ representatives in the coordination of language/homestay programs for international students here in the U.S. and for Americans abroad.

EDUCATION & TRAINING

B.A., cum laude, Education, minor in Psychology, City University of New York, NY
Graduate studies in Psychology, John F. Kennedy University, Orinda, CA

Ongoing Coaches Training, The Coaches Training Institute, San Rafael, CA

Professional Certified Career Coach, Career Coach Institute

Key Executive Seminars with CEOs from major corporations worldwide,
led by John Donovan, Cambridge Executive Enterprises, Inc., Cambridge, MA

Coursework in Conflict Resolution, Mediation, and Entrepreneurship,
The Amos Tuck School of Business Administration, Dartmouth College, Hanover, NH

PROFESSIONAL AFFILIATIONS

International Coaches Federation
Marin Coaches Alliance
Career Coach Institute
Hewlett Packard Alumni Association
Association Auxiliary Board, University of California, San Francisco

WWW.DREAMJOBCOACHING.COM

JOEL GARFINKLE

6918 Thornhill Drive
Oakland, CA 94611
510-339-3201
joel@dreamjobcoaching.com
www.dreamjobcoaching.com

CAREER TRANSITION COACH
&
FOUNDER, DREAM JOB COACHING (1997) AND GARFINKLE EXECUTIVE COACHING (2003)

PROFILE

- Recognized as one of the top 50 coaches in North America.
- Background in executive coaching, performance improvement, and change management.
- Consultant for two of the top consulting firms in the world – Ernst & Young in Hong Kong and Accenture in San Francisco.
- Frequent speaker at national and international conferences; has appeared on ABC News and National Public Radio and is often featured in local and national media.

EXECUTIVE AND CAREER COACH

- Inspired thousands of people to reach personal and professional fulfillment and career transformation.
- Provide: Individual, group, and executive coaching
  Workshops
  Consultations to organizations
- **With individuals,** help executives advance up the corporate ladder quickly through increased exposure, visibility, and self-promotion.
- **With corporations,** increase retention, improve profitability, enhance communications, boost productivity, elevate morale, improve employee relationships, and support teams in working together more effectively.

Partial list of clients:

Hewlett-Packard	Nissan	Aetna	Microsoft
Charles Schwab	Accenture	Deloitte	Visa International
Cisco Systems	Peoplesoft	Oracle	Pricewaterhouse Coopers
Bank of America	Intuit	Coldwell Banker	Marriott Hotels
Eli Lilly	Shell Chemicals	Sapient Corporation	Google
Gap Inc.	Citibank	Electronic Arts	Starbucks

AUTHOR

- Authored three powerful transformative books, read in more than 25 countries:
  Land Your Dream Job*: The Last Career Search Book You'll Ever Need*
  Love Your Work*: Make the Job You Have the One You've Always Wanted*
  Find a Job in 14 Days: *A Practical Guide and Process for Finding the Job You Need Fast!*
- Publish a free, weekly email newsletter, fulfillment@work, which is delivered to over 10,000 people.

— CONTINUED —

WWW.DREAMJOBCOACHING.COM

JOEL GARFINKLE

— PAGE TWO —

PROFESSIONAL SPEAKER

- Keynote Speaker, Pennsylvania Chamber of Commerce statewide Annual Human Resources Conference: *How Do You Keep Your Stars? Twenty Surefire Strategies to Help Your Employees Love Their Work!*
- Speaker, Kentucky Society of Human Resource Management: *Love Your Work and Help Others Love Theirs! The Secrets to Unlocking Our Gifts and Potential at Work*
- Regular Guest Lecturer, San Francisco State University
- Keynote Speaker, University of California Alumni Career Expo
- Presenter, Commonwealth Club of California
- Presenter, Haas School of Business MBA program

INTERNATIONAL CHANGE MANAGEMENT CONSULTANT

- Background includes extensive experience in executive coaching, performance improvement, and change management.
- Broad understanding of business, organizational behavior management, and personal dynamics. Help individual clients make transitions into the work they are meant to be doing and to guide them to more fulfillment in their current career.

EDUCATION AND MEMBERSHIPS

B.A., Psychology, San Diego State University
Coaching Certificate, Coach University

Member, International Coach Federation
Member, Bay Area Chapter, International Association of Career Management Professionals
Member, National Speakers Association

Regina Andrews

123 Sprockett Way • Houston, TX 12345 • (123) 555-8888 • randrews@bamboo.com

OBJECTIVE

Enrollment Counselor, Rangeley College of the Law, University of Texas

SUMMARY OF QUALIFICATIONS

- Organized and motivated, with more than 10 years of success in cultivating rapport with people from diverse cultural backgrounds.
- Excellent listener; able to assess needs, synthesize and articulate information, and assist clients in making appropriate choices to fulfill their goals.
- Motivated and focused; able to work independently and as part of a team to complete tasks within strict deadlines.

PROFESSIONAL EXPERIENCE

2004-06 **Texas State University,** Houston, TX *Student*

- Worked closely with professors, advisors, and top-level administrators in Admissions, Financial Aid, and Arts & Sciences to submit transcript and financial aid requirements, and ensure complete and accurate paperwork.
- Advised and informally advocated for fellow students, providing suggestions to make wise academic decisions, fulfill requirements, and excel in their university experiences.
- Collaborated with students of varied ages and ethnicities to develop questions for tests, and co-wrote mid-term and final exams.
- Wrote extensively, with a focus on critical thinking and analysis, clarity of thought, and grammatical accuracy.

2000-04 **Adherent Components, Inc.,** Longchester, TX *Sales Manager*

- Interviewed clients to assess needs and limitations; identified products for optimal fit.
- Communicated effectively with clients in Europe and Asia, despite differences in language and culture.
- Conducted site visits, built strong relationships, and delivered convincing presentations to improve client loyalty and retention.

1999-00 **True-Time Merchants, Inc.,** Louisville, KY *Sales Account Manager*
1999 **Interstate Hotels, Inc.,** Huntsville, KY *Front Office Manager*
1994-99 **Express Inn,** Crainacre, KY *Guest Services Supervisor*

EDUCATION / AWARDS

B.A., English Literature, Kentucky University, Lexington, KY, 2006

Graduate, Champlain College Preparatory School, Champlain, KY, 1991
Studies included Forensics, Parliamentary Process, and Oratory Skills

Grant Frost, LICSW

123 Peachmont Dr., Birmingham, AL 12345, (123) 555-8888, gfrost@bamboo.com

SUMMARY OF QUALIFICATIONS

- MSW, LICSW, and postgraduate training in advanced child/adolescent psychotherapy.
- Provide EAP assessment, crisis intervention, counseling, and psychotherapy to individuals, couples, families, and groups.
- Particular expertise in:

Depression	Physical/sexual abuse	Family transitions
Anxiety	ADD and PTSD	Medical issues and loss
Addictions	Eating disorders	Chronic illness

- Experience coordinating among multiple-treatment settings: community mental health, hospital, schools, legal systems, and inpatient psychiatric and outpatient clinical settings.

EXPERIENCE AND ACCOMPLISHMENTS

Counseling, Therapy, and Crisis Intervention

- Provide brief and long-term psychotherapy for individuals, couples, and families.
- Conduct short-term psychotherapeutic and educational groups on eating disorders.
- Offer crisis intervention for abused teens, elders, and victims of domestic violence.
- Conduct family therapy and discharge planning as part of multidisciplinary treatment team on inpatient psychiatric unit.
- Present at Clinical Case and Masters Conferences; offer multicultural training for nurses.
- Complete assessments, crisis stabilization, interagency coordination, and referrals.

Child Welfare

- Counsel expectant birth parents in the adoption process; offer transracial adoption seminars to potential foster parents.
- Work closely with substance-abusing mothers during and after pregnancy.
- Advise parents of children who are hospitalized facing surgery or born with birth defects. Provide support, education, and advocacy.
- Supervise supportive services to leaders of Spanish-speaking teen parenting group.

PROFESSIONAL HISTORY

1996-present, Psychotherapist, Marriage & Family Therapy Partners, Birmingham, AL
1996-1997, Field Instructor, Alabama University School of Social Work, Crossville, AL
1995-1996, Psychotherapist, Hillside Mental Health Agency, Crossville, AL
1994-1995, Psychiatric Social Worker, Interdenominational Medical Center, Hillcrest, AL
1993-1994, Clinical Social Worker, St. Joseph Family Hospital, Lewiston, AL
Year II, Social Work Intern, Alabama Mental Health Center, Birmingham, AL
Year I, Social Work Intern, Uptown Clinic, South Birmingham, AL

LICENSING

LICSW, Licensed Independent Clinical Social Worker, State of AL, 1996

EDUCATION AND AFFILIATIONS

Post Graduate Certificate in Advanced Child and Adolescent Psychotherapy
Alabama University School of Social Work, Crossville, AL

MSW, Eirhart School of Social Work, Birmingham, AL, 1993

BS in Human Services, Pearmont College, New Hampton, GA, 1991

Member, Society of Eating Disorder Professionals, Toulaire, GA
Member, National Association of Social Workers (NASW)

Eduardo Ortiz

123 Blake Circle • Anaheim, CA 12345 • (123) 555-5555 • edortiz@bamboo.com

JOB OBJECTIVE

Customer Service Representative

HIGHLIGHTS OF QUALIFICATIONS

- History of representing organizations with professionalism, poise, and integrity.
- Adept at maintaining a positive atmosphere in the workplace and resolving problems with calm and grace.
- A hard-working team member who gets along well with everyone.

PROFESSIONAL ACCOMPLISHMENTS

2003-pres. Henderson Motor Club, Anaheim, CA
Customer Care Representative

- Handled member concerns with diplomacy, and followed through to ensure resolution.
- Recognized by management for superior service to the company.
- Trained new customer care reps to appreciate and clearly communicate membership benefits and promotions.
- Cultivated excellent long-term relationships with members using a friendly approach to questions and problems.

2000-03 Main Street Library, Santa Barbara, CA
Assistant Librarian

- Assisted patrons with various levels of technical ability to use the library's public computers.
- Showed extreme patience and interest when answering questions and helping patrons from diverse backgrounds.
- Received regular, outstanding feedback from Head Librarian.

1999-00 Pro Pet Products, Los Angeles, CA
Marketing Assistant

- Presented products and addressed questions from prospective customers at trade shows.
- Interacted daily with team members to synchronize completion of projects.

EDUCATION

Ongoing coursework in Intercultural Studies
Anaheim University, Anaheim, CA

COMMUNITY SERVICE

2001-pres. KidPride, Teen Mentor
2000-02 Disaster Relief and Prevention, Neighborhood Coordinator

Page 1 of 1

Leanne Sayer

123 Fleury Street
Joplin, MO 12345

123-555-5555
leannesayer@bamboo.com

Job Objective
Customer Service Representative

Highlights of Qualifications

- Experience developing and maintaining strong relationships with customers and co-workers from diverse backgrounds.
- An effective problem-solver who promptly responds to customer needs.
- Highly developed interpersonal skills; open minded and perceptive.

Professional Achievements

CUSTOMER SERVICE

- Provided initial contact to customers at Wise Company, responding quickly and diplomatically to concerns to ensure superior service and satisfaction.
- Fielded a high volume of client calls for Corbett Communications, including catalog requests and customer complaints.
- Provided excellent customer service to guests at Grand Hotel, and answered their questions about local events and services.
- At Teen Time, inspired teens to create life goals and supported them in conflict resolution among their peers.
- Earned praise for my ability to work as part of a customer service team at each of my last two positions.

ADMINISTRATIVE

- Developed many clerical skills as a volunteer at Connor County Humane Society.
- Keep an extremely well-organized home office, where I manage volunteer and family matters.

Work History

2003-pres. Receptionist and customer service positions through Amy's Temp. Agency

	Clients include:	Wise Company, Joplin, MO
		Corbett Communications, Greenleaf, MO
		Grand Hotel, Greenleaf, MO
2003	Waitress	Grant's Restaurant, Madison, MO
2000-03	Food Server	Boyer School, Quinby, MO

Education

Administration Skills Training
White Vocational School, Joplin, MO

Community Service

2000-pres.	Office Volunteer	Connor County Humane Society, Joplin, MO
2004-pres.	Mentor	Teen Time, Joplin, MO

Page 1 of 1

KATE WASHBURN

123 Commerce Street
San Jose, CA

(123) 555-8888
kwashburn@bamboo.com

CUSTOMER SERVICE SPECIALIST

- ☐ More than 10 years as a Customer Service Professional.
- ☐ Focused on service excellence.
- ☐ Creative and supportive team player.
- ☐ Skilled at resolving interpersonal and technical problems.

PROFESSIONAL EXPERIENCE

2001-PRESENT FRONTLINE BOOKS, SAN JOSE, CA

Customer Service Specialist

- ☐ As front-of-store bookseller, assist customers from diverse backgrounds, in person and on the phone.
- ☐ Created store map to help customers easily navigate this 3,000-square-foot retail outlet filled with thousands of books.
- ☐ Created and maintain Best Seller bulletin board to help customers with their shopping decisions.
- ☐ Won numerous service and attendance awards.

1995-2001 REASONS FOR SEASONS, SAN JOSE, CA

Supervisor, Client Services Technical Support, 1999-2001

- ☐ Supervised the technical support team, which won many service awards at this retail store selling weather-related merchandise.
- ☐ Created weekly internal newsletter to improve employee knowledge and customer service efficiency.

Telephone Help Desk Support, 1995-1999

- ☐ Managed the Help Desk that supported PC and Mac hardware and software customers.
- ☐ Repaired computers, and installed hardware and software.
- ☐ Trained new employees.
- ☐ Created and maintained award-winning Help Desk tracking system.

1994-1995 FIRST REPUBLIC BANK, SAN JOSE, CA

Telemarketer

- ☐ Assisted bank customers with their accounts.

EDUCATION

BA, Liberal Arts, Hunter College, St. Paul, MN

JOYCE FAVOR

123 Farley Avenue
Dallas, TX 12345
(123) 555-5555
joycefavor@bamboo.com

JOB OBJECTIVE

A position in the Accounting Department

SUMMARY

- ✓ Four years' experience performing accounting duties.
- ✓ Developed computer skills; able to quickly learn new technologies and systems.
- ✓ Meticulous organizational habits.

PROFESSIONAL EXPERIENCE

2002-pres. **Sears Company, Dallas, TX**
Accountant's Assistant

- ✓ Assisted manager with overall department supervision, including training of new hires.
- ✓ Coordinated preparation and timely dissemination of financial reports for department managers.
- ✓ Met multiple daily deadlines for processing checks and ensuring proper routing, clearance, imaging, and statement rendering.
- ✓ Ordered and monitored inventory of accounting supplies.

2001-02 **FastForward, Plano, TX**
Bookkeeper

- ✓ Entered accounts receivable information in database, paying close attention to accuracy in this high-pressure, time-sensitive environment.
- ✓ Created spreadsheet to track accounts payable to ensure bill payment.
- ✓ Cultivated and maintained strong relationships with co-workers and other departments.

1999-00 **Bishop Autos, San Antonio, TX**
Sales Support

- ✓ Handled reproduction and timely distribution of sales materials.
- ✓ Used database and word processing programs to organize and maintain company records.

EDUCATION

A.S., Accounting, 2001
University of Dallas, Dallas, TX

John Blitzer
123 Ford Street, Plymouth, IN 12345
123-555-8888, jblitzer@bamboo.com

OBJECTIVE

Position in Accounting in the Insurance Industry

SUMMARY OF QUALIFICATIONS

- Experienced using QuickBooks, Peachtree, and other accounting software.
- Two years of experience in accounting in the insurance industry.
- Energetic self-starter with strong communication skills; work well independently or on a team.
- Highly productive managing projects; a creative problem solver who rapidly adapts to changing demands.

ACCOUNTING & COMPUTER SKILLS

QuickBooks	Accounts Payable	Vendor Management
Peachtree	Accounts Receivable	Producer Commissions
Quicken	Finance Agreements	Payroll
MS Office	Collections	Benefits Administration

WORK HISTORY

2002-present **Hugh and Grant Insurance Inc., Plymouth, IN** **Comptroller/IT Manager**

- Managed: Accounts Receivable
  Accounts Payable
  Automation of Accounts
  QuickBooks

2001-2002 **Family Therapy Associates, Wilkinson, IN** **Bookkeeper**

- Handled: Insurance Billing
  Customer Billing
  Vendor Management
  Banking

1998-2001 **Littleton Bank of the West, Promise, IN** **Business Systems Analyst**

- Administered network and data warehouse security ids for employees.
- Designed and implemented various databases to manage information.
- Coordinated vendor activity.

1996-1998 **Timely DataGathering Inc., Promise, IN** **Office Manager**

- Managed: Accounts Receivable
  Banking
  Customer Service
  Vendor Management

EDUCATION

Bachelor of Science in Business, Highland College, West Fork, IN

LILLY L. CARVER

123 Princeton Ave. • Trenton, NJ 12345 • (123) 555-1234 • lcarver@bamboo.com

OBJECTIVE Position as Office Manager / Bookkeeper within the Construction industry

SUMMARY OF QUALIFICATIONS

- A highly organized and dedicated office manager and bookkeeper, with more than 10 years' experience providing excellent support to both management and customers.
- Analytical and accurate. Computer skills include: MS Word, Excel, ACT, and QuickBooks. Notary Public.
- A resourceful and creative self-starter who takes initiative to complete projects. Able to prioritize effectively to accomplish multiple tasks within tight deadlines.
- Personable and professional, with a strong customer focus and the ability to collaborate with team members to ensure customer satisfaction.

PROFESSIONAL EXPERIENCE

2004-pres. **NEW JERSEY HEAT AND AIR, INC.,** Trenton, NJ *Office Manager / Bookkeeper*

- Perform full charge bookkeeping using QuickBooksPro, including A/R, A/P, payroll, job costing, bank reconciliations, Trial Balance, and financial statements.
- Prepare calendaring for two owners and eight technicians performing HVAC repair and installations. Act as first contact with customers; set all service and follow-up calls. Respond to inquiries and complaints, and build excellent relationships with customers.
- Work closely with owners to develop sales and cost projections and strategic business plans. Develop and manage budgets, including costs for workers' compensation, additional vehicles, and inventory.
- Manage additional administrative duties, including word processing, ordering of equipment and parts, answering telephones, and handling correspondence.

2000-04 **OVERVIEW PAINTING,** Atlantic City, NJ *Business Manager / Bookkeeper*

- Completed all company correspondence and performed full charge bookkeeping with QuickBooksPro and QuickBooks Construction Premier.
- Refined ACT client database and maintained computer programs and networking, using Windows 2000 and XP.
- Assisted Project Coordinator and Estimators with bid preparation and with assuring customers of a positive and pleasant painting experience.

1990-00 **PRESLEY SERVICES, INC.,** Atlantic City, NJ *Business Manager / Bookkeeper*

- Scheduled appointments and service calls, dispatched service personnel, and ensured the complete, accurate, and timely preparation of bids.
- Coordinated workflow, consulted with general contractors, and provided support to 25 employees in two divisions.
- Priced and ordered equipment for residential contracting projects, including heat pumps, air conditioners, compressors, and other equipment.
- Monitored and maintained all insurance contracts, including health, auto, general liability, and workers' compensation to ensure proper coverage and eliminate extra costs.
- Organized submittal manuals, operations manuals, and as-builts for each project. Drafted Safety Manual per New Jersey code, which is still used by all employees. Researched, selected, and installed new DataBasics bookkeeping system.

EDUCATION B.A., cum laude, Psychology, Princeton University, Princeton, NJ

Dave J. Ross

123 Newbury Street • Boston, Massachusetts 12345 • (123) 555-1234 • djross@bamboo.com

JOB OBJECTIVE: Staff Accountant in a public accounting firm

SUMMARY OF QUALIFICATIONS

- Successfully completed **Uniform CPA Examination** in 2004.
- Four years' experience in all levels of the accounting process, including:

A/R	Internal audits	Individual returns	G/L
A/P	Quality assurance	Partnership returns	Budget management
Payroll	Inventory control	1120S	C. Corporation

- Well-organized, focused, and productive with proven ability to complete projects on time.
- Track record of developing strong client relationships, anticipating customer needs, and providing timely, proactive service.
- Commitment to furthering the success of team members, as well as delivering quality individual performance in a high-pressure environment.
- Knowledgeable in the use of Excel and professional accounting software.

EDUCATION & CERTIFICATIONS

Certificate in Accountancy, Bentley College, Waltham, MA
BS in Accounting, Babson College, Wellesley, MA

RELEVANT ACCOMPLISHMENTS

ACCOUNTING

- Consistently met deadlines in preparing financial data for private clients, Ross Jewelers, and Polaroid, including:

Payroll	Compilations	Tax returns
Reviews	Financial statements	

- Tracked inventory worth more than $4 million for Ross Jewelers.
- Reduced client tax obligation by effectively communicating with management and accounting departments.

BUSINESS DEVELOPMENT & MANAGEMENT

- Managed installation and conversion from manual ledgers to an in-house computerized accounting system at Ross Jewelers.
  - Researched and selected the system and software.
  - Communicated with software consultants to successfully resolve problems.
  - Trained staff and coordinated troubleshooting on the new automated system.
- Devised a marketing program for Ross Jewelers that expanded the customer base and increased profitability.

WORK HISTORY

2004–pres.	Accounting Consultant	
2003-04	Medical Technologist	Massachusetts General Hospital, Boston, MA
1995-03	Medical Technologist	Boston City Hospital, Boston, MA
1992-95	Staff Accountant	Ross Jewelers, Boston, MA
1991-92	Staff Accountant	Polaroid, Cambridge, MA

HARRY CONDUTTORI

123 Tulari St., Eugene, OR 12345 Home: 123.555.1234 / Cell: 123.555.2345 harryc@bamboo.com

OBJECTIVE: Senior Level Financial Risk Management Position

HIGHLIGHTS OF QUALIFICATIONS

- Highly successful career in financial marketing, planning, and trading.
- Strong knowledge of foreign exchange and capital markets; CFA, CCM, and MBA.
- Customer focused and proactive; skilled in cultivating new and lucrative business.
- Goal oriented and highly motivated professional who excels in high-pressure situations.
- Excellent communication and interpersonal skills; a leader and team player.

CERTIFICATIONS & EDUCATION

CFA (Chartered Financial Analyst), AIMR, 2006

CCM (Certified Cash Manager), AFP, 2004

MBA, Finance & Accounting, Oregon State University, 1999

BA, Business Economics, University of Washington, 1996

PROFESSIONAL EXPERIENCE

First Bank, Eugene, OR & New York, NY 2002-pres.

VICE PRESIDENT, FOREIGN EXCHANGE MARKETING (2004-pres.)

- Currently rebuilding bank's Foreign Exchange presence in western United States. Tripled client base of middle to large cap customers and increased earnings by over 200%.
- Work closely with clients' executive officers in the management of financial strategies, following through to successful outcomes and ensuring customer satisfaction.
- Identify and quantify clients' accounting and economic cash flow risks, then develop and execute custom solutions, utilizing foreign exchange tools.
- Structure and execute spot, forward, and option contracts in accordance with customers' cash management forecasts.
- Work with clientele in the construction and accounting evaluation (FASB 133) of interest rate and currency derivative products.
- Perform extensive research on the web to develop economic and political profiles pertaining to foreign currencies.
- Generate technical analyses including economic models, forecasts, and projections.

ASSISTANT VICE PRESIDENT, FOREIGN EXCHANGE TRADING (2002-04)

- Worked as Senior Spot Trader for Asian and London markets.
- Built highly productive working relationships with 180+ foreign corporate and institutional clients.

- Continued on Page 2 -

HARRY CONDUTTORI

- Page 2 -

PROFESSIONAL EXPERIENCE

ASSISTANT VICE PRESIDENT, FOREIGN EXCHANGE TRADING - FIRST BANK (continued)

- Quoted prices and provided overview for clients of Asian and London market developments.
- Developed supportive team structure on trading floor, fostering cooperative efforts in highly dynamic and oftentimes volatile environment.
- Provided liquidity for trading desk and covered currency prices in absence of primary dealer.
- Continually increased and maintained large relationship base in Asia and Europe.

USNationalBank, New York, NY 1999-02

FOREIGN EXCHANGE SPOT TRADER (2000-02)

- Provided liquidity for trading desk in spot USD/DEM.
- Quoted prices on interbank basis, developing relationships in Europe, Asia, and North America.
- Solicited new order business.

FOREIGN EXCHANGE TRADER - DERIVATIVES GROUP (1999-00)

- Traded in the forward risk for the global OTC and Exchange Options Books.
- Assisted in pricing of options.

College Intern, Chicago, IL & Paris, France 1998-99

Treasury Department, Chicago (1998-99)

- Assisted City Controller in management of pension and cash funds.

Foreign Exchange, USNationalBank, France (1998)

- Developed strong working knowledge of Foreign Exchange Market by assisting in all aspects of currency trading.

AFFILIATIONS, SKILLS & CONTINUING EDUCATION

Active Memberships:

Eugene Society of Financial Analysts, AIMR Local Chapter 2006

AIMR, National Chapter 2004

AFT, National Chapter 1999

Coursework in Preparation for CPA Exam: 2006-pres.

Oregon State University - Accounting, Auditing, Tax, Accounting Information Systems

Information Systems Skills:

- Bloomberg - Reuters - FENICS - EBS - Microsoft Office - Internet

Personal Accomplishments:

Second Degree Black Belt, Isshin-Ryu Karate

LEE CHIN
123 Patterson Street, Queens, NY 12345
(123) 555-5555
leechin@bamboo.com

OBJECTIVE
Human Resources Specialist

HIGHLIGHTS
- Experienced in prioritizing effectively to manage multiple tasks under tight deadlines.
- Compelled to meet and surpass management-set objectives.
- Skilled at using word processing and data entry applications.
- Gifted at making contact with and reading all types of people.

HISTORY
Volunteer Coordinator, 2002-present
Queens Hospital, Queens, NY
- Recruit and train volunteers in program delivery and leadership.
- Provide motivation and evaluation to foster staff development.

Human Resources Specialist, 2000-02
A&C Management Group, Queens, NY
- Established reputation for applicant screening skills that produced excellent candidate selection ratio.
- Conducted extensive Internet research on online recruiting programs, reporting findings to HR manager.
- Initiated changes to data entry of electronic resumes, resulting in faster identification of job candidates.
- Educated new employees, answering questions and clearly conveying company policies.

Administrative Assistant, 1997-99
Fieldstone & Johnson, Brooklyn, NY
- Provided superior administrative support for Sales department composed of two managers and three salespeople.
- Processed client profiles and organized office systems to ensure smooth workflow.

EDUCATION
B. A., Business Administration
Queens College, Queens, NY

BRENT CASTLETON

123 Main Street East, Bedford, MA 12345
123-555-5555, bcastleton@bamboo.com

OBJECTIVE
Position in Human Resources with emphasis on Recruitment Management

HIGHLIGHTS
- Ten years of management experience, with particular interest in employee recruitment and development.
- A confident, result-oriented professional with a proven track record of success in personnel management.
- A focused team player with a positive attitude and highly developed interpersonal skills.

RELEVANT EXPERIENCE

Recruiting
- Recruited and mentored entry-level retail team members who have since become department managers in J. Perth Fine Clothing.
- As member of management team, worked closely with other managers to identify key human resources issues in response to organizational growth of J. Perth Fine Clothing.
- Recruited 13 excellent sales representatives for Morse Manufacturing; trained new reps in sales techniques, policies, and procedures.
- Met periodically with human resources manager to address hiring needs for Sales Department at Indigo Corporation.
- Led staff and volunteer recruitment at Gatewood, a state-wide employment agency.
- Reviewed resumes, interviewed candidates, and hired numerous employees throughout my professional career.

Administrative
- Served on team that wrote and reviewed strategic proposals for reorganization of management at J. Perth Fine Clothing.
- At Morse Manufacturing, completed government paperwork to ensure compliance with OSHA standards.
- Provided database management for individual and team sales achievements at Indigo Corporation.

HISTORY
Manager, 2001-present
J. Perth Fine Clothing, Harrison, MA

Sales Supervisor, 1998-2001
Morse Manufacturing Company, Brookline, MA

Administrator, 1996-1998
Indigo Corporation, Boston, MA

EDUCATION
M.A., 1995, Boston University, Boston, MA

VOLUNTEERISM
Board Member (2004-2005), Steering Committee Chair (2005-present)
Gatewood Employment Agency, Bedford, MA

SUSAN BLEEKER
123 Main Street
San Francisco, CA 12345
(123) 555-1234
suebleeker@bamboo.com

OBJECTIVE: An Administrative/Management position in Human Resources focusing on Project/Database Management

SUMMARY OF QUALIFICATIONS

- Eight years' experience in management and administration, with a reputation for high quality service to both internal and external clients.
- Exceptional organizational skills; able to integrate details and coordinate tasks to accomplish overall project goals.
- An excellent manager; able to match candidates with specific positions and encourage development of career and company objectives.
- Experience in database management, administration, and coordination.

PROFESSIONAL EXPERIENCE

HUMAN RESOURCES MANAGEMENT & ADMINISTRATION
PeopleSoft

- Assessed organizational needs and guided staff in the development of skills and core competencies to further individual and organizational growth.
- Recruited, hired, and trained top candidates for customer service positions.
- Created new-hire orientation and training procedures. Facilitated training of all new hires.
- Directed departmental changes resulting in a self-supporting and cohesive work group structure.
- Consistently inspired excellent staff performance and respectful relations in a pressurized, multi-tasking environment.
- Oversaw the delivery, registration, and administration of 100 programs per year.

— Continued —

SUSAN BLEEKER

Page Two

PRODUCT DEVELOPMENT & PROJECT MANAGEMENT

PeopleSoft

- Co-leader in the design and development of custom software to automate administrative, tracking, and financial management/reporting processes.
- Project director of membership program: Analyzed market research, developed strategies to attract and retain clients, initiated and implemented innovative programs for members and prospects.
- Assisted in creation of online registration form to enhance client accessibility to services via the Internet.
- Managed database to ensure integrity and quality of data, and timeliness of targeted mailings.

EMPLOYMENT HISTORY

1996-pres.	PeopleSoft, Pleasanton, CA	
	Human Resources Director	***2003-pres.***
	Education Manager	***2000-03***
	Customer Service Coordinator	***1999-00***
	Customer Service Representative	***1996-99***
1994-96	Clear Concepts, Santa Fe, NM	
	Retail Management & Sales	

EDUCATION & TRAINING

B.S. Business Administration - University of Massachusetts, Amherst, MA
Computer skills include: MS Word, Excel, FoxPro, FileMaker Pro, and Internet

Sandra Cole

123 Kendall Street, #1 San Francisco, CA 12345
(123) 555-1234 scole@bamboo.com

OBJECTIVE

A Supervisory position in Human Resources Administration

QUALIFICATION HIGHLIGHTS

- More than four years' experience in Human Resources Administration, with two years of hands-on supervision and training.
- Highly organized, with a dual focus on big picture issues and details; skilled at following through to accomplish simultaneous objectives within deadline-driven environments.
- Able to anticipate concerns and provide quick solutions using effective communication tools.

PROFESSIONAL EXPERIENCE

KXYZ-TV, SF TV, San Francisco, CA 1999-present
Project Coordinator, 2004-present
Local Programming Coordinator, 2000-03
Viewer Liaison/Public Relations, 2000
Administrative Assistant, 1999-00

Supervision & Training

- Recruited individuals for production positions and internships at SF TV, coordinating with universities and recruiters to secure top candidates.
- Scheduled and conducted interviews; hired new employees and coordinated with Human Resources, MIS, and Telecommunications departments to ensure complete orientation to the organization.
- Trained and coached production assistants and interns in administrative and production support. Matched new staff with supervisors for optimal team results.
- Conducted weekly staff meetings and evaluated employees and interns; recommended promotion or termination based on review.

Management & Organization

- Created and implemented an information distribution system to effectively communicate new Human Resources and management policies to all SF TV employees, resulting in streamlined operations and greater consistency.
- Acted as liaison between Human Resources department and SF TV staff, ensuring the organization, completeness, and compliance of all documentation.
- Developed and maintained budgets for capital improvements and operations. Advocated for department staff in negotiating budgetary needs with top management.
- Managed $3MM annual payroll for 200+ employees of SF TV; oversaw bi-weekly verification and coding processes to ensure accuracy and meet strict payroll deadlines.

EDUCATION/PROFESSIONAL DEVELOPMENT

B.A. in progress, Communications, San Francisco State University, San Francisco, CA

Professional Development seminars include: Conflict Management Skills for Women, Money Sense – Corporate Budgets & Payroll

Computer proficiencies: MS Word, Excel, Meeting Maker XP, Schedule+, Project, Exchange, Netscape Navigator, FileMaker Pro, PowerPoint

NORA JONES

123 Tillman Avenue • Memphis, TN 12345 • (123) 555-1234 • njones@bamboo.com

OBJECTIVE: Paralegal position

SUMMARY OF QUALIFICATIONS

- More than six years as a paralegal with both civil litigation and criminal defense experience, including three years of experience working for the State of Tennessee.
- Independent and self-directed professional, able to cultivate strong relationships with individuals from diverse organizational and cultural backgrounds, and collaborate effectively with team members to achieve overall organizational objectives.
- Computer skills include: MS Word/Excel/Access, Lexis/Nexis, Westlaw, FileMaker Pro, Concordance, Summation and extensive Internet research.

PROFESSIONAL EXPERIENCE

2001-04 **OFFICE OF THE STATE PUBLIC DEFENDER,** Memphis, TN ***Legal Analyst***

- Conducted comprehensive research and document collection from government and academic institutions, medical facilities and community organizations to develop compelling arguments to mitigate sentences for Death Row inmates.
- Oversaw the analysis, distillation, and synthesis of 10+ years of research, resulting in more than 20 volumes (300 pages each) of relevant exhibit materials.
- Performed extensive fieldwork to gather relevant information. Interviewed government officials, community members and expert witnesses during each case. Collated and prepared materials for review by expert witnesses.
- Conducted juror and witness interviews and drafted declarations for signing.
- Wrote letters to hospitals, schools, Boards of Education, police, prisons, jails and the Tennessee Youth Authority to preserve and present documentation for use in critical cases.
- Collaborated with team of legal and professional experts to discuss elements and develop mitigation strategies for the case.
- Summarized copious amounts of information for attorneys and recommended next steps in case development. Maintained case files and databases.

1998-01 **STANLEY AND KELPER, LLP,** Memphis, TN ***Litigation Paralegal***

- Supported litigation attorneys in a diverse array of high-profile legal cases, including contract dispute resolution, intellectual property, labor/human rights issues, civil rights litigation, a *habeas corpus* Death Row Appeals case and a federal criminal investigation.
- Prepared witnesses, trial exhibits and deposition testimony for a patent infringement case and conducted research for post-trial briefs.
- Met with trial witnesses and testifying experts in preparation for depositions as part of complex arbitration between the City of Memphis and its professional basketball team.
- Lead paralegal on a *pro bono* civil rights case against the State of Tennessee in which we were co-counsel with the ACLU.
- Performed extensive legal research via multiple media, drafted briefs and collated evidence for presentation at hearings. Obtained critical documents to support the charge that race bias was a key element in stops by THP officers.

EDUCATION

B.A., History, minor in Environmental Science, University of Tennessee, Memphis, TN, 1998

SOFIA A. GIOVANNI

123 Santa Maria Place • San Francisco, CA 12345 • (123) 555-1234 • giovanni@bamboo.com

OBJECTIVE

Position as Legal Counsel in Workers' Compensation
focusing on litigation and legislative change

SUMMARY OF QUALIFICATIONS

- More than 15 years of experience providing legal expertise in litigating workers' compensation cases for diverse industries.
- Extensive knowledge of workers' compensation laws and related issues, with the ability to communicate them effectively to non-legal audiences.
- Excellent reputation with the California workers' compensation bench and bar; known for high ethical standards, integrity and ability to handle complex cases.
- Dedicated to active involvement in developing and legislating improvements in the California workers' compensation system.

PROFESSIONAL EXPERIENCE

1995-pres. **DVI, INC.,** San Francisco, CA
A 100,000-employee import/export company traded on the NYSE.
Assistant Vice President / Deputy General Counsel of Workers' Compensation

- Actively litigate caseload of 110-120 workers' compensation files, including third-party cases. Handle all stages of litigation, including depositions, settlement conferences, workers' compensation hearings and civil jury trials.
- As Vice Chair of California Coalition on Workers' Compensation, work with key figures in the State Administration and Legislature and industry stakeholders to develop legislation to improve the workers' compensation system.
- Collaborate with Human Resources staff on shared cases, including ADA and other disability-related issues.
- Monitor outside counsel and coordinate communications between counsel, internal claims examiners and field operations to streamline litigation process and ensure accuracy and consistency of information.
- Work closely with District Attorney and Department of Insurance to investigate and prosecute fraud cases.
- Design and deliver dynamic and interactive training to operations staff.
- Hired and supervised Sacramento legal staff of two attorneys and two secretaries: Reviewed litigation strategies, resolved personnel issues and conducted performance reviews.

-continued-

SOFIA A. GIOVANNI
PAGE TWO

1993-95 **LEGAL COMPENSATION ASSOCIATES,** San Francisco, CA
Associate

- Successfully litigated a full caseload of workers' compensation files, including third-party cases.
- Cultivated positive relationships with existing clients and developed new business through networking.
- Developed and delivered presentations and training to labor law firms and insurance companies on workers' compensation issues, laws and strategies.

Previous experience includes:

Associate, Labor & Employment Dept., Jordan, Johnson & Jones, Los Angeles
In-House Counsel, New World Insurance Company, Sacramento

EDUCATION

J.D., Stanford University School of Law, Palo Alto, CA, 1990
B.A. with Honors, International Relations
Georgetown University, Washington, DC, 1986

Internships:

California State Assemblyman Willie Brown, Sacramento, CA, 1985
U.S. Senator Alan Cranston, Washington, DC, 1984

AFFILIATIONS

Member, California State Bar, 1990-pres.
California Coalition on Workers' Compensation, 2002-pres.
Vice Chair, Board of Directors
Executive Committee
Policy Advisory Committee

Darrell J. Kramer, JD, MPA

123 62nd Avenue, San Francisco, CA 12345 123-555-1234 djkramer@bamboo.com

CAREER PROFILE

- Environmental attorney specializing in federal, state, and local environmental laws for water, air, solid waste, and hazardous materials.
- Skilled at administrative law and transactions such as reviewing and drafting construction contracts and consulting agreements.
- Experience as legal counselor, mediator, and facilitator for parties including community organizations, corporations, and government agencies.
- Adept at dispute resolution, both internal and external to an organization.

EDUCATION

Columbia University, New York, Masters of Public Administration, 2003
National Urban Fellow, 2002, 2003

Hastings School of Law, San Francisco, Juris Doctor, 1997
New California State Regents Professional Scholar, 1995, 1996
Clinical Internship, USEPA, Office of Regional Counsel, Region II, Fall 1996-Spring 1997

Boston University, Massachusetts, Bachelor of Arts, Political Science, 1992

BAR AFFILIATIONS

California Bar: passed exam, 1997; admitted, 1998
New York State Bar: passed exam, 1997; admitted, 1998

EXPERIENCE

2002-pres. OAKLAND INTERNATIONAL AIRPORT, Oakland, CA

Environmental Manager, 2003-pres.

Developed and direct the Environmental Program, which ensures environmental compliance of medium-hub airport servicing 12 million passengers annually. Program includes:

- Fueling systems oversight
- Recycling and reuse
- Air quality permitting
- Groundwater remediation
- Hazardous materials management
- Storm Water Pollution Prevention Program
- Underground and aboveground storage tanks
- Tenant and employee training and multi-medium inspections

- Implement the mitigation measures required of the airport's $3 billion master plan.
  - Execute systems and policies for landside and airside operations.
  - Negotiate tenant/permittee commitment to the program.
  - Act as project manager for construction of alternative fuel infrastructure and procurement of vehicles.
- Interpret environmental regulations and respond to internal inquiries regarding airport environmental issues.
- Serve as regulatory contact for the airport to outside agencies and professional organizations.
- Create and administer contracts; write consulting agreements; develop and oversee environmental section workplan, staff and budget.

Special Assistant to the Director of Aviation, 2002-03

Assisted Director of Aviation in management of international commercial operations and personnel.

- Advised administrators on federal environmental and transportation laws and regulations.
- Resolved disputes and provided dispute resolution training for management and staff.

—Continued—

Darrell J. Kramer, JD, MPA, page 2

1998-02 CA ENVIRONMENTAL JUSTICE ALLIANCE, San Francisco, CA
Counsel and Executive Director
Served as Counsel to San Francisco communities during negotiations with local, state, and federal Environmental and Transportation Agencies.

- Analyzed and evaluated compliance with federal and state environmental laws including SEQRA, NEPA, RCRA, CERCLA, CAA, FWPCA, FSWA, and ISTEA.
- Advised clients about environmental enforcement, compliance, siting, risk management, permitting, and land use; and negotiated with government agencies on clients' behalf.
- Planned and directed projects and policies in the areas of solid waste, water quality, air quality, Brownfield development, and alternative fuels.
- Testified at national and local hearings and lobbied state, city, and federal governments for transportation and environmental regulations.
- Served as Principal Investigator (2000-02) to the CA Environmental Worker Training Program to develop a federally sponsored superfund waste site and emergency response operation job training program. Training included:
  - Asbestos removal
  - Lead abatement
  - Environmental site monitoring
  - Confined space entry
- Interacted with environmental remediation and construction businesses to place 100% of trained students from the Environmental Worker Training Program.

2000-01 SAN JOSE STATE COLLEGE, San Jose, CA
Adjunct Professor, Federal Environmental Law and Policy

RELEVANT COMMITTEES

American Association of Airport Executives, 2003-pres.
California State Bar Association: Environmental Law Section, 1995-02
The Association of the Bar of the City of San Francisco: Transportation Committee, 1999-02
San Francisco City Environmental Benefits Fund: Board Member, 2000-02
Department of Environmental Conservation Comparative Risk Project, 2001-02
Mayor's Task Force on Brownfields, 2001-02

CHARLES C. GILROY

123 Harrington Ave. • Brady, Nebraska 12345 • (123) 555-1234 • gilroy@bamboo.com

Civil Litigation Attorney

SUMMARY OF QUALIFICATIONS

- More than 12 years' experience litigating personal injury, business, employment and insurance cases for a diverse clientele, plaintiff and defendant, as both principal litigator and litigation team member.
- Excellent verbal and written skills; able to offer clear counsel to clients and deliver persuasive arguments in court.
- Skilled in assessing client needs, evaluating cases and developing appropriate litigation strategies for each case.

PROFESSIONAL EXPERIENCE

1995-pres. **PEIDMONT & GRANGER,** North Platte, Nebraska
Partner, 2004-present *Associate, 1995-04*

- Represented diverse clients in civil litigation matters, including:

Catastrophic injury	Business disputes
Premises liability	Product liability
Vehicle accidents	Professional malpractice
Insurance coverage & bad faith	Employment matters

- Met with clients and developed litigation strategy based on client needs and assessment of each case.
- Litigated each case, including depositions, discovery, law and motion practice, research and briefing, settlement negotiations, mediation, arbitration, trial and appeal.
- Consistently achieved favorable results for clients, including four verdicts and settlements in excess of $1 million.
- Responsible for overall management of firm, including support staff of six.

1993-95 **PILSNER, HIDELY, BILSMORE & HEIDLEMAN,** North Platte, Nebraska
Associate

- Handled own caseload of insurance defense matters.

1992 **HUNTER, SILLY, KRAMER & TANN,** North Platte, Nebraska
Summer Associate

1991-92 **HUCKLEBERRY & COSTANZA,** North Platte, Nebraska
Law Clerk

EDUCATION / PROFESSIONAL DEVELOPMENT

J.D., Midwestern School of Law, Chicago, Illinois, 1993
Top 20% of Class

Admitted to the Nebraska Bar, 1993

Author, "To Media and Win…" 21 Mw.L.Rev. 123, 1993

American Jurisprudence Book Awards: Civil Procedure I and II, and Comparative Law, Outstanding Achievement Award – Civil Procedure

Member: Law Review / Moot Court / Student Bar Association

B.A., Political Science, Nebraska State University, North Platte, 1990

Jared Burke

45 French Avenue • Elmira, NY 12345 • (123) 555-5555 • jaredburke@bamboo.com

JOB OBJECTIVE

Marketing Communications Manager
in the Construction Industry

EDUCATION

MBA, Marketing, 1996
University of Buffalo, Buffalo, New York

SUMMARY

- 13 years of combined experience in marketing and the construction industry.
- Led team to develop strategic business plan for market penetration, including analysis of organization's strengths, weaknesses, and competition.
- Skilled at providing clear, concise communication to team members.

PROFESSIONAL EXPERIENCE

Marketing Communications Director
HEMPHILL CONSTRUCTION, INC., Elmira, NY, 2001-present

- Developed, managed, and tracked communications budget of $260K.
- Negotiated with vendors to improve quality of service and resolve complaints, resulting in a 90% customer retention rate.
- Restored company's presence in Singapore as a major construction supplier by customizing promotional materials for the Asian market.

Marketing Team Leader
FREMONT BUILDERS, INC., Avon, NY, 1997-01

- Coached and directly managed marketing staff to ensure budget compliance, daily operations, and prompt resolution of issues.
- Developed and implemented marketing strategy for new merchandise program, resulting in significant sales growth.

Training Specialist
YARROW & WHITE CONSTRUCTION, Buffalo, NY, 1994-97

- Set up and ran training sessions; communicated results to management team.
- Served as liaison between staff and clients, earning their confidence with reliable follow-through and clear communication.

COMMUNITY SERVICE

Elmira Chamber of Commerce, Fundraiser, 2000-present
Construction Kings of America, Board Member, 2003-05

Page 1 of 1

Sally Romerez
Marketing Professional

123 Kramer Street · Rapid City, South Dakota 12345 · (123) 555-1234 · sallyr@bamboo.com

SUMMARY OF QUALIFICATIONS

- Over ten years' management experience in marketing, with over five years in the technology industry.
- Highly regarded for building strong partner relationships and generating innovative solutions that achieve quantifiable results.
- Thorough and committed; exceptional organizational and team leadership skills.

MARKETING ACCOMPLISHMENTS

2000-2006 **High-Tech Communications,** Rapid City, SD
MANAGER, STRATEGIC MARKETING *(2005-2006)*

- Collaboratively developed strategies with senior management that drove market leadership in emerging Bandwidth Trading market.
- Developed consistent, well-positioned marketing messages in seamlessly coordinated executive briefings, conferences, trade shows and customer meetings.
- Spearheaded production of major marketing videos, DVDs, online campaigns and internal sales launch to support sales team in applying High-Tech's marketing message and increase product sales.
- Orchestrated the Industry Communications Financial Summit 2005, focusing on advising industry professionals on critical telecommunications finance issues. Achieved over $28M in addressable revenue.

MANAGER, GLOBAL EVENTS *(2004-2005)*
MARKETING PROGRAM MANAGER *(2000-2004)*

- Planned and executed inspiring and well-attended seminars on Lucent products, collaborating with product groups to develop content; identified speakers and industry experts, and created outbound marketing materials.
- Generated over $1.5B in expected revenue and 15,000 leads.
- Skillfully nurtured partner relationships with exceptionally clear communication.
- Coordinated innumerable logistics, ensuring that complex scheduling and presentation technology flowed smoothly at key industry trade shows.
- Managed direct marketing campaigns, which resulted in over 4% response rates and the highest number of qualified leads achieved to date.
- Developed and implemented seminar programs through direct mail, web marketing and telemarketing, launching solutions and exceeding projections by 100%.

1994-2000 MARKETING CONSULTANT

- Team-developed marketing plan for **'RoundTheWorld Communications, Inc.** that evolved into the focal point of venture capital solicitations for this reliability and scalability software company.
- Oversaw software upgrade marketing campaign for **Computer Publishing Corporation,** increasing net sales.
- Served as the interim Direct Marketing Director of **Get Hip Clothing** and re-launched $5M catalog business.
- Oversaw feasibility study and participated in President's Roundtable on Direct Marketing, Advertising and Database Marketing strategies.

EDUCATION: BA, Political Science, University of South Dakota, Rapid City, SD

SANDRA O'MALLEY

123 Stonebridge Court, #2 • Los Angeles, CA 12345 • (123) 555-1234 • somalley@bamboo.com

OBJECTIVE: A Marketing Communications position within the high-tech industry

PROFILE

- A highly creative team member, able to brainstorm new ideas and deliver marketing concepts and presentations with clarity, enthusiasm, and humor.
- A skilled listener, able to assess needs and develop programs and products that achieve results for a diverse clientele.
- An organized and detail-oriented professional with solid software skills and familiarity with dynamic high-tech environments.

SELECTED ACCOMPLISHMENTS

Marketing Communications & Sales

- Pitched creative ideas and "outside the box" projects to experts at Los Angeles Design Group; discussed methods for realization and project improvements.
- Created an entirely new product line for UC students based on thorough research and perceived need, and completed all regulatory requirements and copyright procedures to ensure successful product launch.
- Quickly responded to in-person and telephone inquiries at Barnes & Noble, assisting customers with product selection and maintaining excellent relations within a fast-paced environment.

Technical

- Taught Adobe Photoshop, PageMaker, PowerPoint, and MS Office Suite to diverse customers at Multimedia Graphics, Inc.
- Utilized 3D Studio MAX to develop innovative urban park in Los Angeles and created animation for UC's School of Automated Design project.

- continued –

Sandra O'Malley

Page Two

Project Management

- Managed design, development, and production of new product for College of Architecture students, which raised 40% of yearly funds.
- Completed project entitled "Digital Dynamics: A Live/Work Environment for a Software Designer":
  - Conducted research and established priorities, tasks, and workflow to meet strict deadlines.
  - Created an integrated high technology environment designed for optimal space utilization and productivity.
  - Designed and delivered impressive multimedia presentation to UC faculty, students, and invited experts, utilizing 3D Studio MAX and AutoCAD 13.

WORK HISTORY

2003-pres. **Sales Associate**
Barnes & Noble, Los Angeles, CA

1998-03 **Full-Time Student**
University of California (UC), Berkeley, CA

1998 **Architectural Intern**
Los Angeles Design Group, Los Angeles, CA

Additional experience includes: **Lab Assistant** for Multimedia Graphics, Inc. **and Research Team Member at** Stanford University **and** University of California, Berkeley.

EDUCATION

Bachelor of Architecture, cum laude, **University of California,** Berkeley, CA, 2003

ROXY JEAN KENNEDY

123 Jones Street, #1 • Miami, FL 12345 • (123) 555-1234 • rkennedy@bamboo.com

CAREER GOAL

A position in Marketing & Promotions with an emphasis on Sales

SUMMARY OF QUALIFICATIONS

- Five years' experience in marketing, promotions, and sales, with a flair for communicating effectively with people from diverse cultures.
- A highly organized and creative events coordinator.
- Flexible and energetic; skilled in multitasking to accomplish overall goals.

PROFESSIONAL EXPERIENCE

TECH TRAINING INTERNATIONAL, Palm Beach, FL Sales & Marketing Consultant 2003-pres.

- Collaborated with promotional teams to coordinate grand opening events at new training facilities in Tampa, FL and Atlanta, GA.
- Built strong relationships with software vendors and negotiated agreements for customized training.
- Worked with marketing consultants to create incentives, generate leads, and attract new clients.
- Researched local trends and competition to identify opportunities for nationwide advertising spots and secure optimal market positioning.

BIG 5 INTERNATIONAL, LLP, New York, NY Human Relations Specialist 2002-03

- Acted as primary liaison for international employees from Europe, Africa, and Asia Pacific: Secured visas, coordinated logistics, and guided the transition into U.S. culture and employment at the firm.
- Devised strategies and implemented both team-building and corporate-sponsored events, including Bay to Liberty, Home Chef, and Friday massage.
- Created and maintained an Intranet Web site for use by all employees.

KHAKIS R US, Hong Kong, China Sales Representative / Merchandiser 2001-02

- Analyzed daily sales reports to identify market trends. Selected point-of-service marketing materials and created eye-catching displays for top-selling locations.
- Coached sales associates on key selling points of seasonal merchandise, and prepared products for presentation at national sales meetings.

ENTERTAIN U, Vienna, VA Talent and Production Coordinator / Event Planner 2000-01

- Coordinated travel and performance logistics for national circus events, including an 18-elephant salute for the "Salute to Congress."
- Supported four Vice Presidents simultaneously in accomplishing multiple tasks within a high intensity, deadline-driven environment.

EDUCATION

B.A., Merchandising, Marymount University, Arlington, VA
Marketing emphasis, Digby Stewart College, London, England
Computer: MS Word, Excel, PowerPoint, Access, PeopleSoft, Lotus Notes

Sandi Patterson
123 Fordham Road
Beaufort, Georgia 12345
123-555-5555
spatterson@bamboo.com

JOB OBJECTIVE

Marketing Manager

HIGHLIGHTS

- Experienced manager with more than five years in Marketing and Sales.
- Robust record of success in managing product launches and ongoing marketing campaigns that exploit new technologies.
- Able to motivate others to realize potential and meet organizational objectives.

EDUCATION

MBA, Marketing, 2005
Franklin University, Atlanta, Georgia
Thesis: Internet Marketing Strategies for Profit and Nonprofit Organizations

SELECTED ACHIEVEMENTS

At Mandrake Company

- Increased quarterly revenues to $1.7M within first year of launching email marketing service, establishing company as the leading online marketing provider.
- Launched a cooperative marketing product, gaining 34 clients and significant revenue in the first 4 months.
- Initiated innovative strategies to increase company's name recognition in new markets.
- Created and executed strategic and tactical sales/marketing plans for key accounts.
- Hired, trained, and supervised sales/marketing team; delivered periodic performance evaluations, apportioning raises, stock options, and bonus grants.

HISTORY

Hopkins Incorporated, Beaufort, GA, 2006-present, Sales Manager
Mandrake Company, Atlanta, GA, 2002-2006, Sales Manager
Edelweiss & Sons, Columbia, SC, 2000-2002, Sales Associate
Verity Corporation, Birmingham, AL, 1997-2000, Corporate Trainer

COMMUNITY SERVICE

Events Promotions Volunteer, Festive Occasions, 2004-present
Member, Environmental Board, 2000-2004

Shawn Larkin
123 Savoy Street
Atlanta, GA 12345
123-555-8888
slarkin@bamboo.com

Arts Administrator

HIGHLIGHTS

- Over 25 years of managerial experience with arts, governmental, and nonprofit organizations.
- Innovative project designer and implementer whose plans become reality, on budget and on time.
- Creative and powerful communicator.
- Lifelong learner who converts passionate interests into successful businesses.

EDUCATION

M.A., Arts Administration, University of Georgia, Atlanta
M.B.A., Marketing, Haas School of Business, University of California, Berkeley

ARTS MANAGEMENT EXPERIENCE

- Doubled the state portion of the budget with the creation and support of 50 community-based arts agencies; wrote 10 grants that brought in $400,000. (National Foundation for the Arts)
- Raised program's profile significantly with coverage in music publications. (Southeast Performing Arts Program)
- Instrumental in formulating orchestra's vision, market positioning, and strategies to identify and reach target audiences. (Georgia Orchestra)
- Mentored fundraising staff in the following areas: cold calling, direct mail, and event production. (Atlanta Women's Chorus)
- Manage a used classical record business for collectors. (personal business)

WORK HISTORY

1999-2006 Manager, Manchester Hotel, Atlanta, GA
1998 Administrative Director, Atlanta Women's Chorus, Atlanta, GA

Previous Relevant Experience
1 year Project Director, Southeast Performing Arts Program
1 year Facilitator, National Foundation for the Arts
2 years Director, Georgia Arts Commission
2 years Coordinator, Georgia Orchestra

Eunice Graves

123 Emerson Street • Gary, IN 12345 • (123) 555-5555 • eunicegraves@bamboo.com

OBJECTIVE

Director of a Nonprofit Organization serving the homeless and disadvantaged

PROFILE

- Seasoned professional who understands the dynamics of nonprofit culture.
- Creative visionary who brings ideas to fruition.
- An extraordinary ability to build close-knit teams and elicit loyalty.
- Committed to improving the lives of children, families, and communities.

EXPERIENCE

INSIDE, Gary, IN 2001-present
An organization dedicated to providing shelter and job training to the homeless
Assistant Director

- Recruited diverse team and cultivated collaboration through numerous team-building projects.
- Instituted training and programs that achieved measurable improvement in job placement for clients.
- Researched and recommended specific vendors for improved facilities management, resulting in reduced costs and more efficient operations.

KELLY'S, Indianapolis, IN 1996-01
A nonprofit retail outlet selling used items to raise funds for its parent nonprofit organization
Program Manager

- Consistently developed successful programs within strict deadlines and budgets.
- Maintained daily contact with volunteer sales associates to communicate goals, measure progress, and maximize performance.

HAVE A HEART, Indianapolis, IN 1993-96
The city's only animal shelter with a no-euthanize policy
Program Coordinator

- Trained up to 15 volunteers in the safe and humane care of dogs and cats, some of which were housed in the shelter for as long as 18 months before being adopted.
- Implemented and monitored a puppy training program that encouraged teens to be volunteer trainers once a week.

Prior relevant experience:
ELDERCARE, Gary, IN
A senior center for low-income citizens
Recreation Facilitator

- Gained understanding of the great need for nonprofit organizations that support our society's disadvantaged elderly.

EDUCATION

Humanities
St. John Fisher College, Rochester, NY

SYLVIA E. FARLOW

123 Green Street, NW • Honolulu, HI 12345 • (123) 555-1234 • sefarlow@bamboo.com

OBJECTIVE

A Management position within a nonprofit organization, with a focus on team building and community relations

SUMMARY OF QUALIFICATIONS

- Fourteen years' experience providing leadership in managing diverse programs and teams, collaborating with government, community organizations, businesses, and private citizens.
- A skilled strategic thinker, able to plan and implement programs that achieve organizational objectives.
- Focused, organized, and direct. An articulate and persuasive communicator able to reach individuals and groups from all backgrounds, constituencies, and organizational levels.
- A dynamic team leader and mentor, able to accurately assess candidates, match individuals with specific positions, and motivate team members to work cohesively and fulfill overall goals.

PROFESSIONAL EXPERIENCE

1992-pres. **CITY OF HONOLULU**, Honolulu, HI

Deputy City Manager / Director of Administrative Services — *2002-pres.*
Assistant City Manager — *1997-02*
Administrative Assistant to the City Manager — *1992-97*

Team Building / Personnel Management

- As Personnel Director, hired, trained, and mentored employees for diverse positions, utilizing a direct approach to address issues specific to each team member's needs.
- Supervised staff development, including salary negotiations, labor relations, Workers' Compensation incident review, grant writing, and safety/ergonomics.
- Initiated successful personnel programs, including an employee newsletter, wellness programs, an online job application, and financial counseling.
- Conducted Comprehensive Classification/Compensation Study: Met with staff and negotiation team, recommending salary adjustments based on results.
- Co-chaired the Employee Action Committee to address staff concerns and improve customer service, actively engaging team members in program recommendations and problem solving.
- Performed an internal survey of all city employees to address and improve Purchasing Department functions. Implemented changes based on survey data.
- Developed in-house, self-paced computer training for staff, and coordinated workshops in meeting facilitation, safety and ergonomics, and career building.
- Rewrote the comprehensive manual of rules, regulations, and procedures for all city employees, to improve clarity, consistency, and effectiveness.

-continued-

Community Relations

- Received award for the development and coordination of a collaborative, 10-month Leadership Program to engage business, government, and community leaders in discussion and debate regarding issues critical to Honolulu County.
- Managed daily operations of Honolulu Career Works, a joint effort between the city, county, and statewide agencies, providing job search, training, computer skills, and other services to job seekers.
- Created online availability of the City's Municipal Code for citizens and internal staff, including search capacities for specific needs.

Program Management / Operations

- Established and directed the Environmental Affairs Division and managed operations of Technology, Personnel, Housing Authority, Community Development Block Grants, Housing Rehabilitation Loans, Workers' Compensation, Insurance, and Purchasing.
- As Director of the Honolulu Housing Authority, managed an 11-member staff, created an internal accounting function and administered a $5M annual budget, and developed a strict Administrative Plan that carefully screened candidates for eligibility and improved the program's credibility.
- Coordinated with disparate entities and constituencies, including the Housing Authority, the Department of Public Health, the Community Block Grant Program, and statewide agencies, to develop an effective lead prevention program.
- Initiated and oversaw the first-ever transition from the county to state retirement system, acting as primary negotiator and liaison between parties.
- Directed team in development, implementation, and maintenance of new website, despite extremely limited funding and personnel resources.

Previous experience includes: **Legal Extern** for the Honolulu County Public Defender, and **Patient Rights Advocate** for Honolulu County Mental Health, Honolulu, HI.

PROFESSIONAL & COMMUNITY AFFILIATIONS

Elected President of Community Services Department, League of Hawaiian Cities
Chair, Honolulu County Leadership Program, Honolulu County
Board of Directors, Junior Achievement, Honolulu City College, Honolulu, HI
Staff Liaison, Community Advisory Commission, City of Honolulu

EDUCATION

J.D., University of California, Davis, CA

A.B., University of California, Berkeley, CA

Lionel Lamberdini

123 Frost Street • Piedmont, NJ 12345 • 123-555-1234 • lionell@bamboo.com

JOB OBJECTIVE

An administrative management position in a nonprofit organization.

SUMMARY OF QUALIFICATIONS

- Master of Nonprofit Administration with honors, June 2006.
- Five years' nonprofit experience and over ten years in business management.
- Strategic thinker with a strong development orientation; able to identify and achieve priorities.
- Natural gift for networking, collaboration, and bridging class and culture.

RELEVANT ACCOMPLISHMENTS

2003-06 **LifeInTheWild** (wildlife rehabilitation clinic), Piedmont, NJ

PROJECT CONSULTANT, 2004-06

- Created a management information system for development department, utilizing Funder's Edge database, which included:
  - Constituent identification and management
  - Problem and cost identification
  - Information flow, maintenance, and security procedures
  - Employee training
- Conducted a marketing audit and review, evaluating the organization's marketing opportunities, including recommendations to the board.

VOLUNTEER COORDINATOR, 2003-04

- Coordinated 400 volunteers, collaboratively wrote volunteer policy manual, created docent education program, recruited and trained volunteers, and streamlined volunteer training system as a popular coordinator with the tongue-in-cheek nickname, "Toughy the Volunteer Slayer."

2004-05 DEVELOPMENT ASSOCIATE, **Camden Primary & Middle School,** Camden, NJ

- Created much-needed annual giving plan, including case statement, readiness goals, gift chart, action plans, and implementation calendar.
- Organized and maintained Funder's Edge database, and configured advanced options for expansion coinciding with the organization's needs.
- Served as liaison between board and both parent and volunteer groups, identifying prospects for major donor campaign, and providing information about best practices in nonprofit operations and management.
- Assisted with annual auction and provided right-hand support to interim development director.

- Continued -

Lionel Lamberdini
Page Two

2004 ADVISORY COMMITTEE MEMBER, **Online Nonprofit Network,** Camden, NJ

- Created analysis and action plans for strategic planning, ED recruitment, and board development to assist a new nonprofit aiming to make digital technology available to all segments of society.

1999-05 **Tradeshow Exhibits,** Piedmont, NJ
MANAGEMENT CONSULTANT, 2003-05

- Ensured full, smooth leadership transition.

OPERATIONS MANAGER, 1999-03

- Managed daily operations and up to 30 employees to build trade show booth company from $500K to $1.25M annually.
- Forged strong working relationships with clients and staff, coordinated complex scheduling and events, oversaw major projects, analyzed financial data, managed budgets, identified goals, and allocated tasks to accomplish them.
- Established efficient infrastructure for accounting, project management, and HR, including policies, manuals, data tracking, and computer systems.
- Passed audits with flying colors and reduced Workers' Compensation costs by 45% through safety programs and renegotiated insurance agreements.

1993-99 OPERATIONS MANAGER, **Auction International Inc.,** Medford, NJ

- Led staff of 20 in three offices to package and ship art and antiques valued at up to $6M to international locations in collaboration with premier auction houses.
- Coordinated complex timelines and resolved innumerable logistics, insurance, and security issues under rigid time constraints.
- Skillfully built trust and personal rapport with VIP clients, establishing reputation for expertise in handling every type of personality with proactive implementation of their very specific requirements and deadlines.

Previously: SPECIAL EVENT COORDINATOR, **New Jersey League of Conservation Voters**
FUNDRAISER, **New Jersey League of Conservation Voters**
INTERN, **Friends of the Planet**

EDUCATION & TRAINING

Master of Nonprofit Administration, University of New Jersey, Camden, NJ
Fundraising & Management Certifications, Onward Progress, Camden, NJ
Bachelor of Arts, Political Science, University of New York, New York, NY

AFFILIATIONS

Association of Grant Writers
Association for Nonprofit Organizations and Volunteerism

PEARL SANCHEZ

123 Larkspur Avenue, #111 • San Francisco, CA 12345
(123) 555-1234 • pearls@bamboo.com

OBJECTIVE

Arts Program Associate
focusing on youth and community outreach and program development

SUMMARY OF QUALIFICATIONS

- A visual artist with more than 5 years' experience working with youth, educational, and community groups in arts programming.
- An enthusiastic and personable communicator, skilled in delivering creative presentations and developing positive relationships with students, artists, clients, and colleagues from diverse backgrounds and interests.
- An organized and resourceful team leader, able to prioritize effectively, motivate team members, and follow through to ensure on-time project completion.
- Dedicated to providing arts access and education to youth and communities, with a comprehensive knowledge of local artists, art and community organizations, exhibition spaces, and resources.
- Proficient in MS Word, Excel, Outlook, PhotoShop, database programs, and Internet applications.

PROFESSIONAL EXPERIENCE

2004-pres. **MENLO COLLEGE OF ARTS & CRAFTS**, Menlo Park, CA
Recruitment Counselor

- Developed recruitment strategies and cultivated relationships with Bay Area high schools, community colleges, and agencies to identify and recruit students for admission. Sponsored Portfolio Days to attract out-of-state candidates.
- Assisted Director of Admissions with coordination and management of the Ambassador Program and the Pre-College Program:
  - Coached student participants in telemarketing methods.
  - Trained Administrative Assistant in database, FAQs, and school policies.
- Designed and delivered dynamic multimedia presentations on art, artists, and career opportunities in the visual arts at diverse locations throughout the Bay Area and nationwide.
- Met individually with high school and community college students, answering questions and providing guidance about furthering their educational goals.
- Reviewed hundreds of portfolios and provided feedback to students to enhance their opportunities for admission into arts schools. Assessed artwork and applications; determined admissibility for each student.
- Counseled students on applications and financial aid process, following through to completion and satisfaction.
- Conducted informative school tours for prospective students and their families, artists, and industry leaders.

-continued-

PEARL SANCHEZ
PAGE TWO

2002-04 **CITY COLLEGE OF SAN FRANCISCO,** San Francisco, CA
Admissions Representative

- Recruited visual artists into B.F.A., Extension Education, and Young Artist Programs through exciting presentations at schools and individual counseling with prospective students.
- As member of Scholarship Committee, evaluated applications and portfolios to determine eligibility and amount of award.
- Built excellent relationships with faculty, students, and administrators at target schools.
- Coordinated and managed special marketing events, including Open Houses and Portfolio Days.

2000-02 **SAN FRANCISCO MUSEUM OF MODERN ART,** San Francisco, CA
Gallery Technician / Registration Assistant

- Assisted Gallery Director and staff with sales and rentals, show installations, and fostering positive relationships with Bay Area visual artists.
- Coordinated installation of monthly shows, working closely with artists to ensure proper handling and placement of pieces.
- Maintained and updated extensive database for use in promotional mailings.
- Developed visual database of SFMOMA's permanent collection, including scanning, cataloguing, color correcting, and balancing of visual images.

2000-02 **INDEPENDENT INSTALLATION TECHNICIAN,** San Francisco, CA
(concurrent)

- Collaborated with local artists in writing a successful grant for Art In Public Spaces, resulting in funding for the following projects:
  - ***GoGirl:*** Worked with Bay Area teenage girls at established community organizations to create original poster "Art in Transit" displays in Market Street kiosks.
  - ***Susan B. Anthony High School:*** Worked with high school students in creating stop motion animation films and xerography books.
- Managed installation and de-installation of "New from Old," a large traveling exhibition of visual art and art objects on recycled art at the Oakland Museum of California.
- Supervised installation of group shows of local artists at the Walnut Creek Community Gallery, fielding calls and responding to inquiries about the gallery, shows, and artists.

Additional experience includes: **Graphics & Print Production Intern,** NYC Press, New York, NY; and **Recruiter,** Women's Health Program, SUNY, Ithaca, NY.

EDUCATION

B.F.A., School of the Art Institute of Chicago

Loretta King
123 Main Street
Westfield, NH 12345
(123) 555-8888
lking55@bamboo.com

OBJECTIVE: Career Center Director

HIGHLIGHTS

- Twelve years' experience as director of a college career center
- Counseled hundreds of students in all aspects of career development
- Sensitive and caring career counselor who believes in the value of change as a means of personal growth

PROFESSIONAL EXPERIENCE

1994-present Director of Career Development and Placement
COLLEGE OF LAMONT, Westfield, NH
Directed all aspects of the college's career development center

Administration

- Created and implemented on-campus recruiting program. Tripled the number of students interviewing with companies.
- Increased use of career center by 50% in the first two years.
- Partnered with Wheels Rent-a-Car to sponsor "Lunch with a CEO" and developed paid internships for students.
- Scheduled and staffed 12 units of career development courses a year.
- Developed and administered budget.

Counseling and Teaching

- Counseled students and alumni at all academic levels and from a wide variety of backgrounds.
- In academic undergraduate and graduate classes, made numerous presentations on all aspects of career development.
- Created and taught a class (for credit): "Career Strategies for the Working Professional."

EDUCATION

M.A., Career Development, University of New Hampshire, Durham, N.H.
Member, Eastern Association of Colleges and Employers

JAMES CARPENTER
123 Bank Street
Hartford, CT 12345
(123) 555-5555
jamescarpenter@bamboo.com

Public Relations Professional

PROFILE

- More than 10 years of outstanding public relations experience.
- Straightforward and persuasive communicator; able to tailor approach to meet the needs of specific audiences.
- Highly motivated and self-directed; able to work independently and as part of a team to achieve organizational goals.

EXPERIENCE

2000-06 **Sierra Country Club, West Hartford, CT**
Public Relations Manager

- Acted as spokesperson on radio and television programs to promote the Club's annual charitable ball.
- Planned and coordinated numerous public relations events, resulting in a significant increase in membership.
- Wrote and persuasively presented proposal to collaborate with Windsor Golf Club in putting on a golf tournament, which resulted in more than twice the publicity of previous tournaments.
- Acted as liaison between departments, working closely with staff to meet organizational goals.

1995-00 **ACT Agency, Meriden, CT**
Public Relations Specialist

- Managed publicity campaigns for more than 30 clients a year.
- Established a strong client base by maintaining superior client-focused service.
- Met regularly with team to discuss concerns and develop solutions for specific client needs.

1993-95 **Quigley Office Products, Danbury, CT**
Marketing Representative

- Worked closely with sales department to develop marketing materials for new products.
- Collaborated with tradeshow committee members to plan and produce marketing events such as welcome receptions and VIP parties.

Previous Stellar Communications, Danbury, CT, Sales/Marketing Representative

EDUCATION

MBA, Marketing
New York University, New York, NY

COMMUNITY SERVICE

Steering Committee Member, Freebird International, 2005-pres.
Spokesperson, Golf Clubs of America, 1999-pres.

Taylor Dawkins
123 Plymouth Avenue • Dover, NH 12345
123-555-5555 • tdawkins@bamboo.com

OBJECTIVE

A position in a Public Relations Agency

SUMMARY

- Experience working in a Public Relations Agency with a diverse client base.
- Personable and open-minded; able to communicate complex ideas in clear language.
- Adept at responding to changing priorities in fast-paced environments.

SELECTED ACHIEVEMENTS

- Collaborated with cross-functional team members to design publicity campaigns for approximately 20 clients a quarter. (Wheeler Communications Group)
- Helped negotiate a contract with a key corporate client, resulting in dramatic increases in revenues. (Creative Concepts, Inc.)
- Developed press releases for a new client; supervisor said she had never heard so much praise from a client. (Randolph & Hurst, Inc.)
- Frequently selected to write client proposals because of my clear, concise writing style and ability to simplify complex details. (Grinnell Corporation)
- Updated and maintained client database, and completely re-organized hardcopy files to allow quick access by entire sales team. (Blackford Marketing Group)

WORK HISTORY

2005-pres.	Administrative (contractual), Dover, NH	
		Wheeler Communications Group
		Creative Concepts, Inc.
		Randolph & Hurst, Inc.
2001-05	P.R. Specialist	Grinnell Corporation
1999-00	Sales Support	Blackford Marketing Group, Preston, NH

EDUCATION

1998 B.A., English, Beckford College, Ambrose, NH

LOUISE TURNER

123 Bryant Street #A • New York, NY 12345 • (123) 555-1234 • louiseturner@bamboo.com

OBJECTIVE: A position in Public Relations / Marketing

QUALIFICATIONS

- A creative and hard-working professional with 3+ years experience in Marketing, Event Coordination, and Public Relations.
- Able to prioritize effectively, consistently achieving project completion while maintaining a professional manner under tight deadlines.
- Strong writing, editing, and presentation skills. Able to work with clients, vendors, and media representatives to ascertain and translate needs into action.
- Knowledge of MS Word, Excel, PageMaker, PhotoShop, and Internet.

PROFESSIONAL EXPERIENCE

2003-pres. **THE NEW YOU, INC.,** New York, NY *Marketing Coordinator*

- Wrote newsletters and press releases to vendors and fashion, beauty, and lifestyle magazines, to introduce The New You line and new products prior to launch.
- Worked closely with Product Development Manager and RKO's Product Placement Coordinator to facilitate placement of fragrance products on RKO's "Nouveau Noir."
- Conducted extensive industry research to keep current with market trends for this top wholesaler of natural skin care and fragrance products.
- Cultivated strong relationships with vendors and media representatives to ensure ongoing product coverage. Coordinated partnership with vendor to design and deliver promotional gifts for specific fundraising events.

2002-03 **FASHION INSTITUTE OF TECHNOLOGY,** New York, NY *Graduate Admissions Coordinator*

- Responded to a high volume of telephone inquiries, providing information and referrals to applicants and prospective students.
- Acted as liaison between Graduate Art and Design departments, reviewing and organizing hundreds of portfolios for the Admissions Review Committee.

1999-01 **METROPOLITAN MUSEUM OF ART, N**ew York, NY *Library Assistant*

- Provided consistent telephone follow-up with magazine and book publishers, advised employees and vendors, and maintained library database.

1997-99 **BERGDORF GOODMAN, N**ew York, NY *Sales Associate, Designer Department*

- Top Salesperson in department. Maintained client book, informed clients of new product offerings, and provided exemplary customer service.

Additional experience includes: Event Planning/Coordination for private New York clients.

EDUCATION

M.A., Art History, Columbia University, New York, NY, 1997
B.A., English Literature, University of California, Berkeley, CA, 1993

FRED HERRINGTON

123 Everett Heights Street • Bismarck, ND 12345 • (123) 555-1234 • fredh@bamboo.com

PUBLIC RELATIONS PROFESSIONAL

SUMMARY OF QUALIFICATIONS

- More than five years' experience developing and executing bold and innovative public relations and marketing communications strategies and tactics that achieve results for consumer, corporate, and technology companies.
- Skilled in building positive relationships with senior executives, media, analysts, clients, customers, outside agencies, and internal team members.
- A direct and articulate writer and communicator, able to present and synthesize complex material into cogent marketing messages for diverse audiences.
- Strong technical background, with the ability to translate technical information for nontechnical groups.

PROFESSIONAL EXPERIENCE

2006 **PUBLIC RELATIONS MANAGER**

YouKnowWho, Bismarck, ND

Providing technology and services for telecommunications carriers worldwide.

- Directed all public relations efforts to drive awareness and build brand identity with targeted audiences. Developed new corporate messaging, positioning, and tagline for U.S. and European markets.
- Hired and supervised outside consultants in the U.S. and Europe: Developed strategies for market entry and delegated tasks to achieve on-time completion.
- Cultivated relationships with media, analysts, and other influencers, including *The Wall Street Journal, Forbes, Fortune,* and *The New York Times.*
- Wrote press releases for new products and strategic partnerships, data sheets, FAQs, and marketing materials.
- Researched trade shows and secured speaking engagements for CEO at top industry events. Supported trade shows and sales presentations.

2005 **PUBLIC RELATIONS / MARKETING CONSULTANT**

Enrich Corporation, Bismarck, ND

Marketing/Advertising targeting online financial banking customers.

GoHunt, Inc., Bismarck, ND

- Developed corporate identity, messaging, and positioning, managing internal staff and outside Public Relations and Design agencies. Wrote press releases.
- Researched market segments, conducted competitive analysis, and developed launch strategy based on results. Managed marketing budget of $1,000,000.
- Built media and analyst relations; coordinated press/analyst tours, meetings and TV/radio opportunities prior to and during company launch. Secured over 10 speaking engagements for CEOs.
- Collaborated with customers and partners to build case studies, generating testimonials for placement in targeted publications.
- Company partnered with several top 10 U.S. banks.

-continued-

FRED HERRINGTON
PAGE TWO

2002-2005 **SENIOR ACCOUNT EXECUTIVE**
Looking Forward, Inc., South Bismarck, ND

- Led multiple Public Relations teams of up to seven members each and managed budgets of $2,000,000 in implementing aggressive high-tech PR campaigns for public and pre-IPO companies.
- Launched over 10 companies and more than 50 products and services.
- A partial list of clients includes:

Pacific Bell	**AOL**	**Cisco**
Intel	**Microsoft**	**IBM**

- Consulted with clients to assess needs and led process in developing long-term strategic plans and tactics, including company positioning and messaging.
- Created programs to dramatically increase visibility and build relationships with analysts and media.
- Wrote backgrounders, FAQs, press releases, case studies, and other collateral.
- Managed speaker placement process, including placement at *PC Forum, DEMO, Businessweek,* and *Forbes.*
- Facilitated weekly meetings to discuss issues and monitor progress for each campaign/project.
- Developed new business through extensive market research and excellent relationships with key industry contacts.

2001-2002 **ASSISTANT ACCOUNT EXECUTIVE**
Heines and Filbert, Los Angeles, CA

- Developed and executed media relations plans for this worldwide PR agency.
- Wrote and edited public relations materials and prepared reports.
- Clients included: Copy Mat, Chrysler, and biotech companies.

Additional experience includes:
Public Relations Assistant, Boulder Museum, Boulder, CO
Public Relations Consulting for private clients

EDUCATION

J.D., Dean's List, Syracuse University School of Law, Syracuse, NY, 2002

M.A., Public Relations
Syracuse University S.I. Newhouse School of Public Communications, 2002

B.A., History, Jackson University, Jackson, MI, 1999

Lettie Perkins

123 Commons Drive
Sarasota, FL 12345

(123) 555-5555
lperkins35@bamboo.com

SALES PROFESSIONAL

Highlights of Qualifications

- Successful sales professional with a history of making positive change.
- A persuasive communicator with a gift for tact and diplomacy, sense of humor, and a good memory.
- Highly organized and enthusiastic; able to prioritize effectively and reach sales goals under pressure.

Professional Achievements

2005-pres. **Contempo Furniture Company, Sarasota, FL**
Sales Associate

- Consistently achieved sales objectives by attending closely to customer needs and developing personable relationships with them, which generated repeat business.
- Worked with entire retail sales team to develop a friendly, service-oriented atmosphere on the floor.
- Received "Employee of the Year" for 2005.

2003-05 **Woods Home Decor, Inc., Tampa, FL**
Sales Representative

- Received annual Sales Award for achieving highest net sales in 2004.
- Trained new sales team members on effective closing techniques and client protocol.

Concurrent with education:
2002-03 **HomeHelpers USA, Tampa, FL**
Fundraiser

- Conducted weekly phone solicitations to raise more than $2,000 a month for this nonprofit that relies entirely on donations for its financial support.
- Wrote persuasive direct mail pieces, clearly expressing the organization's services and financial needs.

Education

A.A., 2003
University of Tampa, Tampa, FL

Personal Pursuits

Team sports such as volleyball, basketball, and soccer
Individual challenges such as rock climbing and triathlons

Page 1 of 1

TINA R. GELB

123 5th Street, San Francisco, CA 12345 (123) 555-1234 tgelb@bamboo.com

OBJECTIVE: A sales position within the high-tech industry

PROFILE

- Eight years' experience as a consistently top-ranked sales professional, known for the ability to quickly acquire new product knowledge.
- Highly skilled in developing excellent relationships with key decision makers and business partners to support overall sales and marketing objectives.
- Computer skills include: MS Word, Excel, PowerPoint, Internet, and customized software applications.

SELECTED ACCOMPLISHMENTS

Sales & Marketing

Major Markets

- Designed and implemented comprehensive business plan: Developed sales projections, conducted detailed market analyses, and determined optimal sales tools to achieve plan goals. Managed $2.3MM territory.
- Promoted to district product co-champion for EverGuard, based on product knowledge and sales results. Ranked in the top 10% in the nation for EverGuard sales.
- Attended national and international industry trade shows: Set up booth displays, promoted company products, and generated a high volume of sales leads.

Premium Growth

- Managed $1.8MM territory. Promoted to Territory Specialist within two years due to excellent sales performance.
- As one of the top six national sales representatives, selected to act as liaison between sales staff, management, and outside marketing consultants in the development and implementation of a new product launch.

Business Development & Client Relations

Major Markets

- Established and maintained strong, collaborative relationships with world-renowned research leaders:
  - Discussed up-to-the-moment changes in new product development.
  - Facilitated promotional events and speaking engagements for industry experts.

Premium Growth

- Built a loyal client base by providing consistent support and product information.
- Conducted informative lectures and demonstrations, and facilitated hands-on training seminars for clients on new products and methodologies.

WORK HISTORY

2003-pres. **Sales Representative**
MAJOR MARKETS PHARMACEUTICALS, San Francisco/Peninsula Territory

1996-03 **Sales Representative**
PREMIUM GROWTH LABORATORIES, San Francisco Territory

1992-96 **Assistant Buyer / Manager, Apparel Department**
MACY'S, INC., Portland, OR

EDUCATION

B.S., Business Administration with a concentration in Marketing
Oregon State University, Portland, OR, 1991

Cynthia Lau

123 Lesson Blvd.
Napsville, VA 12345

123-555-1234
cynthialau@bamboo.com

SUMMARY

- A top sales professional with 15 years in local media.
- Major strengths: new business development, product design, and client retention.
- Additional experience in sales management.
- An optimistic self-starter who mentors and leads by example.

HIGHLIGHTS

At MSN – Local

- MSN Local Presidents Award, 2005
- #1 contracts sold SE Region, 2004, 2005
- #2 percent over budget nationally, 2004
- #4 qualified sales nationally, 2004
- #21 in gross sales nationally, 2005
- Opened Atlanta and Lexington markets

At RBO – AT&T Media Service

- RBO Presidents Award, 1999
- $1,000,000 sales, 1999 – 2001
- Exceeded revenue budget, 1997 – 2001
- Won five new business contests
- Earned four promotions, 1997 – 2002
- Opened new zone office, 2001

SALES ACHIEVEMENTS

MSN.COM – LOCAL, Williamburg, VA **2003 – 2006**
Account Manager

- Generated one or more new sales per week for the first 12 weeks on the job, sparking the efforts of the sales team and lifting office morale.
- Designed vertical advertising packages that increased local sales and were adopted for use in local markets nationally.

RBO – AT&T MEDIA SERVICES, San Francisco, CA **1997 – 2003**
Local Sales Manager / Team Leader / Senior Account Executive

- Developed package template for quick and easy use, resulting in streamlined sales process.
- Created annual programs that addressed the needs of the advertiser and maintained the highest level of long-term business.

CINCINNATI TRIBUNE, Cincinnati, OH **1991 – 1997**
Account Executive – Direct Mail

- Designed several new direct mail and FSI products resulting in increased sales.
- Coordinated a network of Northern Ohio direct mail and newspapers, resulting in several long-term partnerships with large advertisers needing coverage outside the Cincinnati area.

EDUCATION

BA, Psychology and Sociology, Kent State University, Kent, OH

COMMUNITY SERVICE

Board of Directors, Napsville Chamber of Commerce, 2000 – 2003

FRANK GETTY

123 Fifth Street • San Jose, CA 12345 • (123) 555-1234 • fgetty1@bamboo.com

Sales / Marketing Professional

QUALIFICATIONS

- An experienced high-tech professional with a broad base of industry knowledge, including OEMs, channels, end users, and competitors.
- Skilled at product positioning and developing strategies for successful market penetration.
- Able to deliver dynamic sales and marketing presentations to diverse audiences.

PROFESSIONAL EXPERIENCE

2002-pres. **IBM,** San Jose, CA *Disk Drive Marketing Executive*

- Developed strategic plans based on customer needs, and trained business partners to penetrate target markets and increase market share.
- Delivered informative and convincing presentations on IBM storage strategy and business initiatives to business partners and end users.
- Coordinated and communicated daily marketing messages, promotions, and incentives to business partners and end users.

2001-02 **AMDAHL,** San Jose, CA *Storage Systems Sales*

- Collaborated with mainframe client representatives to increase mid-range storage and server revenue within targeted accounts.
- Used knowledge of competitive products to determine successful sales and marketing strategies.

1999-01 **OPTI, INC.,** San Jose, CA *Regional Sales Manager*

- Designed and implemented the Optimum Value Partner Program, which included lead generation, direct marketing, and co-marketing tools, for VARs and distributors throughout the United States and Asia Pacific.
- Coordinated business development projects, product positioning, incentives, and motivational tools for channel sales team. Built Asia Pacific sales by 50%.

1997-99 **PREMIUM MICRO,** Palo Alto, CA *District Sales Manager*

- Generated $3.2M in sales of optical storage solutions within one year.

1995-97 **SYMBOL TECHNOLOGY,** San Mateo, CA *District Sales Manager*

- Planned and coordinated bi-weekly marketing seminars to educate end users at Fortune 500 companies on aspects of the data capturing industry. Followed through to cultivate strong business relationships and to close sales.

EDUCATION & TRAINING

B.S., Marketing Communications, Yale University, New Haven, CT, 1995
Additional studies at Heidelberg University, Germany; and Imperial College, London, England
Certificate, Top Gun Storage Training, IBM

Melissa Vasquez

123 Third Street • Portland, ME 12345 • (123) 555-5555 • melvasquez@bamboo.com

CAREER OBJECTIVE

Chief Executive Officer

PROFESSIONAL PROFILE

- A hands-on entrepreneurial professional, skilled in growing new businesses and leading teams to success.
- Seven years' progressive leadership of product development and production.
- An inclusive, team-oriented manager who effectively communicates company goals to staff and leads by example.

CAREER ACCOMPLISHMENTS

PRIDE PHARMACEUTICALS, Portland, ME 2004-present

CEO and Board Member

- Recruited to create and direct this pharmaceutical firm that produced $17M in its first year.
- Grew the organization through successful recruiting and management building, achieving a 95% retention rate for direct hires.
- Developed and implemented strategic plans for successful launch and promotion of new products.
- Met daily with management team to facilitate problem solving and maintain clear channels of communication.

CRANIUM COMPUTER SALES, Bangor, ME 2002-04

General Manager

- Directed production meetings, generated forecasts, and set performance milestones to ensure accuracy and timeliness of deliverables.
- Spearheaded business development opportunities and strategic partnerships with vendors.
- Motivated staff to perform at their best and reach their goals by offering incentive programs and training seminars.

ACE MANUFACTURING COMPANY, Bangor, ME 1999-02

General Manager

- Recruited, hired, and supervised staff, providing support and leadership in individual career and overall company growth.
- Consistently exceeded goals for sales, inventory management, and productivity.

EDUCATION

MA, Business Psychology, 2003
University of Bangor, Bangor, ME

BA, Organizational Development, 1996
Nazareth College, Rochester, NY

JOSEPH THURGOOD

123 Robin Hills, Chatham, NJ 12345, 123-555-8888, jthurgood@bamboo.com

OBJECTIVE

A senior-level position in management in the wood products industry

SUMMARY OF QUALIFICATIONS

- 20+ years of experience as a leader in the wood products business, with a broad network of contacts.
- Experienced public speaker, writer, and community liaison; able to articulate complex ideas to diverse audiences and build strong relationships with corporate, academic, governmental, and nongovernmental organizations.
- Skilled furniture craftsman.

PROFESSIONAL EXPERIENCE

1976-2006 **SUSTAINABLE DESIGN,** Chatham, NJ
A high-end office furniture manufacturing company.
Chief Executive Officer

Strategic Planning & Organizational Management

- Founded and expanded business from 1 to 50 employees and from $0 to $6M in annual revenues.
- Led senior management team in the development of annual strategic business plans.
- Worked closely with graphic designer and marketing director to develop new company brand identity.
- Analyzed market research and developed new products to fill market niche, particularly in meeting the needs of the emerging "green" market.
- Coordinated team effort in design of new manufacturing facility, which supported the company's aesthetic and environmental brand identity.

Marketing & Public Relations

- Developed and presented hundreds of multimedia training seminars on environmental and technical issues related to forestry and wood products.
- Established strategic alliances within the industry as well as with international environmental organizations, governmental agencies, and academic institutions.
- Authored magazine articles, newsletters, press releases, training materials, brochures, advertising copy, and web content.

-continued-

JOSEPH THURGOOD
PAGE TWO

- Frequent lecturer at schools and architecture firms on sustainable forestry issues.
- Acted as community liaison and spokesperson on social and environmental issues integral to the company's mission.
- Collaborated with design team to develop marketing materials for company capabilities and new products, including photography, brochures, and website.
- Interviewed by and published in *New York Magazine* and numerous trade publications.
- Initiated the "1/2% for the Forest" program, in which the company donated 1/2% of all revenues to organizations working to promote sustainable forestry.

PROFESSIONAL DEVELOPMENT

Kent State University, Kent, OH, 1972-1974

Training in Team-Based Management, Leadership, Financial Analysis & Management, Millwork Estimating, and Project Management.

Traveled extensively to investigate forestry practices in North America, South America, Europe, Australia, and Asia.

BOARD AFFILIATIONS

- Architectural Woodwork Institute
- Certified Forest Products Council – Board Chair
- Certified Wood and Paper Association
- Good Wood Alliance
- Forest Mountain Watch – Treasurer & Legal Liaison
- Tropical Forest Foundation

Maria Sedgewick

123 Parting Way Westchester, NY 12345 123-555-1234 msedgewick@bamboo.com

Information Technology Executive

Summary

- More than 25 years of IT experience, including 20 years of management experience.
- Developed and implemented IT systems and applications on a wide range of platforms.
- Strong leadership, communication, and presentation skills.
- Selected twice as one of the "Inner Circle" of top leaders in AccountBase.

Professional Experience

eTECHS, London, England

President – U.S. Operations **2005-present**

Spearheaded the U.S. start-up of this e-commerce consulting business.

- Created the B2B operational structure, including sales and delivery in the United States.

AccountBase, New York, NY

Account Executive for Major Communications Client **2004**

Managed a team of 400 AccountBase employees that provided benefits administration to the 200,000 employees of the client, including applications, data center, and call desk.

- Assumed control over an account in trouble, turned around a dispirited employee team, and increased the employee morale based on AccountBase Employee Satisfaction Index.

Account Executive for Food Retail Client **2002-2004**

Managed a team of 150 AccountBase employees that provided full outsourced Information Technology services to the client, including data center, applications, wireless WAN, and help desk.

- Took over an account that had lost 40% of its personnel the previous year, rebuilt the team, reduced turnover to 15%, and dramatically increased employee morale based on AccountBase Employee Satisfaction Index.
- Met or exceeded revenue and profit targets.
- Renegotiated the contract to expand business and revenue.
- Provided excellent customer service and received a 6 out of a possible 7 on the AccountBase Customer Service Index for this client.
- Created the vision and plan for this account and then taught the planning techniques used at the AccountBase Leadership Training Program.
- Communicated with the client by conducting regular briefings for the executives, and by creating end-of-year summary documents detailing all accomplishments for the year.
- Created CRM system for the client with shopping cards, tailored marketing, and data warehouse analysis to increase customer loyalty.

Account Manager for Food Manufacturing Client **1999-2001**

Managed a team of 100 AccountBase employees that provided outsourced Information Technology services to the client, including data center, network, desktop, help desk, and applications.

- Helped grow revenue from $10M to $45M in 18 months for a new division by leading this flagship account, creating a referenceable client, providing pre-sales and post-sales support, and training and providing leaders for new accounts.
- Met or exceeded revenue and profit targets on the flagship account.
- Established the most referenced client out of 8,000 AccountBase clients.

Continued

Maria Sedgewick
Page 2

- Created Continuous Replenishment Process, which allowed the client's customers to reduce inventory by 50% and reduce stock outs from 3% to less than 1%.
- Dramatically decreased response time by implementing a Frame Relay Network.
- Enabled the client to close remote sales offices and improve productivity by implementing a Sales Office Automation System.
- Created Internet Promotion Planning and Tracking system, which allowed the client to reduce Promotion spending by more effectively using every promotion dollar.
- Developed the account personnel and provided opportunities for advancement on other accounts for the account leaders.

Manager, Database and Technology for Food Client 1997-1999

- Created comprehensive technology strategy that matched the business plan, and implemented Frame Relay network, Mainframe and Unix databases, CASE, and desktop tools.
- Provided 24/7 database support, data warehouse, and Enterprise Application Integration.

KRAFT FOODS, San Francisco, CA
Manager, Database and Technology 1991-1997

Managed the Database Team, with responsibility for Database, Data Warehouse, CASE Administration, and General Technology Direction.

- Wrote and implemented software and processes to streamline the Supra Database administration.
- Implemented the Kraft Data Warehouse, which enabled business people to write queries against the Kraft data, allowing quicker access to data and freeing up IT resources.
- Installed DB2 and implemented the first production system.

Sedgewick Consulting, Inc., Philadelphia, PA
Consultant and CEO 1982-1991

Started and ran a successful consulting business. Consulted with mostly Fortune 500 companies in project management, structured methodologies, applications systems development, and database administration.

- Marketed and sold new engagements and grew the business each year.
- Created a steady stream of repeat business by providing excellent customer service.
- Managed a project for an oil company to implement new technology and rewrite all on-line systems.
- Resolved a major customer issue for a database software company by resolving problems, writing utilities, and providing service to their customer.
- Prepared and presented a training program for a manufacturing company on project methodology and structured techniques to increase productivity of new employees.
- Presented a seminar for DataPro entitled "Recruiting, Training, and Motivating IT Personnel."

Education and Training

B.A., Duke University, Durham, NC, summa cum laude
Graduate Studies, Duke University, Durham, NC
Leadership Training Program, AccountBase
Technical Courses in the areas of Network, Database, Internet technologies, and Desktop

HENRY HAUSER

123 First Avenue #123 • Rapid City, SD 12345 • (123) 555-1234 • hhauser@bamboo.com

OBJECTIVE

A Management position in Operations

Product Management **P&L Responsibility** **Team Leadership**

SUMMARY OF QUALIFICATIONS

- A focused and energetic management professional with 10+ years of broad-ranging experience in diverse industries and a keen interest in operations and product management.
- Extensive experience in financial analysis, risk management and budgeting.
- Skilled in establishing strong, ongoing relationships with clients and co-workers at all organizational levels and cultural backgrounds. Language skills include: Spanish, Hebrew, French, Portuguese.
- A respected team leader, able to set clear goals, recruit top candidates for specific positions and foster cohesiveness in achieving results.

PROFESSIONAL EXPERIENCE

2004-2006 **ICLIMB, INC.**, Rapid City, SD

Founder and CEO

- Identified target markets and set goals for innovative online brokerage offering life insurance products.
- Secured and allocated appropriate resources for product development and management. Recruited and led experienced team of senior executives.
- Consulted with industry leaders to determine product focus and features and to generate funding for development.
- Negotiated strategic partnerships with major insurance companies and real estate brokerages.
- Supervised operations team in setting goals and reaching budget objectives.

2002-2004 **HIGHTRAIN ENTERPRISES**, Atlanta, GA & San Juan, PR

Vice President of Corporate Development

- Opened and operated San Juan office during initial phase of industrial manufacturing project.
- Negotiated with financing sources and participated in development decisions for a $100M high-end office complex.
- Hired and supervised management company in the development of a championship golf course, including planning, construction and alignment of goals to meet bottom-line objectives.
- Developed business plan, financial goals and corporate support structure; negotiated franchise agreement with national restaurant chain.
- Conducted financial analyses for each project and developed appropriate metrics to set goals, evaluate results and ensure budgetary accuracy.

-continued-

HENRY HAUSER
PAGE TWO

PROFESSIONAL EXPERIENCE (continued)

2001 **CITYBANK BOSTON,** Philadelphia, PA, & Mexico City, Mexico
Investment Banking Summer Associate

- Created complex financial model to project costs and financial returns for a $400M toll road in Mexico.

1999-2000 **HERRINGTON MEXICO,** Mexico City, Mexico
Investment Banking Analyst

- Collaborated with cross-functional team to develop a creative financing mechanism to restructure $400M in non-performing assets.
- Handled highly confidential materials and projects, prepared board reports, coordinated audits and managed treasury operations.
- Advised Mexican manufacturing company in its sale to a U.S. firm.

1998 **CASA DE RAMOS,** Mexico City, Mexico
Manager of International Affairs, Office of the Chairman

- Contacted potential investors and coordinated due diligence in the successful sale of the company to a U.S. financial institution in the company's first post-NAFTA transaction in Mexico.

1995-1998 **INTERNATIONAL BANK OF TRUST,** Los Angeles, CA
Financial Analyst / Internal Auditor

EDUCATION

Harvard Business School, Cambridge, MA, 2002
M.B.A., Certificate in Global Management
Winner of 2002 NAIOP Real Estate Challenge

Hebrew University of Jerusalem, Jerusalem, Israel, 1998
Visiting Graduate Student in Economics

University of California, Berkeley, 1997
B.A., Economics, Phi Beta Kappa, Cum Laude
Minors in Biology, Chemistry, Judaic Studies

Lorene Lincoln

123 Primary Lane • South Hampton, NH 12345 • 123-555-1234 • llincoln@bamboo.com

JOB OBJECTIVE

Executive Manager or Director of Major Business Projects/Initiatives.

SUMMARY OF QUALIFICATIONS

- Twelve years of progressive leadership of major business projects.
- Exceptional team management in critical collaborative contexts.
- Robust record of success in achieving complex objectives and timelines.
- Dynamic, articulate, analytical, and results-oriented; I love a good challenge.

PROFESSIONAL EXPERIENCE

1999-pres. Home Entertainment Solutions, Boston, MA

Director, Project Management Department, 2003-pres.
Led multimillion-dollar business initiatives and created a highly effective new department including an intranet and training program; dramatically reduced time to market with a new project management process.

- Planned and launched distribution in 4,000 retail stores in 60 days.
    - Selected and led cross-functional team from 16 departments, and served as point person, ensuring high levels of synergy between companies.
    - Established and attained detailed action plan, milestones, and timelines, and created efficient documentation system available to all involved via intranet.
    - Ensured installation of 4,000 in-store kiosks and live demo units on tight time schedule.
    - Won internal support with inspiring presentation of objectives and benefits.
    - Resolved countless questions daily, weighing costs and benefits, creating solutions, and consulting with others; provided weekly executive updates.
- Wrote and persuasively presented proposal to executive team, and directed initiative for a major e-Business program projected to save $20M per year.
    - Created online functionality in troubleshooting, ordering, account activation, installation scheduling, and bill payment, updating to an entertainment theme with new hosting and content management.
- Oversaw development, beta, and launch of three new products with other companies, including a digital video recording product and the largest interactive television platform in the U.S. with over 3 million customers.
- Managed $1.5B partnership with MSN, implemented acquisition and integration of Broadwide (a broadband service).

Senior Project Manager, Media Company Acquisition, 2002
Directed smooth transition planning for technically complex migration of 3 million customers following $2B acquisition, achieving high retention.

- Continued -

Lorene Lincoln, Page Two

Senior Project Manager, Media Company Acquisition, 2002

- Led steering committee of key department heads from both companies and three critical vendors to develop and implement an elaborate plan for a very risky customer migration of 100,000 customers per day for 31 days.
- Negotiated sensitive vendor agreements, and managed $30M transition budget.
- Held daily conference calls and weekly meetings to track and troubleshoot progress, frequently creating multi-layered contingency plans.
- Comprehensively evaluated business management and personnel strengths to consolidate operations, and elegantly arranged transition assignments.

Senior Project Manager, Customer Service, 2001
Launched joint technical call center handling 300,000 calls per month, consistently meeting specified performance metrics.

Project Manager, Home Entertainment Solutions Japan Launch, 2000
Selected by CFO to collaborate with five Japanese partners on enterprise start-up.

- Developed policies, procedures, and processes for all aspects of operations, including dealer approval, sales, customer support, and billing.

Senior Project Specialist, Financial Planning, 1999
Led multi-department finance team to develop support process for sales and marketing promotions, and served on vendor selection team.

- Negotiated and managed vendor contracts, and launched two employee programs.

1998-99 HEALTH INSURE CORPORATION, Boston, MA
Corporate Insurance Analyst
Managed $500M portfolio of 12 Fortune 500 clients, consistently achieving high returns.

- Led re-engineering team to dramatically improve operating efficiencies.

1994-98 FUNDCORP, INC., Chicago, IL & Detroit, MI
Senior Financial Analyst, 1996-98
Successfully managed projects such as forecasting, profitability analyses, a General Ledger upgrade, and five-year strategic planning.

- Reconciled $3M inventory, evaluated capital spending, and implemented inventory process controls program that increased warehouse efficiencies by over 20%.

Financial Analyst, FundCorp Financial Development Program, 1994-96
Selected for financial management training program, managed budgets of $10M, consolidated financial plans for 15 facilities, and assisted with special projects.

EDUCATION

B.S., Business Administration, 1994, Loyola University, Chicago, IL

GARY T. WILSON

123 Center Street, Sophia, WV 12345 (123) 555-1234 gwilson@bamboo.com

OBJECTIVE: Management Position in Healthcare Field

HIGHLIGHTS OF QUALIFICATIONS

- Highly experienced Practice Administrator and ACMPE Certified Medical Practice Executive.
- Opened Neurosurgery group; coordinated expansion of Cardiology and Neurosurgery groups.
- Proven skill in change management implementation of workflow processes and technology systems.
- Adept in all aspects of medical practice administration, organization, and supervision.
- Effective communicator, presenter, and negotiator; resourceful, perceptive decision maker.

HEALTHCARE MANAGEMENT EXPERIENCE

WEST VIRGINIA NEUROSURGERY, L.L.C., Beckley, West Virginia 2002 to present
Practice Administrator

- Accomplished opening of a Neurosurgery practice within a one-month timeframe:
  - Located and leased interim facility.
  - Set up computer systems (Electronic Medical Records, Peachtree Accounting, and Mysis practice management system), network configuration, and telephone system.
  - Planned and executed large publicity campaign for new opening.
- Coordinated office relocation, expansion, and remodeling in 2004.
- Performed buy vs. lease analysis and made recommendations for office relocation.
- Instrumental in rapid growth of practice: Patient numbers grew from 0 to 8,000 since opening in 2002 with average of 3,000 active at any one time, and $4.7M annual receipts for 2004.
- Maintained A/R collections at a high of 89% of net receipts (national average = 52%).
- Trained, oversaw, and audited staff on use of surgical claim coding, CPT, and ICD-9.
- Integral part of Human Resources function:
  - Recruited two surgeons and Nurse Practitioner, negotiated contracts, and publicized new hires.
  - Hired support staff, including over 20 management, clerical, and clinical personnel.
  - Oversaw administration of payroll processing and benefits package.
- Collaborated with hospital's Director of Neurosciences Program, Neurosciences Marketing Manager, and CEO in the development and opening of three clinics in rural Wyoming.
- Ensured and sustained low clinic overhead costs at 32% of net receipts (national average = 45%).

WEST VIRGINIA CARDIOPULMONARY SERVICES, P.C., Beckley, West Virginia 1982 to 2002
Administrator (1992 to 2002)

- Active participant in management team that developed short-range and long-range strategic plans.
- Liaison between practice and hospital, maintaining ongoing and positive relationships between physicians and hospital's executive committee.
- Steering committee member of hospital's Cardiac Program, servicing 70% of the state of Wyoming.
- Coordinated all aspects of design and construction of new office facility (9,650 sq. ft.), working directly with general contractor.
- Participated in the design of new facility's interior space and handled office relocation.

- Continued on Page 2 -

GARY T. WILSON

- Page 2 -

HEALTHCARE MANAGEMENT EXPERIENCE

Administrator (West Virginia Cardiopulmonary Services - Continued from Page 1)

- In 2001, directed construction and design of a 6,670-sq.-ft. addition to office facility.
- Planned and oversaw installation of the area's first two-story file system; then created and implemented policies and significantly improved workflow processes.
- Facilitated and implemented new processes in Total Quality Management (TQM) and Teamwork.
- Initiated and increased outreach program that grew from 0 to 14 clinics; situated, staffed, and marketed the program.
- Upgraded practice's software and communications systems:
  - Coordinated and oversaw two conversions/upgrades to Reynolds and Reynolds PAR PM system in 1992 and +Medic practice management system in 1999.
  - Involved in installation of new hardware/equipment for all computer systems.
  - Evaluated and implemented AT&T Legend telephone system and trained staff on voice mail.
  - Handled installation of Peachtree Accounting system that recorded/generated Accounts Payable, General Ledger, financial and cost accounting statements and reports, and on-demand spreadsheet analyses.
  - Initiated and coordinated upgrade to automated medical transcription system in WordPerfect with electronic signatures and electronic faxing of physician referrals.
- Supervised 18 staff members in office with RN, PA, and four cardiologists:
  - Trained staff on all new systems, processes, and procedures.
  - Taught staff CPT and ICD-9 coding.
  - Developed and implemented Human Resource policies and procedures.
  - Hired and retained new personnel; handled new physicians' contract negotiations.
- Marketed practice, physicians, and clinics to region via press releases and advertisements.

Office Manager, West Virginia Cardiopulmonary Services (1982-1992)

- Recruited, trained, and supervised up to six medical staff members as clinic grew from two cardiologists to four cardiologists and two cardiac surgeons.
- Involved in outreach clinic program, developing six new sites while improving workflow processes.
- Actively worked with programmer to customize computer system.

EDUCATION, CERTIFICATIONS & MEMBERSHIPS

Certified Medical Practice Executive - ACMPE 1999 to present

A.S., Business Management, Beckley College, WV 1992

Continuing Professional Education: 1992 to present

MGMA Med Series - Management Education & Development (160 credit hours)
MGMA, Kellogg Institute - Group Practice Governance Leadership Group (32 credit hours)
University of West Virginia, Beckley College Upper Division, WV - Business courses

Notary Public, State of West Virginia 2004 to 2007

Memberships:

American College of Medical Practice Executives (ACMPE) 1991 to present
Medical Group Management Association (MGMA) 1991 to present

BRENDA R. LINCOLN

123 Lexington Ct. • Lindsay, NV 12345 • (123) 555-1234 • blincoln@bamboo.com

OBJECTIVE

Senior Business Analyst position within a regulated environment
with a focus on the Healthcare and Pharmaceutical industries

SUMMARY OF QUALIFICATIONS

- More than 10 years' experience combining technical expertise in software development with economics background and business acumen within the healthcare field.
- Adept at building positive relationships and communicating effectively with both clients and colleagues, with particular skill in translating across technical and nontechnical arenas to ensure client understanding and satisfaction.
- Strong organizational abilities with astute attention to detail to ensure top quality in meeting client requirements; able to keep projects on track and achieve success within scope, budgets, and deadlines.
- A driven and dedicated leader and team member who takes initiative and learns new skills, systems, and processes quickly.

PROFESSIONAL EXPERIENCE

1999-pres. **RESEARCHINTENSIVE, INC.,** Lindsay, NV

Associate Director, Systems Compliance	*2002-pres.*
Associate Director, IVR Programming	*2002*
Manager, IVR Programming	*2001-02*
Manager, IVR Production Support	*2000-01*
CIS Analyst/Senior Analyst, IVR	*1999-00*

- Actively participated in Corrective Action Plan (CAP) and 21 CFR Part 11 analysis to address federal regulations related to the pharmaceutical industry.
- Initiated and conducted compliance review of all project documentation for products used by physicians in clinical trials of new pharmaceuticals.
- Worked closely with Interactive Voice Response (IVR), Data Management, and Biostatistics departments to ensure compliance with internal SOPs.
- Analyzed issues and discrepancies for each review and worked closely with team members to redefine priorities, resolve specific issues, and develop additional staff training to ensure proper compliance in the future.
- Completed eight reviews for each department per year. Wrote reports and quarterly summaries of findings for senior management.
- Directed a team of up to 16 programmers and analysts in IVR development. Created and implemented change orders for existing systems and plans for six new systems per month, including timelines, requirements, and cost estimates. Supported 50 active projects simultaneously.
- Defined and documented user requirements for internal projects. Created development, installation, and testing plans, and consistently met stringent deadlines, quality standards, and CSV requirements.

-continued-

PAGE TWO

- Oversaw Computer System Validation (CSV) efforts for in-house development and OTS software, including Inform, Captiva, Remedy, and LiveLink.
- Member, IVR Change Management Committee, 2000-present; Committee Chair, 2000-01. Worked with cross-functional committee members to ensure accuracy and completeness of all documentation prior to production.
- Member, Risk Assessment Committee, 2002-present. Reviewed RFPs and protocols for clinical trials to determine optimal approach for building a system to meet user requirements, including timelines and potential risks.
- Conducted periodic demonstrations of system functionality and proposal defense presentations to clients.
- Identified and anticipated special problems and developed recommendations for the client for specific design adjustments and improvements.
- Hired, trained, and directed team members. Conducted performance evaluations and maintained all training records.

1990-99 **HIGHHEALTH HEALTHCARE (FORMERLY HEALTH COMPUTER SYSTEMS),** Lindsay, NV

Senior Software Analyst 1996-99
Programming Supervisor 1994-96
Programmer/Analyst 1990-94

- Directed projects, trained users, and supported office management system for physicians, clinics, and healthcare facilities nationwide, including diagnosis, scheduling, billing, budgeting, accounting, reporting, and database administration.
- Developed customized software components to address the specific needs of managed care and urgent care environments.
- Tracked and maintained new software releases, installations, and revisions to ensure accuracy and consistency for 70+ diverse versions available in the field.
- Won President's Award for Outstanding Performance as Programmer/Analyst.

1988-90 **PRINCETON UNIVERSITY,** Princeton, NJ

Research Assistant, Economics Department & Business School

- Conducted extensive research for project involving both Economics and Business School Professors.
- Created computer questionnaire to assess health concerns of a diverse array of individuals in the Princeton area and beyond.
- Recruited and trained outside organization to conduct surveys to wider audiences and significantly increase participation in the project.
- Gathered, reviewed, and synthesized data, worked closely with professors to determine optimal types of data analysis, and presented analysis reports.

EDUCATION / PROFESSIONAL DEVELOPMENT

M.A., Economics, Princeton University, Princeton, NJ, 1989

B.S., Economics, minors in Mathematics & Computer Science, St. Albans College, Green, MT, 1987

Additional training through ResearchIntensive:
FDA Audits and Computer Software Validation
Communication Skills

Member, Drug Information Association (DIA)

Frank Ford
123 Main Street
Lake Forest, IL 12345
(123) 555-5555
frankford55@bamboo.com

Senior Management Consultant

EDUCATION

Masters in Business Administration, 2004
University of Chicago, Chicago, IL

HIGHLIGHTS

- A creative Senior Management Consultant with management experience in diverse workplace environments.
- Strategic thinker, leveraging analytical skills with an in-depth understanding of management to develop business solutions.
- An excellent communicator who can identify opportunities and establish strategic alliances.

SELECTED ACHIEVEMENTS

2005-06, Business Consultant, Horvath Corporation, Chicago, IL

- Significantly improved administration of deliveries from 70% to over 95% by developing efficient processes and relevant, timely reporting.
- Conducted research, created detailed business models, and delivered strategic recommendations that resulted in significant savings to the company.
- Evaluated and redefined job descriptions, resulting in greater efficiency and a reduction in annual costs.
- Facilitated communication and cooperation among departments, resulting in increased productivity and reduction in overhead.

2001-04, Operations Manager, CoFix Industries, Chicago, IL

- Smoothed interdepartmental operations by developing and implementing a series of checks and balances.
- Utilized extensive knowledge of and skill in production logistics to significantly improve assembly and shipping departments.
- Developed strong relationships with managers and staff, creating a cohesive and productive team in a deadline-driven environment.

1999-01, Production Manager, Best Products, Erie, PA

- Developed policies, procedures, and processes for all aspects of operations.
- Rapidly promoted to higher level based on quality of work, speed in acquiring new skills, communication, and team leadership.

Kate Warren

Paramount College • 44 Main St. • Cambridge, MA 12345
123-555-8888 • kwarren@bamboo.com

JOB OBJECTIVE

To obtain a research position with a biotechnology or pharmaceutical company in the research and development division.

PROFESSIONAL EXPERIENCE

PARAMOUNT COLLEGE, Cambridge, MA, 2005-present
Research Assistant

- Collaborated on research to assess potential angiogenic factors.
- Performed migration and proliferation assays; maintained cell cultures.
- Applied synthetic organic chemistry to produce 13-HODE, using purification techniques including TLC and HPLC.

THE CANCER RESEARCH LABORATORY, Greenville, ND, summer 2005
Research Assistant

- Isolated and partially characterized gene on mouse chromosome 13.
- Utilized techniques including PCR, cloning, gel electrophoresis, DNA extraction and purification, Southern blot, and phage library screening.
- Drafted final paper and presented results at Summer Student Symposium.

HILLSDALE HOSPITAL, Hillsdale, MN, January 2004
Medical Technology Intern

- Completed rotation through hematology, urinalysis, chemistry, microbiology, and blood bank.
- Observed patient procedures.
- Learned to perform and interpret tests used for medical diagnostics.

EDUCATION

Paramount College, Cambridge, MA

- B.A., Biochemistry/Chemistry, anticipated 2007
- In addition to introductory courses, completed two semesters of organic chemistry with experimental organic chemistry lab, one semester physical chemistry with lab, advanced inorganic chemistry with lab, and microbiology with lab.

AWARDS

Paramount Foundation Award recipient, 2004 and 2005
Dean's List, fall 1997-fall 2005
Presidential Scholarship (based on GPA)
Crooper Scholarship (awarded the top 10% of entering class)

AFFILIATIONS

American Chemical Society
Beta Beta Beta National Biological Honor Society

Paul Herkimer
123 Pleasant Street
San Diego, CA 12345
123-555-8888
pherkimer@bamboo.com

OBJECTIVE: A position in visual merchandising

QUALIFICATIONS

- Experience as a visual merchandiser in retail industry.
- Very good oral and interpersonal communication skills; a team player.
- Talent for visual design, proven through increased sales and loyal clientele.
- Creative, analytical problem solver; skilled in sketching and prop construction.

EDUCATION

Fashion Merchandising coursework, City College of San Diego, CA, 2000-present

Internships:	2005-present	Dresser at Fashion Shows, Bollerton's for Women
	2005	Dresser at Fashion Shows, Macy's

Graphic Design from Tripp College, Santa Fe, NM, 2001
Interior Design, College of the West, San Diego, CA, 2000

EMPLOYMENT
(concurrent with education)

2004-present **Sales/Visual Merchandise Associate**
Granger's Department Store, San Diego, CA

- Design and maintain all store presentations and displays of luxury linens under the supervision of the department manager.
- Assist department manager in maintaining inventory of department fixtures and props.
- Built exclusive clientele through successful presentations and valuable recommendations of tasteful linen arrangements and merchandise.
- Manage and support new product rollouts within the department.
- Increased sales of linen lines by 10% through a creative consultative sales approach.
- Major brands: Christopher Lowell, Ralph Lauren, and Fossil.

2003-2004 **Graphic Designer**
Grisham Bank, Grisham, CA

- Created original artwork, layout, and copy for training manuals and textbooks.
- Produced dynamic presentation materials for Grisham Bank VPs and Directors of Marketing Research Organization for use in meetings and client presentations.
- Worked with Grisham Bank channel partners and clients one on one and in groups.

2001-2003 **Desktop Publisher**
State Auto Club, San Diego, CA

- Analyzed client's data and needs to create customized textbooks and manuals.
- Developed visually interesting and easy-to-follow PowerPoint presentations.
- Improved style guides for development standards in technical manuals and online guides.
- Resolved production-related problems during pre- and post-production processes. Always kept within the time frame and scope.

Janine Borelli

Laney College
Herstville Rd. #1234
Greener, LA
123-555-8888
jborelli@bamboo.com

Objective

To obtain data-entry work for summer 2006

Profile

- A vision-oriented and energetic individual.
- Demonstrates ability to motivate and work with others to achieve reachable goals.
- Strong organizational, interpersonal, and communication skills.

Education

Laney College Greener, LA
Anticipated graduation: May 2008
Majors
- Business Administration
- French

Activities
- Student Government Representative-at-Large
- Class Cabinet Events Coordinator
- Student Union Planning Committee
- Fall 2005 - Resident Advisor of Dormitory

Work Experience (concurrent with Education)

Dr. Mary Hall, Rheumatology, Summer 2005 Greener, LA
Office Support
- Provided extensive keyboarding to assist in office management of this busy medical practice.
- Typed and filed medical forms for insurance and hospital records.

Fresh Donuts, Summers 2003 - 2005 Herstville, LA
Customer Service

Powerton Library, Summers 2001 - 2004 Powerton, LA
Data-Entry
- Performed data-entry for this small library with 300+ patrons, monitoring new acquisitions and "retired" books.
- Helped patrons find publications, showing them how to use the library's hardcopy index card filing system.

Luis M. Riskala
lriskala@bamboo.com

College address:
123 Terrace Street, Apt. 221
New York, NY 12345
123-555-1234

Permanent address:
123 Stratford Road, Flat 7
London SW2Y6ET UK
001-555-1234

JOB OBJECTIVE

A strategic planning position in multimedia and Internet business

SUMMARY OF QUALIFICATIONS

- An ambitious student of multimedia and Internet business strategies and management.
- Creative training with solid foundation of computer knowledge.
- Strong ability to achieve goals in cross-cultural environments: Europe, United States, and the Middle East.

EDUCATION

Columbia University, New York, NY
B.A., Visual and Media Arts, concentration: New Media, anticipated May 2006

- Worked with Colcom, the marketing communication agency at Columbia serving the school's newspaper, *The Word.*
- Participated in the 2004 summer abroad program at U.S. Intercontinental University in London. Compared the cultural advertising methods of UK and the U.S.

PROFESSIONAL EXPERIENCE
(Concurrent with education)

Fall '05 WEB SOLUTIONS, New York, NY
New Markets Research Intern

Web Solutions provides web-based applications to venture capital businesses, real estate businesses, and other clients including those in the Wireless Application Protocol (WAP) industry.

- Developed prospect quality check lists of client sites, used to generate add-on business.
- Helped develop Web Solutions' PR kit.
- Researched website functionality of new client, JumpJack (jumpjack.com/fp.asp), a wireless gaming application company.
- Conducted research for the president on possible new B2B venture: distributed computing, a new software product that conserves hard drive memory.

Fall '04- Spring '05 LOGON.COM, New York, NY
Strategic Consultant

A small web design start-up company.

- Collaborated with designer, programmer, and content writer to determine website feel and content for ResumesThatWork (www.resumesthatwork.com).
- Researched and wrote proposal on viability of creating an Internet portal to appeal to the intellectual market.

SKILLS

PC and Mac operating systems: Adobe Photoshop, Adobe Indesign, Adobe Premiere, Adobe ImageReady, Adobe Illustrator, Adobe AfterEffect, Media 100, ProTools, Media Cleaner Pro, Flash, Director, Dreamweaver, Netscape Communicator, Internet Explorer.

Languages: Arabic, English, and Italian

Charlotte E. Williams

123 Michigan Avenue, Apt. C • Chicago, IL 12345
(123) 555-1234 • charwilliams@bamboo.com

OBJECTIVE

An audit position

SUMMARY OF QUALIFICATIONS

- A highly organized and detail-oriented achiever with a thorough understanding of accounting principles and systems.
- An enthusiastic and personable team player, able to communicate effectively with people from diverse cultures. Fluent in Mandarin.
- Dedicated, known for consistently giving 110% to get the job done.
- Computer skills include: Microsoft Excel, Word, Access, PowerPoint, Peachtree Accounting.

EDUCATION

University of Chicago, 2002-pres. Graduation date: December 2006
Bachelor of Science with an emphasis on Accounting
Accounting GPA: 4.0 **Cumulative GPA:** 4.0

President, Beta Alpha Psi, 2005-06
National Honor Society for Financial Information Professionals

AWSCPA Scholarship Recipient, 2006
Scholarship awarded based on scholastic performance

EXPERIENCE

2002-pres. **UNIVERSITY OF CHICAGO,** Chicago, IL *Accounting Student*

- As President of Beta Alpha Psi, coordinated between students, alumni, administrators, and accounting firm representatives to orchestrate successful meetings, educational and networking sessions, and community service events.
- Created financial statements for numerous diverse projects, including integration of international accounting standards into GAAP.

2005 **MIDWEST CAPITAL CORPORATION,** Chicago, IL *Accounting Intern*

- Conducted extensive research for the CFO of this venture capital firm and contacted potential investors.
- Worked with Accounting department to update general ledgers, securities accounts, and Access database.
- Completed bank reconciliations for five subsidiary companies.

2003-04 **PAINE WEBBER,** New York *Financial Consulting Intern*

- Assisted private financial consultant with development and delivery of financial seminars and daily administrative operations, acting as first point of contact for clients and prospects.

2001-03 **CHINA PUBLISHING CORPORATION,** Taipei, Taiwan *Administrative Assistant*

- Provided administrative and translation assistance to this publisher of major international publications throughout Asia.

George Benicio
123 Cramer Avenue • Nashville, TN 12345
(123) 555-5555 • georgebenecio@bamboo.com

OBJECTIVE
Corporate Trainer

SUMMARY

- Five years of corporate training experience, combined with a strong background in teaching and sales.
- A creative communicator and presenter; able to establish rapport with individuals and groups at all organizational levels.
- Succinct, honest, and energetic, with unusual social ease, a solid commitment to follow-through, and a good sense of humor.

EXPERIENCE

2001-pres. ***Trainer, Product Sales***
Med-Way Corporation, Nashville, TN
One of the leading manufacturers of medical equipment.

- Helped turn around sales force to leap from $150M to $164M in annual revenues, through weekly sales training and coaching.
- Facilitated onsite training of sales reps for new product rollouts, with a particular focus on sales performance.
- Wrote technical sales guides and provided one-on-one training to instill a high level of confidence in each salesperson.

2000-01 ***Adult Education Teacher***
Carson County School, Nashville, TN
A public school offering night and weekend classes to adults at very low fees.

- Conducted dynamic and enjoyable English as Second Language classes for students of diverse backgrounds.

1998-00 ***Sales Associate***
Looks for Less, Cleveland, OH
A Mom-and-Pop store that was well known locally for high quality clothing.

- Worked with a team of seasoned sales professionals who taught me a "customer's needs first" sales philosophy.
- Commended by management for reaching weekly and monthly sales goals.

More experience: Teacher, Cleveland High School, Cleveland, OH; Basketball Coach, Westover Junior High School, Cincinnati, OH; Scout Master, Boy Scouts of America, Cincinnati, OH

EDUCATION

B.A., Education
University of Cleveland, OH

Corporate Training Seminars
Bogart School, Cincinnati, OH

Page 1 of 1

G. Vijayalakshmi

7-8-10/4 Mahatma Gandhi Road
Visakhapatnam, Andhra Pradesh 530003
Phone: 1235558888
vlakshmi_g80@bamboo.com

JOB OBJECTIVE

Accent Trainer for International Call Center

HIGHLIGHTS

- Experience training customer service employees in using clear and diplomatic communication skills by telephone and in person.
- Fluent in English, Spanish, Telugu, and Sanskrit.
- Speak English with an American accent, understand proper written English grammar, and am fluent in American casual conversation, including American slang.
- Excellent computer skills, including MS Office, spreadsheets, and the Internet.

SELECTED ACHIEVEMENTS

- Lived and educated in the United States until age 16.
- Trained clinic personnel in the correct procedures for answering the telephone, booking appointments, and taking accurate messages.
- Authored and illustrated a children's book in English, which was selected for the Young Author's Competition by a select panel of English Teachers in the U.S.
- Received an Award for Excellence in Reading from the Greenwich Board of Education for a reading competition of English books.
- At the Hotel Brundavan, the Human Resources Manager requested that I facilitate a Spoken English Class for management.

HISTORY (concurrent with education)

Intern, Human Resources Management Research Project, summer 2004
Hotel Brundavan, Visakhapatnam, Andhra Pradesh

Part-Time Head Receptionist, 2000-2005
Harshavardhan (Eye Clinic), Visakhapatnam, Andhra Pradesh

Part-Time Receptionist and Clerical Support, 1998-1999
Eye Associates, Greenwich, CT, USA

EDUCATION

Bachelor of Business Management, 2005
College of Management Studies, Gandhi Institute of Technology and Management
Gandhi Nagar Campus, Rushikonda, Visakhapatnam, Andhra Pradesh

Commerce, Economics, Civics, 2002
Bharatiya Vidya Kendra Junior College, Visakhapatnam

Greenwich High School, Greenwich, CT, USA

COMMUNITY SERVICE

Volunteer for Clean and Green, Janma Bhoomi (Chief Minister Chandra Babu Naidu's project for beautification and ecological preservation of Andhra Pradesh)

Enrique Murillo

123 45th Avenue • New York, NY 12345
(123) 555-1234 • emurillo@bamboo.com

Business Trainer

International Business • Cross-Cultural Relationships • Management • Marketing

SUMMARY OF QUALIFICATIONS

- More than 15 years' experience in business training. Skills include:

Curriculum development	Presentations	Theater
Train-the-trainer	Negotiations	Writing
Race and gender relations	Team-building	

- Proven ability to "think on my feet" and adapt curriculum to meet individual and company goals.
- Outstanding command of language: written, oral, and nonverbal.
- Quickly build rapport with individuals from diverse backgrounds and experience at all organizational levels.

PROFESSIONAL EXPERIENCE

1999-pres. BUSINESS TRAINER
Business English Teacher, Center for U.S. Studies, New York, NY (2004–pres.)
Business Trainer, FYCSA, Madrid, Spain (2000-04)
English Professor, University of Spain, Malaga, Spain (1999-00)

- Trained executive, technical and administrative staff from all over the world in:
  - Building cross-cultural business relationships
  - The language and culture of U.S. business
  - Achieving personal and business goals
  - Negotiations and presentations
- Bridged intercultural prejudices by focusing on cultural similarities, maintaining an open demeanor, and communicating with honesty and respect.
- Created a flexible, innovative curriculum—tailored on-the-spot to individual and group needs—that challenged clients to interact through role-plays and multi-media.
- Guaranteed repeat business for FYCSA in a highly competitive market when curriculum and improvisational style generated consistent enthusiastic client response.
- Taught practical communication skills, which:
  - Improved the negotiation abilities of executives and government officials.
  - Increased sales.
  - Reduced communication errors and technical staff time by transforming technical language into "plain English."
  - Strengthened company reputations in foreign markets.

1998 Independent Study–Cross-cultural teaching methods

- continued -

Enrique Murillo
Page Two

PROFESSIONAL EXPERIENCE, continued

1980-97 SUPERVISOR, Retail sales and customer service divisions
Barney's of New York, New York, NY

- Managed up to 30 sales and customer service staff.
- Sought out by manufacturers to provide expert consultation on intracultural marketing strategies.

EDUCATION & TRAINING

Teaching Accreditation, University of Cambridge, New York, NY

BA (degree pending) in International Relations and Broadcast Communications, University of New York, New York, NY

LANGUAGES

Fluent Spanish; basic Finnish

COMMUNITY SERVICE

Broadcast Journalist, Radio Free Europe, Munich, Germany

Chair, Iberian Council of New York, New York, NY

President, Spanish Society, New York, NY

Jason Manriquez

123 Central Avenue • La Habra, California 12345 • (123) 555-1234 • jmanriquez@bamboo.com

Elementary School Teacher

PROFILE

- Elementary School Teacher with experience working with culturally and linguistically diverse students.
- Expert at designing and implementing Whole Language programs.
- Fluent in Spanish.
- Currently applying for Language Development Specialist Certificate.

EDUCATION AND CREDENTIAL

California State Multiple Subject (Elementary) Teaching Credential, 2000

M.A., Educational Psychology, 2000
Developmental Teacher Education Program
CALIFORNIA STATE UNIVERSITY, Fullerton, CA

B.A., Cultural Anthropology, 1998
NEW COLLEGE OF CALIFORNIA, San Francisco, CA

TEACHING EXPERIENCE

2000-pres. **Elementary School Teacher,** EUCLID SCHOOL, Fullerton, CA

- Taught primary grade classes in this State Compensatory Education School with diverse student populations including:

Latino	European American	Pacific Islander
Filipino	African American	East Indian

- Designed and implemented developmental, student-centered, integrated curriculum covering all subject areas.
- Created and taught Whole Language program, including Writers' Workshop.
- Used Sheltered English and bilingual (Spanish) instructional techniques to help students of diverse linguistic backgrounds build content knowledge.
- Conducted parent conferences in both Spanish and English.
- Served as Master Teacher for five Fullerton State University student teachers.
- As a member of Euclid's Leadership Team, helped write four-year improvement plan and conducted staff in-services.
- Played active role in developing and writing Patterson's Achieving Schools proposal which was chosen one of fifteen in California for review in national competition.
- Planned and conducted staff in-service on teaching the concept of multiplication throughout the grade levels.

— Continued —

1999 **Student Teacher,** six months, ARROWHEAD ELEMENTARY SCHOOL, Anaheim, CA

- Participated in an innovative university/public school liaison project.
- Worked extensively with Spanish- and Cantonese-speaking students, grades 1-6, using Sheltered English as an instructional technique.
- Implemented on-going dialogue journal writing for first grade Cantonese-speaking students to increase English literacy.
- Conducted research and wrote Master's Project on the use of games to facilitate the development of emotional intelligence.

1998-99 **Student Teacher,** six months, BREA ELEMENTARY SCHOOL, Brea, CA

1998 **Student Teacher,** five months, BALDWIN PARK ELEMENTARY SCHOOL, Baldwin Park, CA

1998 **Student Teacher,** two months, BURBANK ELEMENTARY SCHOOL, Burbank, CA

1998 **Student Teacher,** two months, ROWLAND ELEMENTARY SCHOOL, Rowland, CA

1996-97 **Teacher,** ten months, FULLERTON STATE UNIVERSITY CHILDREN'S SCHOOL, Fullerton, CA

- Participated in team instruction of children, ages six through eight.
- Planned and executed activities in the areas of language arts, math, science, computers, art, and dramatic play.
- Adapted and tested a language arts curriculum for children in the primary grades.

ADDITIONAL EXPERIENCE

1999 **Instructional Assistant,** ARTISTIC TALENT DEVELOPMENT PROGRAM, Los Angeles, CA

- Co-taught a poetry class for gifted and talented primary students.

1999 **Research Assistant,** CALIFORNIA STATE UNIVERSITY, Fullerton, CA

- Assisted in educational research by conducting experimental sessions and confirming data.

1998 **Teaching Assistant,** CALIFORNIA STATE UNIVERSITY, Fullerton, CA

- Taught section of undergraduate cultural anthropology course. Supervised students and conducted review and study sessions.

Matthew Crosby

123 Clipper Street, Hazeltown, ND 12345 (123) 555-8888, mcrosby@bamboo.com

Elementary School Music Educator

Summary of Qualifications

- GRAMMY Award 2002 for excellence in music education
- Experience in evaluating teachers and students with a positive critical eye
- Superlative evaluation skills and the ability to communicate need for improvement

Professional Accomplishments

HAZELTOWN ELEMENTARY SCHOOL, Hazeltown, ND, 2000-present
Choir Director (grades 3-8), **Music Teacher** (grades K-2)

- Develop excellent vocal production, and prepare for school and community concerts.
- Offer Kodaly-based curriculum with Orff and Dalcroze incorporated.
- Prepare 60 3rd-graders for May Pole celebrations, and 120 1st- and 2nd-graders for spring concert.
- Develop Music Education lessons, which incorporate activities for special learners.
- Awarded grant for the music department from the Philanthropic Ventures Foundation.

BRUSHMOOR CHILDREN'S CHORUS, Brushmoor, ND, 2000-2001
Music Director and Kodaly Specialist for Training Choir (ages 5-8)

- Taught in-tune singing, memorization, posture/breath support, and solfeggio sight singing.
- Prepared singers for winter and spring concerts.
- Worked with all levels from beginners to advanced chamber choir.
- Communicated weekly with parents.

GRAIGMONT SCHOOL, Leechmere, ND, 1996-2000
General Music Teacher, Drama Director (grades PK-8)

- Conductor for annual All School Concert.
- Prepared middle-school students for MENC vocal competitions.

Education

Master's in Music Education (Kodaly), St. John's College, Berring, ND, 2001
North Dakota Credential Program, St. John's College, Berring, ND (Professional Clear), 2000
Whiley College, Windham, ND, Orff Schulwerk Graduate Level Certification Program, Level I, 1997
Bachelor of Music, Music Education, Honor Student, University of Kansas, Kansas City, 1995

Professional Development

CLAD certification program, University of North Dakota, 2004
TRIBES Learning Community Training, Center Source Systems, Hazeltown, ND, 2002
Attendance to OAKE National Conference, 2000 and 2004
Attendance to ACDA National Conference, 2002

Awards/Honors

NDAKE Scholarship to attend OAKE National Conference, April 2000
St. John's College Kodaly Graduate Fellowship, 1998, 1999, 2000
University of Kansas, Music Department Scholarship, 1993, 1994, 1995
Pamela A. Hastings Scholarship for excellence in the performing arts, 1992
State of North Dakota Single Subject Credential (Music) grades PK-12
State of Kansas Beginning Educator Certificate (Music) grades PK-12

Affiliations

MENC, Music Educators National Conference
OAKE, Organization of American Kodaly Educators
NDAKE, North Dakota Association of Kodaly Educators, Board Member (Membership)

Walter Crumb

123 Pike Street
Rancho Vista, VA 12345
123-555-8888, wcrumb@bamboo.com

Objective

Basketball Officiating for High School Playoff Games

Professional Experience

Current Assignments

- Full 2004-05 pre-season and league high school schedule: girls and boys fresh/soph, JV & Varsity competition
- Regular National High School Basketball (NHSB) assignments
- Appointed new referee trainer for the Basketball Officials Society (BOS)

Top Assignments

- Terrance versus Lynnwood men's college game, Lynnwood College, December 1, 2004
- Rancho Vista basketball, 8th grade club tournament, Rancho Vista, September 2004
- Santa Questa Brofest, St. Clare Valley High School, Rancho Vista; worked JV girls and boys contests, August 2004
- Talley City J.C.C. summer league, freshmen and sophomore boys games, 2004
- JV summer tournament, Cruville High School, ND; two-day competitive event, June 2004
- Rancho Vista Pirates basketball tournament, Sinclair Middle School, Titenville; worked an up-tempo girls 8th grade division, May 2004
- AAS girls division, Lynnwood College, Lynnwood, May 2004
- Redeemer tournament, College of Bruno, March 2004
- NHSB "All-Net" boys, Clairmont High School, February 2004
- Middle School boys and girls 8th grade squads, Trooper Middle School and Rancho Vista Middle School, including playoffs, 2003-04 season

Camps & Clinics

- BOS, three training sessions, 2004
- PBOS, new points of emphasis clarification; NGHS 2004-05 rules certification
- Introductory Meeting and Floor Evaluation Clinic, NCBOS, Pinesnook City, April 2004

Affiliations

- Basketball Officials Society, Clairmont, VA, 2003-05 seasons
- Valley Basketball Officials Society, Rancho Vista, VA, 2004
- National Association of Sports Professionals, Parchland, ND, 2004
- Superior Coaching, Tillman University Athletics, Amherst, ND, 2004
- Amherst United Methodist Church, Board of Trustees, Amherst, ND, 2000-pres.

Education

- B.A., English Literature, Rancho Vista University, 2004

Kerry Wainwright

123 Porter Street, Denver, CO 12345
(123) 555-8888
kwainwright@bamboo.com

SUMMARY

More than 10 years' programming and application development experience, including:

Dynamic database-backed websites	Real-time data collection
Content Management Systems (CMS)	Web crawling

COMPUTER SKILLS

Languages

- Java, C, C++, PERL, JavaScript, Pascal, Fortran, Modulo2, SED, AWK, C/bourne/korn/bash shells, XSLT, XML, HTML, SGML, and various other data-defining methodologies.

Software

- Database: SQL, ESQL, ODBC, JDBC, MySQL, Oracle, Access.
- Platforms: Windows XP/2000/NT/95/3.1, VAX-VMS, various UNIX flavors (Redhat Linux, Solaris, HPUX), Mac-OS.

EXPERIENCE

WEB PROGRAMMER/SOFTWARE ENGINEER

InterRef, Denver, CO, 2004 - present

- Developed Java applications for the DOI infrastructure.
- Developed database-backed web servlets for customer website.
- Managed company website and features.

CONTRACT SOFTWARE ENGINEER

Seamless Systems, Denver, CO, 2003

- Managed several MySQL databases (design, creation, transaction programming).
- Developed features for websites and Content Management Systems, using Java, PERL, JavaScript, and/or XSLT.

SENIOR SOFTWARE ENGINEER

RiteInfo Inc., Boulder, CO, 2002 - 2003

- Designed and built Internet and real-time newswire data acquisition and processing.
- Developed news service system on Linux, including a real-time messaging system.
- Built applications to crawl customer websites.

SENIOR SOFTWARE ENGINEER

Spectrum Technology, Denver, CO, 1996 - 2002 (acquired by RiteInfo, Inc. in 2002)

- As part of the original start-up team, developed and built various systems, including data aggregation, processing, testing, loading, and staging systems.
- Developed original systems and testing tools for real-time news service.
- Developed data management system (structure, processing and management tools, and data warehousing system).

PROGRAMMER

WINSCO Publishing, Denver, CO, 1992 - 1996

- Developed various data conversion programs and production process and test tools, written in C.
- Provided production support to teams building CD-ROM and Internet products.
- Built and maintained tools and performed troubleshooting of production processes.

EDUCATION

B.S. in Electrical Engineering, University of Utah, Salt Lake, UT, 1991

RYAN SEYMOUR

123 Pillar Street, #1 (123) 555-8888
Kansas City, KS 12345 rseymour@bamboo.com

Multimedia Developer and Web Designer

- Self-motivated technical/creative professional.
- Enthusiastic and cooperative team member.
- Advanced knowledge of computer systems and applications.
- Quickly and intuitively comprehend complex systems.

PROFESSIONAL EXPERIENCE

1998-present Web Design and Multimedia Consultant

www.reliefinsite.com, 1998-present

- Redesigned and added video content to a comedy website, increasing traffic 20%.

www.themansion.com, 1998-present

- Created informational website for Island Mansion and Spa, increasing business and reducing event coordinators' workload.

www.experthere.com, 1999-2002

- Created prototype website for Internet consultant startup to attract venture capital.

www.ress.com, 1999

- Updated and added video to Regional Energy Services website.

1990-1998 Kansas Automobile Club (KAC), Kansas City

Multimedia Developer, 1997-1998

- Consulted with internal departments on corporate Internet and Intranet website multimedia projects.
- Created RealAudio website cataloging KRGO radio spots, which increased the effectiveness of company website.
- Created KAC website for *Auto magazine*, working with creative directors and writers.
- Developed Instant Info website, providing local information and maps to KAC members.
- Digitized corporate video for Intranet distribution, reducing costs and promoting employee communication.
- Designed, illustrated, co-wrote, and published booklet that supported frontline decision making, improving customer service and company efficiency.
- Created and maintained MS Access database of marketing projects and a calendar of marketing events for executive staff. Saved money by eliminating redundant campaigns and improving the planning process.
- Created and maintained MS Access database of over 6,000 KAC employees' phone numbers, titles, and addresses for company phone book. Created PDF phone book and HTML version for the Intranet, saving printing and distribution costs.

—Continued

Ryan Seymour

Kansas Automobile Club (continued)

Supervisor, Client Services Technical Support, 1993-1994

- Supervised hardware and software support specialists. Created computer user-groups, which improved employee knowledge and efficiency.
- Oversaw newsletter supporting computer users.

Presentation Support Specialist, 1990-1992

- Worked with the executive staff to create multimedia, including digital video, 35mm slides, and overheads to support their business presentations to the Board of Directors.
- Created animated video, informing managers-in-training about Information Services and promoting better relations with internal clients.
- Produced video that documented workflow of claims adjusters, resulting in new and efficient claims procedures.

Technology and Application Expertise

BBEdit	Painter	SoundEdit	Lingo
Dreamweaver	Final Cut Pro	Acrobat	ShockWave
PhotoShop	MediaCleaner	Distiller	MS Access
Illustrator	RealMedia	Director	Mac/Win/NT

Education

MA, Creative Writing, Kansas State University, Kansas City, KS
BA, English, Hollindale State College, Priceline, KS

Graham Phelps

123 Provence Drive • New Orleans, LA 12345 • (123) 555-1234 • gphelps@bamboo.com

OBJECTIVE

A senior IT project management position, with a focus on
System Administration Manufacturing Engineering Customer Support

SUMMARY OF QUALIFICATIONS

- 10+ years of progressive responsibility in IT for global organizations.
- Highly analytical, with particular skill in maintaining a strong customer focus while providing expert technical problem solving.
- A dynamic project manager, skilled in creating realistic project plans, prioritizing and delegating effectively, and tracking progress to ensure accurate, on-schedule completion.
- Experienced in building solid relationships and communicating articulately to build bridges between customer needs and engineering/technical team requirements. Fluent in Japanese.

PROFESSIONAL EXPERIENCE

1992-pres. **Notable Graphics Inc. (NGI)**, U.S. and Asia locations

Global Product Support Engineer, New Orleans *2004-pres.*

- Conduct in-depth analysis and offer technical support and guidance to 150 System Support Engineers (SSEs) worldwide. Provide third-level support to U.S. customers and second-level support to international customers.
- Consult with engineering team members when necessary to resolve complex technical issues. Manage customer relationships, expectations, and escalations, effectively balancing customer needs and engineering requirements.
- Maintain strict adherence to customer turnaround times, consistently achieving on-time completion of system repairs.
- As Support Expert, prepare and deliver dynamic, interactive presentations to educate frontline support team on new products.

Manufacturing Test Engineer, New Orleans and Tokyo *1999-04*

- Designed and implemented test processes for mid-range desktop product and high-end server proprietary software product, serving as primary contact among Quality, Field, and Support teams for all issues during system manufacturing.
- Worked closely with Production Schedulers to prioritize tasks and projects, allocate resources, and ensure on-time completion and ISO9001 compliance.
- Met regularly with Quality Group to identify, analyze, and resolve discrepancies and problems with components. Utilized the Integrated Product and Process Development (IPPD) approach to improve the quality of new products while reducing costs and time-to-market.
- Project-managed 15-member Engineering Group in Tokyo, including Mechanical, Quality, Test, and Board-level Engineers. Delegated and matched team members with specific tasks to achieve optimal performance.

-continued-

GRAHAM PHELPS
PAGE TWO

- Trained team members on the production floor for upcoming builds, and acted as liaison between Engineering, Planning and Finance departments.
- Facilitated conference calls between the U.S. and Japan manufacturing and engineering groups to address problems and keep current with technical issues.
- Prepared test procedures and documentation in both Japanese and English for high-end systems and desktop products.
- Received 2001 Employee Excellence Award for outstanding performance, the only native English speaker to ever win this award.

Field Technical Analyst / System Support Engineer, Boston, MA *1992-99*

- Provided ongoing technical support, responded to SSE questions, and traveled to customer locations where necessary for escalation management.
- Promoted to Field Technical Analyst based on excellent performance.

1984-92 **PRIMARYTECH,** Boston, MA

Network Analyst / System Administrator *1989-92*

- Primary System Administrator to the Vehicle Analysis Branch at Boston Tech Research Center. Supported numerous networked systems, resulting in increased efficiency, productivity, and communication.
- As Network Analyst, responded to user questions and quickly diagnosed and resolved network problems.
- System Administrator for the Network Support Office's Sun computers.

Programmer *1984-89*

- Lead programmer on the Simulation, Monitoring, Analysis, Reduction, and Test System acceptance team for a U.S. military support contract. Designed and tested bug fixes and system upgrades.
- Designed and coded C programs and Bourne shell utilities to support the Cray systems, the world's fastest supercomputers at the time.
- Received two Outstanding Achievement Awards for work in support of the project.

EDUCATION / PROFESSIONAL DEVELOPMENT

B.S., Computer Science, Louisiana Tech, New Orleans, LA

Completed Kempner-Tregoe Project Management Training

Technical skills: Unix, C, shell scripting, PERL, Linux, JavaScript, PHP, MS Excel, Word, and PowerPoint

Former member, IEEE

PATRICIA GONZALEZ

123 Russell Avenue, Pittsburgh, PA 12345 • 123/555-1234 • pgonzalez@bamboo.com

E-COMMERCE PROJECT MANAGER

SUMMARY

- Over seven years' technical project experience, seven years in relationship management, and over two years e-commerce project leadership.
- MBA and MS, Engineering (South American equivalents).
- Proven ability to target and reach high standards; widely perceived as a technical resource.
- Exceptionally precise yet comprehensive thinker; strong team builder; skillful negotiator.
- International, cross-cultural experience, and fluency in five European languages.

PROFESSIONAL EXPERIENCE

PayTime, Pittsburgh, PA **2000-present**
PROJECT MANAGER
Managed multiple IT projects for an e-payment provider with 20% monthly growth.

E-COMMERCE TECHNOLOGY
Developed e-commerce product allowing websites to accept online payments and establish credit relationships of up to $3M per month with banks.

- Led successful server-side gateway integrations with two large banks and oversaw gateway software integration with over 100 commercial websites.
- Upgraded product with new features, opening code to accommodate customer language and platform preferences, improving interface, and increasing security.
- Conducted thorough stress tests to meet financial industry quality standards.
- Adjusted to the unpredictable loss of a major partner by quickly integrating a new bank.

SYSTEMS DEVELOPMENT
Created extranet-based customer relationship systems allowing partners to track real-time progress of customer application and reducing processing time from 90 to 30 days.

- Built and rolled out branded website for company reseller network increasing lead response volume by 300% within two months.
- Implemented Goldmine sales tracking software, smoothly linking customer relationship systems.
- Dramatically improved customer ease of use and clarity of information.

TEAM MANAGEMENT
Attracted outstanding technical staff and catalyzed strong, eager performance with enticing challenges and responsibilities.

- Encouraged cross-training and peer mentoring, and created team cohesion by involving staff in rollouts and strategic planning.
- Established clear-cut job definitions, filled positions through internal promotion whenever possible, and trained and managed top-notch engineering team of eight.

RELATIONSHIP MANAGEMENT
Maintained high satisfaction among partners, customers, and clients.

- Collaboratively developed new projects with senior managers at partner companies, negotiating and expanding alliance terms along with technical goals and timelines.
- Oversaw technical e-commerce partnerships with major shopping carts (Miva, ECBuilder, ShopSite), completing integrations on time and expanding business opportunities for both partners.
- Championed top-level account service, facilitating the sales success of 15 resellers by ensuring relevant technical support and assistance with client relationship issues.

- Continued -

PATRICIA GONZALEZ

Page Two

Para Force, Caracas, Venezuela **1993-1999**

Managed major accounts and developed engineering improvements for South American stainless steel leader.

VICE SALES MANAGER, 1997-1999

Increased sales by 22% in two years by managing major accounts, joining managers on sales calls, and overseeing product training of account managers from 35 international agencies.

- Won three of Para Force's top ten customers, generating $2.7M annually.
- Designed layout and content of corporate website, conveying product benefits with simple, inviting, and educational images and ideas.
- Reduced errors by over 50% by troubleshooting price quotes and invoicing.
- Saved $1M annually by adjusting price policy to minimize dumping taxes.

PROCESS ENGINEER, 1994-1997

Streamlined operations of stainless steel welded tube factory with process engineering innovations.

- Improved cross-cultural relationship between plants in different countries.
- Designed and implemented concise production management chart, new product classification system, and defect classification chart, providing simple effective tools for plant managers.

IT ENGINEER, 1993-1994

Launched new ERP system on IBM AS 400; installed terminals; tested programs; educated sales force; provided support service; and taught computer-illiterate workforce of 70 how to use a PC.

EDUCATION

MBA, Universite de Caracas, Venezuela, 1993
MS, Industrial Engineering, Universite de Caracas, Venezuela, 1993

SOFTWARE KNOWLEDGE

Proficient in E-commerce, shopping carts, E-payment, HTML, FTP, ShopSite, Goldmine, ECBuilder, Excel, MS Project, PowerPoint, Dreamweaver; familiar with NT, Linux, Unix, Java, Perl, C/C++, cgi, TCP/IP, XML, java-script Transact, Onyx, Saleslogix, Miva

Thomas Perkins
123 Walker Street, Reno, NV 12345
(123) 555-8888, tomperkins@bamboo.com

Objective Sr. Research Associate in the Environmental Energy Technology Division

Education University of Utah, Salt Lake City, B.S., **Mechanical Engineering,** 2006
Graduated with High Honors (3.85 GPA)

University of Nevada, Reno, B.A., **Philosophy,** 2004
Graduated with Highest Honors

Work Experience

2006-present **Project Engineer,** Hyden Associates, Reno
Provide due-diligence services for publicly funded, demand-side management (DSM) programs directed at commercial and industrial customers, including large office buildings, oil refineries, and various manufacturing facilities

Energy Engineering and Analysis

- Oversee metering, measurement, and verification of energy and demand savings
- Monitor data analysis
- Perform and assess energy audits
- Knowledge of end-use technology, including pumps, fans, compressors, condensers, electric motors, variable-speed drives, and fluorescent lighting

Program Management

- Advise participants on energy savings estimates, and measurement and verification methodology
- Write detailed project reviews for utility clients
- Ensure compliance with energy program rules
- Approve applications and savings reports
- Work directly with service providers and customers on projects

Additional Projects

- Reviewed a proposed revision to the Federal Energy Management Program (FEMP) Measurement and Verification Guidelines, chapter on Renewable Energy Projects
- Assisted in developing and implementing measurement and verification plans for projects participating in the Nevada Energy Commission's summer demand initiative

2005 **Research Assistant,** University of Utah Combustion Laboratories, Salt Lake City
Participated in experimental modeling of combustion kinetics; experiments involved shock tube tests with acetylene

Computer Skills

FORTRAN	Excel	Word
MatLab	Pascal	PowerPoint

Technical

BETH BROWN

415-835-2150 bethresumepro@yahoo.com

Professional Resume Writer

SUMMARY OF QUALIFICATIONS

- A successful resume writer for clients in all industries, fields and organizational levels since 1995.
- Skilled in listening carefully and translating information into clear and concise language that illuminates individual strengths and furthers each client's goals.
- Known for excellent spelling/grammatical skills and a sense of humor.

PROFESSIONAL EXPERIENCE

1995-pres. **SUSAN IRELAND'S RESUME TEAM & BETH BROWN RESUMES,** San Francisco, CA
Professional Resume Writer

- Created 1,000+ resumes and cover letters, working collaboratively with a diverse clientele, including more than 300 members of Alumnae Resources/lifeprint career center.
- Provided customized, informative career coaching and interviewing skills training to individual clients.
- Consistently received commendations and referrals from satisfied clients, as well as from Susan Ireland and from Yana Parker, author of *The Damn Good Resume Guide.*
- Completed extensive apprenticeship and training with Susan Ireland, author of *The Complete Idiot's Guide to the Perfect Resume* and *The Complete Idiot's Guide to the Perfect Cover Letter.* Contributed resumes and cover letters to both books.
- Taught monthly resume writing workshops at Alumnae Resources/lifeprint for over three years, utilizing a lively and interactive approach to facilitate learning and enjoyment of resume writing.

1989-95 **TOOLS FOR CHANGE,** San Francisco, CA
Editor / Administrative Assistant

- Offered editorial and administrative assistance to Margo Adair, author of *Tools for Change: Applied Meditation* and *Meditations on Everything Under the Sun.*

Additional experience includes positions in Marketing Consulting, Proofreading/Editing, Teaching/Tutoring, Word Processing and Office Management in diverse settings ranging from Architecture to Healthcare to Technology.

EDUCATION

B.A., English Literature, Washington University, St. Louis, MO

Tawny Hall

123 White Drive • Westchester, NY 12345 • (123) 555-8888 • thall@bamboo.com

JOB OBJECTIVE: Technical Writer

SUMMARY OF QUALIFICATIONS

- Four years' experience writing easy-to-read instructions for technical services, products, and safety procedures.
- Known for quick technical comprehension and clear translation.
- Proficient with Windows and Macintosh word processing applications.

EDUCATION

Bachelor of Science	Leedings College, Westchester, NY
Technical Writing Certificate	Unity Community College, Jamaica, NY

RELEVANT ACCOMPLISHMENTS

WRITING AND EDITING

At Chrysler Bank

- Created Standard Operating Procedures for various responsibilities and tasks.
- Cut customer response time and initial analyst training time by creating an Access database to organize frequently accessed information.
- Designed and implemented a training program for technology phone support.

At Unified Alarms

- Wrote brochures, featuring technical capabilities of wired and wireless systems.
- Reduced customer response time by simplifying complex technical instructions.
- Analyzed process and developed instructions for downloading data from PCS to remote microcontrollers.
- Prepared business proposals for technical installations for up to $25K each.
- Edited manual to demystify instructions for entry-level users.

At Camway Communications

- Cut training time by creating concise instructions and worksheets for operators.

At Leedings College, chemistry, physics, and digital logic classes

- Using scientific third-person format, wrote research and analytical reports.

TECHNICAL

At Chrysler Bank

- Install and troubleshoot phone, pager, and telecommunication networks.
- Provide hardware and software support of bank's computers.

At Leedings College, technical classes

- Programmed in Pascal and Basic; debugged computer programs.
- Built electronic boards, using digital logic diagrams and Boolean formulas.

WORK HISTORY

1998-present	Help Desk Specialist, Chrysler Bank, Westchester, NY
1996-1998	Phone Operator Manager, Camway Communications, Inc., Jamaica, NY
1995-1996	Technical Writer, Unified Alarms, Ltd., White Plains, NY

SUZANNE BRIARLY

123 Wright Street • Harrison, PA 12345 • (123) 555-8888 • suebriarly@bamboo.com

OBJECTIVE: Copy Editor

SUMMARY OF QUALIFICATIONS

- Dedicated and meticulous editor, with rigorous attention to detail, grammar, and style; equally at ease with technical and nontechnical material.
- Adept at working with a broad range of writing styles and cultivating relationships with people from diverse organizational and cultural backgrounds.
- Focused professional; able to work independently and as part of a team to complete writing and editing projects within strict deadlines.

PROFESSIONAL EXPERIENCE

2004-06 HARRISON STATE COLLEGE, Harrison, PA, *Student*

- Wrote extensively, with a focus on clarity of thought, accuracy in grammar, and creative explorations of ideas, perspectives, and topics.
- Proofread and edited papers, providing suggestions and "constructive commentary" to ESL students to clarify ideas and improve writing skills.
- Participated in writing-based forums, interpreting and articulating diverse perspectives through well-crafted written and oral presentations.

2000-04 LEEPAHEAD DISTRIBUTION, INC., Farnsworth, PA, *Sales Manager*

- Wrote in-depth, persuasive reports; summaries of findings; and formal correspondence for clients and senior management. Topics included conclusions regarding new product trials, technical materials, project scope, and results.
- Interviewed clients and prospects to assess needs and limitations, and to identify products for optimal fit.
- Fielded inquiries from vendors and consulted with engineering and manufacturing teams to improve service and delivery based on changing priorities for semiconductor test products.
- Conducted site visits to deliver presentations of products and services.
- Communicated effectively with overseas clients in Europe and Asia, despite differences in language and cultural business practices.

1999-00 INTERACTIVE ELEMENTS, INC., Pittsburgh, PA, *Sales Account Manager*

- Researched electronic components to match client needs and translated technical specifications for nontechnical audiences.
- Supported 40 different product lines and conducted numerous daily calls and client visits to increase sales and maintain superlative customer service.

1999 THE HIDEOUT HOTEL, Pittsburgh, PA, *Front Office Manager*

- Designed, wrote, and delivered training for hotel staff, including "Train the Trainer" modules and training scenarios related to upselling techniques, merchandising, rate integrity, phone etiquette, and professionalism.

EDUCATION / AWARDS

B.A., English Literature, Harrison State College, Harrison, PA, 2006
Gold Medal Champion, Thomas Jefferson Oratory Contest

Maggie McCullough
123 Cramer Street
Chicago, IL 12345
123-555-8888
magmccullough@bamboo.com

Classical Music Journalist

HIGHLIGHTS

- Seven years' experience as a classical music journalist, authoring articles on music festivals and events, interviews with musicians, and reviews of concerts and recordings
- Author of internationally recognized book on London/Decca classical records
- Over 10 years as an administrator of performing arts organizations
- Over 40 years of collecting classical music recordings and attending concerts
- Passionate about the value of classical music in contemporary society

PROFESSIONAL EXPERIENCE

WRITING/PRESENTATIONS

- Authored 187-page book on London/Decca classical records. Favorable reviews in *Grammophone, Stereo Review,* and *International Classical Record Collector*
- Wrote 12 articles for *Instruments Magazine,* which featured summer music festivals and interviews with musicians and music personalities
- Reviewed 33 CDs for *Audiophile Monthly,* an online magazine for record collectors
- Created multimedia presentation on the life of composer Gustav Mahler
- Delivered a presentation on Wynton Marsalis' Jazz Oratorio, *All Rise,* for the Chicago Symphony's Inside Music program

ARTS MANAGEMENT

- As *Project Director of the Regional Arts Planning Study* and *City Spirit Facilitator for the National Endowment for the Arts,* studied and recommended program strategies for regional programming agencies that were successfully adopted
- As *Assistant Manager* for the Chicago Orchestra, developed regional programming and managed their Young People's Concerts
- As *Administrative Director* of the Chicago Girls Chorus, managed budgets and increased chorus enrollment by 20% in five months

Page 1 of 2

Maggie McCullough

WORK HISTORY

Arts Management/Writing Experience, 1971-present:

Columnist	*Instruments Magazine,* Chicago, IL
Owner	Classical Treasures, Chicago, IL
Administrative Director	Chicago Girls Chorus, Chicago, IL
Marketing Consultant	Classical Today, Princeton, NJ
	Musical Providers, Princeton, NJ
Project Director	Regional Arts Planning Study, Chicago, IL
City Spirit Facilitator	National Endowment for the Arts, Washington, DC
Director	New Jersey Arts Commission, Trenton, NJ
Assistant Manager	Chicago Orchestra, Chicago, IL

EDUCATION AND AFFILIATIONS

Member, **Music Critics Association of North America,** 1997 to present
M.A., **Arts Administration,** University of Minnesota
M.B.A., **Marketing,** University of Michigan

PUBLICATIONS

Books

The Arts in the Midwest: A Guide for Regional Planning, 1974
You – The Turning Point, A Workbook for Marketing Your Private Practice, 1984
Full Frequency Sound, A History and Discography of Early Stereo London/Decca *Classical Music Recordings on LP and CD,* 1990

Articles

Conversation with violinist Chee Yun in *Violin Vignettes,* Class Publishing, 2000
12 articles for *Instruments Magazine,* a national magazine for string players
33 reviews of classical CDs and a feature article on Walt Disney Hall for *Audiophile Monthly,* an online magazine for record collectors
Two articles for the *Chicago Times* about Music at Menlo, a chamber music festival

Index

A

B

C

D

E

F

G–H

I

J–K

L–M

N

O

P

Q-R

S

T

U-V

W-X-Y-Z